THE AMERICAN ARMY IN TRANSITION, 1865–1898

Recent Titles in
The Greenwood Press "Daily Life through History" Series

Native Americans from Post-Columbian through Nineteenth-Century America
Alice Nash and Christoph Strobel

Cooking in Europe, 1250–1650
Ken Albala

The Black Death
Joseph P. Byrne

Cooking in America, 1590–1840
Trudy Eden

Cooking in America, 1840–1945
Alice L. McLean

Cooking in Ancient Civilizations
Cathy K. Kaufman

Nature and the Environment in Pre-Columbian American Life
Stacy Kowtko

Science and Technology in Medieval European Life
Jeffrey R. Wigelsworth

Civilians in Wartime Africa: From Slavery Days to the Diamond Wars
John Laband, editor

Christians in Ancient Rome
James W. Ermatinger

The Army in Transformation, 1790–1860
James M. McCaffrey

The Korean War
Paul M. Edwards

THE AMERICAN ARMY IN TRANSITION, 1865–1898

Michael L. Tate

The Greenwood Press "Daily Life through History" Series

American Soldiers' Lives
David S. Heidler and Jeanne T. Heidler, Series Editors

GREENWOOD PRESS
Westport, Connecticut • London

Library of Congress Cataloging-in-Publication Data

Tate, Michael L.
  The American Army in transition, 1865–1898 / Michael L. Tate.
    p. cm. — (Greenwood Press "daily life through history" series,
ISSN 1080–4749) (American soldiers' lives)
  Includes bibliographical references and index.
  ISBN-13: 978–0–313–33212–8 (alk. paper)
  ISBN-10: 0–313–33212–6 (alk. paper)
1. United States. Army—History—19th century. 2. United States.
Army—Military life—History—19th century. I. Title.
  UA25.T27 2007
  355.00973'09034—dc22   2006103475

British Library Cataloguing in Publication Data is available.

Library of Congress Catalog Card Number: 2006103475

ISBN-13: 978–0–313–33212–8
ISBN-10: 0–313–33212–6
ISSN: 1080–4749

First published in 2007

Greenwood Press, 88 Post Road West, Westport, CT 06881
An imprint of Greenwood Publishing Group, Inc.
www.greenwood.com

Printed in the United States of America

The paper used in this book complies with the
Permanent Paper Standard issued by the National
Information Standards Organization (Z39.48–1984).

10 9 8 7 6 5 4 3 2 1

CONTENTS

SERIES FOREWORD

More than once during the military campaigns undertaken by American armies, leaders in both civilian and martial roles have been prompted to ask in admiration, "Where do such people come from?" The question, of course, was both rhetorical and in earnest: the one because they knew that such people hailed from the coasts and the heartland, from small hamlets and sprawling cities, from expansive prairies and breezy lakeshores. They were as varied as the land they represented, as complex as the diversity of their faiths and ethnic identities, all nonetheless defined by the overarching identity of "American," made more emphatic by their transformation into "American soldiers."

They knew and we know where they came from. On the other hand, the question for anyone who knows the tedium, indignity, discomfort, and peril of military service in wartime is more aptly framed, "Why did they come at all?"

In the volumes of this series, accomplished scholars of the American military answer that question, and more. By depicting the daily routines of soldiers at war, they reveal the gritty heroism of those who conquered the drudgery of routine and courageously faced the terrors of combat. With impeccable research and a deep understanding of the people who move through these grandly conceived stories—for war, as Tolstoy has shown us, is the most grandly conceived and complex story of all—these books take us to the heart of great armies engaged in enormous undertakings. Bad food, disease, haphazardly treated wounds, and chronic longing for loved ones form part of these stories, for those are the universal afflictions of soldiers. Punctuating long stretches of loneliness and monotony were interludes of horrific violence that scarred every soldier, even those who escaped physical injury. And insidious wounds could fester because of ugly customs and ingrained prejudices: for too long a span, soldiers who happened to be minorities suffered galling injustices at the hands of those they served, often giving for cause and comrades what Lincoln called "the last full measure of devotion," despite unfair indignities and undeserved ignominy. And sadly, it is true that protracted or unpopular wars could send veterans returning to a country indifferent about their sacrifices, sometimes hostile to the cause for which they fought, and begrudging even marginal compensation to their spouses and orphans. But quiet courage, wry humor, tangible camaraderie, and implacable pride are parts of these stories as well, ably conveyed by these gifted writers who have managed to turn the pages that follow into vivid snapshots of accomplishment, sacrifice, and triumph.

Until recently the American soldier has usually been a citizen called to duty in times of extraordinary crisis. The volunteer army of this latest generation, though, has created a remarkable hybrid in the current American soldier, a professional who nevertheless upholds the traditions of American citizens who happen to be in uniform to do a tough job. It is a noble tradition that ennobles all who have honored it. And more often than not, they who have served have managed small miracles of fortitude and resolve.

Walter Lord's *Incredible Victory* recounts the story of Mike Brazier, the rear-seat man on a torpedo plane from the carrier *Yorktown* in the battle of Midway. He and pilot Wilhelm Esders were among that stoic cadre of fliers who attacked Japanese carriers, knowing that their fuel was insufficient for the distance to and from their targets. Having made their run under heavy enemy fire, Esders finally had to ditch the spent and damaged plane miles short of the *Yorktown* in the rolling Pacific. He then discovered that Brazier had been shot to pieces. Despite his grave wounds, Brazier had managed to change the coils in the radio to help guide the plane back toward the *Yorktown*. In the life raft as he died, Mike Brazier never complained. He talked of his family and how hard it had been to leave them, but he did not complain. Instead he apologized that he could not be of more help.

In the great, roiling cauldron of the Second World War, here was the archetype of the American soldier: uncomplaining while dying far from home in the middle of nowhere, worried at the last that he had not done his part.

Where do such people come from?

We invite you to read on, and find out.

David S. Heidler and Jeanne T. Heidler
Series Editors

PREFACE

The period between the end of the Civil War and the Spanish-American War of 1898 was a time of dramatic change for the U.S. military, one that included the Reconstruction of the South and the fabled Indian wars of the West. This era witnessed the shifting of soldiering duties and led to increased responsibilities, including law enforcement, protection of national parks, building roads and bridges, undertaking exploration and scientific discovery missions, waging war against Indian tribes, defending civilian settlements, conducting relief efforts during national emergencies, and even shielding Native Americans from exploitive white interests. Officers were expected to perform these diverse duties with no more than 25,000 enlisted men, far fewer than the 1.5 million men at arms who had served the Union Army during the Civil War. As the century's end neared, the army faced a new round of retrenchment in manpower and budgets just at the time the nation was acquiring a new colonial empire in the Caribbean Sea and the Pacific Ocean. Simultaneously, veterans of the Indian war era pressed for medical care and increased pension benefits, only to find Congress slow to respond to their demands. While Civil War veterans and their lobbying organizations wielded power in these debates, veterans of the so-called peacetime army went virtually unheralded by a nation that took their contributions for granted.

The American Army in Transition, 1865–1898 describes the soldiers, their duties, their environment and their families in a period of dynamic expansion and settlement of the West. It offers, often in the soldiers' own words, their experiences in the forts, in the treacherous mountains of the Southwest and the expansive Great Plains, and in the complicated political landscape of the South during Reconstruction. Their wives, sweethearts, and children are also heard from, in passages from letters, diaries, and newspapers of the day. Among the many subjects covered in this book, its chapters offer insightful views of the following:

- Recruiting officers and men
- Training and equipping soldiers

- Military law and discipline
- Reconstruction duty in the South
- Western Indian campaigns
- Hardships, including injuries, death, and shortages of supplies
- Family life, including women's roles and observations
- Social life, including gambling, parties, sports, theatrical performances, concerts, and literary societies
- Relationships with nearby civilian communities
- Soldiers' duties in the multipurpose army, including exploring, mapping, assembling scientific materials, delivering mail, and providing telegraphic and weather services for the nation
- Protecting fledgling national parks from private exploitation
- Native Americans, both as adversaries and Indian scout comrades
- Black soldiers facing prejudice and violence in a race-conscious nation
- Passing of the frontier army, including closing posts and seeking pensions for veterans and their families

The book begins with a timeline of the period that allows readers to put the major events into context. It closes with an extensive bibliography, topically arranged, of more than 800 books and articles, about the soldiers and their families. A comprehensive index also aids readers in quickly finding specific information, and numerous photographs help bring the words to life.

Despite the neglect that the so-called Indian-fighting army sometimes suffered, literature about the subject is rich, varied, and sophisticated. Aside from the massive records contained in government documents that serve as the official eye on nineteenth century military life, the writings of veterans themselves are numerous. Officers and their wives published excellent accounts of their experiences, complete with their prejudices and innermost thoughts. Others maintained diaries and assembled large collections of family letters which often provide even more insight into their personal feelings. Because these writings were never intended for publication, they often retain a degree of forthrightness underrepresented in other publications. Fortunately, family members and historians have discovered these valuable documents in more recent decades, have edited and augmented them with further information, and have published them to the delight of researchers and armchair historians.

The authentic voices of enlisted men have not fared as well in the nineteenth or twentieth centuries. Because many of these men bordered on illiterate, they were not likely to write autobiographical accounts for circulation by celebrated publishing houses. Nor were reading audiences interested enough in the lives of these common folk to warrant a spate of their published works. While this earlier myopia in unfortunate, the articulation of enlisted men's viewpoints does exist in alternative sources. Historian Don Rickey, Jr., tapped that resource and located equally obscure primary accounts when he published *Forty Miles a Day on Beans and Hay: The Enlisted Soldier Fighting the Indian Wars* in 1963. The largest stand of letters and reminiscences of nineteenth century army life were found by Rickey in the pages of *Winners of the West*, a newspaper published between 1923 and 1944. The publication, originally intended as a strong lobbying voice to increase federal pensions for Indian war veterans, attracted hundreds of responses from former officers and enlisted men alike.

Published in Saint Joseph, Missouri, by George and Lorena Jane Webb, *Winners of the West* offered a unique forum for veterans to speak of past memories and current financial concerns. The newspaper became the official publication of the National Indian War Veterans organization, which had been chartered in Denver, Colorado in 1911. Dedicated to "The Men Who Protected the Frontier," it attracted donations and mounted a congressional lobbying campaign to eliminate unfairness within the Bureau of Pensions. Furthermore, it encouraged veterans to publish letters and reminiscences within the newspaper to reestablish contacts with former comrades who would see the correspondence. Hundreds of former regulars, including many enlisted men, not only provided pension information to *Winners of the West* but also created a highly personalized record of army life. Their observations appear frequently throughout *The American Army in Transition, 1865–1898*, as do the words of other soldiers who published similar articles in the *Journal of the U.S. Cavalry Association,* the *Army and Navy Journal,* and the *Journal of the Military Service Institution of the United States* during the late nineteenth century.

The goal of this newly published synthesis of life in the army between the Civil War and the Spanish-American War is to correct the notion that this was an unimportant era of military inactivity. Officers and enlisted men served crucial roles—both noble and ignoble—in the development of America during the new industrial age. They were, as historian Francis Paul Prucha reminds us, the right arm of the federal government in its expansionist policies and the most visible symbol of national authority in the West. It is in this larger context that the institution must be evaluated, not through the romanticized cinematic prism of John Ford's "cavalry trilogy," nor through the neglectful eye that has relegated the army to a position of unimportance in more cynical recent decades, as popularized by the disciples of the New Western History.

Above all, this study endeavors to be a good read, edifying to scholars and lay readers alike. It will hopefully sharpen present generations' understanding of military life as it was experienced over a century ago. Utilizing soldiers' own voices where possible, it speaks to the diversity of viewpoints, life styles, and duties experienced by officers and the ranks. It challenges notions of a one-dimensional Indian-fighting army, while simultaneously documenting combat realities that faced all men at arms. Furthermore, it demonstrates that, when *all* of its distinct roles are discussed in a holistic way, the army of the late nineteenth century emerges as a significant institution at the center of important, historical, national change.

TIMELINE

May 1862	Congress passes Homestead Act that will hasten settlement of Great Plains in following four decades and will provoke western Indian tribes to resistance.
November 29, 1864	Massacre of Southern Cheyennes at Sand Creek, Colorado, sets off years of retaliation by Sioux and Cheyennes.
May 1865	Grand Parade of U.S. Army in Washington, DC, to celebrate end of Civil War.
October 1865	United States strongly urges that France withdraw occupation troops from Mexico.
1866	Congress authorizes 10 regiments of cavalry, 19 regiments of infantry, 5 regiments of artillery, and 1,000 Indian scouts, though inadequate funding precluded formation of all authorized units.
1866	Congress authorizes Commissary Department to sell foodstuffs to army personnel at cost to facilitate greater diversity in soldiers' diets.
1866	War on Bozeman Trail leads to Capt. William Fetterman's disaster at Ft. Philip Kearny (December 21) and victory for Sioux.
1866	Army Corps of Engineers begins extensive harbor and reclamation work on Columbia and Willamette rivers, the first of many western river improvement projects by the corps in the decades to follow.
1867	One-third of entire U.S. Army is stationed in the South for Reconstruction duty.
1867	Medicine Lodge Treaty establishes ranges of southern Plains tribes but fails to properly represent their needs.

March 1867	Last French troops leave Mexico, and on June 19, Emperor Maximilian is executed by order of Benito Juárez.
September 1868	Maj. George A. Forsyth and approximately 50 militiamen and scouts hold off superior number of Cheyennes at battle of Beecher's Island in northeastern Colorado before being rescued by elements of 10th Cavalry.
November 1868	Lt. Col. George Custer's attack on Southern Cheyenne village at Washita in western Indian Territory results in death of Peace Chief Black Kettle and others.
1868	Treaty of Ft. Laramie marks Sioux victory as soldiers surrender Bozeman Trail forts, and territories of various northern Plains tribes are designated.
May 1869	Union Pacific Railroad and Central Pacific Railroad meet at Promontory Summit, Utah, linking East and West by transcontinental rail. Army exercised primary role in protecting survey and construction crews.
1870	Col. Albert J. Myer promotes passage of legislation to establish a national weather service through the aegis of the Army Signal Corps.
1870	Congress outlaws "striker system," whereby officers employed enlisted men as cooks and personal servants during their off-duty hours, but the directive generally was not enforced.
1871	Congress ends its treaty making with Indian tribes as tribes are increasingly treated as wards of the government rather than as sovereign nations.
April 1871	Camp Grant Massacre occurs when large force of Tucson, Arizona, civilians attacks peaceful Aravaipa and Pinal Apache camps on reservation and kills 144 Indians, mostly women and children. Lt. Royal Whitman had given his word he would protect the Indians, but he had inadequate troops to do so.
1871	Army performs policing and recovery work in Chicago following the great fire.
May 1873	Col. Ranald Mackenzie attacks Kickapoo and Lipan Apache village near Remolino in Coahuila, Mexico, to prevent further cross-border raiding of southwest Texas.
1873	Brief but bloody Modoc War in northern California results in small Modoc population being forcibly removed to northeastern Indian Territory.
1874	Lt. Col. George Armstrong Custer's massive exploration of Black Hills sets off mining rush and wrath of Sioux and Cheyenne who regard this as sacred Paha Sapa.
1874	First U.S. military prison is opened at Ft. Leavenworth, Kansas, to handle serious offenders within the army.
1874	Congress approves bill to fund army construction of 1,218 miles of military telegraph lines throughout Texas to

	better coordinate military activities and to serve civilian interests.
1874	Soldiers participate in relief efforts following major Mississippi River floods.
1874–1875	Army is victorious in Red River War over Comanches, Kiowas, and Southern Cheyennes in Texas panhandle, thus ending major warfare on southern plains. Major battles and skirmishes include Adobe Walls (June 27), Wichita Agency (August 22–23), Lyman Wagon Train (September 9–14), Buffalo Wallow (September 12), and Palo Duro Canyon (September 28).
1874–1875	Army provides large amounts of food and other supplies to Plains states affected by catastrophic locust invasion.
summer 1876	Three-pronged military offensive against Sioux and Northern Cheyennes leads to Crook's defeat at Rosebud Creek and Custer's debacle at Little Big Horn.
1876–1877	Army's relentless summer through winter campaign against Sioux and Northern Cheyennes forces most onto reservation or temporary escape to Canada. The most important battles are at Warbonnet Creek (July 7), Slim Buttes (September 9), and Red Fork of the Powder River (November 25).
April 1877	President Rutherford B. Hayes begins removing last federal occupation troops from Reconstruction South.
1877	Officers and enlisted men go without pay for five months because of congressional debates about army appropriations bill related to the last phases of Southern Reconstruction.
1877	Henry Ossian Flipper, first black cadet to graduate from West Point, takes assignment with the 10th Cavalry.
1877	Troops sent to El Paso, Texas, to prevent further bloodshed in "Salt War" between Anglo and Hispanic residents.
summer 1877	General Railroad Strike spreads across nation, and army is used to protect federal mail but is accused of supporting railroad management against striking laborers.
1877	Army pursues Chief Joseph and other Nez Percés who had been unfairly forced from their reservation and were fleeing toward Canada. Nez Percé finally defeated at battle of Bear Paw Mountain, Montana, and many sent to small reservation in northeastern Indian Territory.
1878	Lincoln County War in New Mexico sets off wave of violence that provokes intervention by army and allegations of military partisanship in bloody feud.
1878–1879	Northern Cheyennes leave their Indian Territory reservation, where many were dying from harsh conditions, and set out for their homes in Montana. Fight series of running battles across Kansas with civilians and soldiers before

being captured and confined in guardhouse at Ft. Robinson, Nebraska. Their breakout in January 1879 results in more deaths before one group made it to Pine Ridge Reservation and other group eventually reestablished reservation on Tongue River in Montana.

1879   Gen. George Crook sends troops to Hastings, Nebraska, to make sure that cowboy friends of Isom Prentice "Print" Olive do not shoot up the town during Olive's trial for murder.

September–October 1879   Ute uprising in western Colorado leads to death of Agent Nathan Meeker and battle of Milk Creek, where Maj. Thomas T. Thornburgh was also killed. Utes defeated and forced to relocate to new reservations in Utah and southwest Colorado.

1879–1880   Army pursues Victorio and other Mimbres Apaches across southern New Mexico and western Texas until Victorio and many of his people are killed by Mexican militia at battle of Tres Castillos in northern Mexico (October 15–16, 1880).

1883   Congress authorizes army to patrol the three national parks and grants limited power to arrest illegal poachers, miners, grazers, and timber cutters.

1884   *The Soldier's Handbook* is published to help standardize army regulations and to make information more accessible.

1885   Soldiers are sent to Rock Springs, Wyoming, to protect Chinese miners from violent race riot. Followed by similar anti-Chinese riots in Seattle and Tacoma, both responded to by federal troops.

1885   Elizabeth Custer publishes *"Boots and Saddles," or Life in Dakota with General Custer,* the first book in her trilogy that celebrated western military life and lionized her husband.

1886   Final surrender of Geronimo and his small group of Apache followers. They, as well as the Apache scouts who had been so loyal to the government during the pursuit of Geronimo, are sent to confinement in Florida.

1890   Ghost Dance spiritual movement of Wovoka (Paiute) spreads among Great Plains tribes. The message of cultural revitalization and worldy intervention by the Great Spirit are interpreted by some Sioux in a more militaristic way.

December 1890   Sioux police kill Sitting Bull while trying to arrest him, and his death spreads panic among Sioux Ghost Dancers, who flee toward Pine Ridge Reservation.

December 1890   Wounded Knee Massacre of Sioux families at Wounded Knee Creek, South Dakota, marks last major combat of fabled Indian wars. Overreaction by agents, local press, and the army leads to needless deaths of mostly noncombatants.

1891   By this date, the majority of western forts have been closed because the so-called Indian threats have been removed, and Congress forces the War Department to trim its budget.

1891   All-Indian units recruited into regular army, but experiment is terminated in 1897.

1892   Troops are used in Wyoming's Johnson County War to separate feuding groups of cattlemen and homesteaders but are viewed locally as supporters of wealthy cattle barons.

1893   Congress eliminates funding for all contract surgeons and reduces the number of assistant surgeons from 125 to 95, thus marking a substantial decrease in the size of the Medical Department.

1894   Pullman Strike causes dispatch of 2,000 federal troops to Chicago to maintain order and eventually to key railroad towns throughout the West to protect railroad property.

1894   Lacey Act strengthens army power to enforce federal rules in national parks.

1898   Many western forts virtually abandoned as troops march away to Spanish-American War. A significant number are not reoccupied after the war as focus on the so-called frontier era declines.

1 OVERVIEW: RESHAPING THE U.S. ARMY AFTER THE CIVIL WAR

The U.S. Army was born amid adverse circumstances that required the coordination of political and military efforts representing 13 loosely unified governments. Despite the novelty of their independence struggle and their sometimes childish failure to cooperate with each other, the 13 British colonies of North America defeated the world's preeminent power of the late eighteenth century. In the wake of that victory, Americans emerged with two cherished principles regarding the future of their nation. First, they would never tolerate a large standing army, such as the occupying force that Great Britain had imposed on them after 1763. Second, the United States would place its security in the hands of citizen-soldiers like the ones who had emerged from the small-town militias at the time of the battles of Lexington and Concord. Both doctrines therefore guaranteed that the nineteenth-century American military establishment would be relatively small, tightly controlled by congressional budgetary action, and democratically managed so as to encourage the enlistment and promotion of men from all social classes.

Although the beginning of the nineteenth century witnessed two potentially hostile European nations still situated on America's immediate borders, few citizens favored any significant increase in army or navy personnel. When war did break out with Britain in 1812, the nation relied again on militia units composed of state volunteers, a pattern that would be repeated in the subsequent wars of 1846, 1861, and 1898. Following each of these victories, citizens again embraced the concept of citizen-soldiers as preferable to a large and elitist army. At the end of the Civil War, Ulysses S. Grant, a man who had witnessed firsthand the shortcomings of militia units and a fragmented command system, reaffirmed his faith in the supposed wisdom of the Founding Fathers. Writing in his personal memoirs, published in 1886, Grant remarked that men who fought for a cause dear to their hearts and alongside their friends and relatives would always prove to be better soldiers than those professionals who merely served in the ranks for pay or some other material inducement.[1]

A CALL FOR SIGNIFICANT CHANGES IN THE ARMY

Yet the conduct of the Civil War had raised legitimate concerns among a significant percentage of West Point–trained officers. Rather than viewing 1861–1862 battlefield reverses as a reflection of incompetence among senior commanders, these Union officers questioned the overall dynamics of the American system. Leading these postwar critics was Lt. Col. Emory Upton, who attributed many of the tactical blunders to the nation's overreliance on citizen-soldiers, the lack of professionalization of most of their officers, and the continuous interference of politicians into military decision making. In his posthumously published book, *The Military Policy of the United States from 1775* (1904), Upton challenged venerable American myths about the invincibility of minutemen when arrayed against British regulars during the American Revolution. He further objected to the notion that the Continental Congress had steered the colonies to victory by providing the proper political and economic guidance that made military success possible. The well-intentioned but erroneous reliance on militiamen and political interference in command decisions had, according to Upton, endangered American military efforts in the War of 1812, the Mexican War, and the Civil War.

To answer the nation's future military needs, he called for a complete reversal of existing philosophies, one that would forever put away the fear of large standing armies and a professionalized officer corps. In contrast to the questionable performance of state militias in prior wars, he documented how the regular army had achieved a meritorious service record for over a half century.[2] To drive the issue home to his audience, Upton concluded that "regular troops, engaged for the war, are the only safe reliance of a government, and are in every point of view, the best and most economical."[3]

Following his return from a world inspection tour, Upton published *The Armies of Asia and Europe* (1878), in which he challenged fellow citizens to help modernize and expand the American army. In the future, he argued, soldiers would not be performing constabulary duty against small bands of nomadic Indians but rather would be facing large standing armies of hundreds of thousands of well-trained, well-equipped fighting men. To expect that part-time soldiers could somehow rise to this challenge was the height of arrogance, as was the nation's continued reliance on a military supply system that never emerged until long after a declaration of war had been issued. Furthermore, citizen-soldiers would not be able to master the rapidly improving industrial technology that was producing new weapons to make Napoleonic-era fighting tactics obsolete.[4]

Upton also questioned the brief service terms of militia units, sometimes as short as three months. All American wars fought between the Revolution and the Civil War had shown the folly of this policy, he contended. Commanders facing major battles watched helplessly as units completed their terms of service and set out for home, leaving active units vulnerable to enemy attacks. In some cases, senior officers had launched offensives before they were ready because they could not count on state regiments to remain on active duty once their required times had expired.[5]

Finally, in his declaration for modernizing the army, Upton cautioned that the secretary of war, a civilian, should no longer exercise power over purely tactical decisions since these were complex issues for which he had no training. Only in administrative and financial matters should the secretary of war play a significant role, and only after deliberation with senior military officers. Actual command of the army should be entrusted to the general-in-chief, who, by virtue of experience and accomplishment, would best be able to decide the larger issues relevant to achieving victory.[6]

The clarion call by Emory Upton for significant changes in the American military system certainly had relevance to the changing realities of the world, and indeed, his disciples strongly advocated these reforms on the eve of World War I. For the remainder of the nineteenth century, however, most Americans were content to preserve their traditional views of the army's proper place in society. The majority of politicians, thoughtful citizens, and even career officers sided with the philosophies articulated by John A. Logan. As a decorated volunteer officer during the Civil War, subsequently a U.S. Senator from Illinois and Republican vice presidential candidate of 1884, Logan's word carried considerable authority in any forum.

Senator Logan's position on the future of the army was partly a reflection of legitimate ideological concerns and partly attributable to a personal slight he had suffered in the Civil War. During the August 1864 fighting in and around Atlanta, Georgia, Logan had demonstrated courage and leadership as he turned back the assaults of Gen. John B. Hood. The bold actions taken by Maj. Gen. "Black Jack" Logan might well have assured him permanent command of the army, but the reward was not forthcoming. From that time forward, Logan carried with him the deep-seated belief that his promotion was denied simply because he was a volunteer officer rather than a West Point–trained graduate in the regular army. He greatly distrusted any postwar discussion of expanding the professional officer corps or increasing the size of the U.S. Army.[7]

The ultimate expression of Logan's strong beliefs appeared in his 1887 book *The Volunteer Soldier of America.* The ponderous tome, inelegantly written and poorly organized, placed faith in the militia system for guaranteeing success in America's future wars. It ridiculed the West Point officers for hiding behind a self-anointed cloak of "professionalization" when, in fact, most of their education and training made them no more fit leaders than the average officer who had emerged from the state volunteer forces. He paid homage to many specific military heroes, ranging from George Washington and William Henry Harrison to Zachary Taylor, all of whom had risen to illustrious careers without ever attending the U.S. Military Academy. Devoid of quantifiable proof, Logan also argued that West Point officers who graduated at the bottom of their class tended to do better in the field than those who performed admirably in the classroom. In short, the best officers of the future might well come from the public school system, where they would undertake rigorous physical training and learn the drill of an infantry soldier as a minimum exposure to military life. Citizen-soldiers would thus remain the protectors of America's future, just as they had been the guarantors of national security in the past.[8]

Logan's view prevailed, and the army of the late nineteenth century therefore closely resembled its antebellum predecessor in terms of structure and mission. Historian Robert Utley best described the reality for both eras when he concluded that "the United States Army was not so much a little army as a big police force."[9] True enough, it engaged in other activities, such as exploration, coastal defense, relief work for suffering civilians, and occasional suppression of civil insurrections, but none of these tasks necessitated the creation of a grand army on the scale of those seen in Europe. Despite all of its diverse contributions to society, the army's primary occupation remained the same as it had been when first created during the presidency of George Washington—to control the Indians on the western frontier.

THE CONFLICTING ROLES OF THE ARMY

In essence, the army had two seminal roles to fill: (1) protect settlers from Indian raids and (2) protect Indians from illegal advances of white people. The twofold effort was never a balanced one because federal officials yielded to stronger public pressures with each new generation and demanded that Native Americans surrender more of their land base and tribal cultures. Caught between the hammer of increased pressures to force all Indians onto reservations and the anvil of well-intentioned reformers who demanded civilian control over Indian affairs, the army could not satisfy either party. In the former case, frontiersmen berated army officers for allowing so-called renegades to use reservations as sanctuaries, from which they could sally forth and massacre innocent families and then return to the protection of the reservation. On the other hand, many reformers categorized soldiers as trigger-happy and vengeance-seeking martinets of special interest groups that wanted to quickly secure Indian lands by violent means.

In spite of the wave of criticism that came from both sides, the late-nineteenth-century army did learn from its frontier experiences to innovate new methods by trial and error. Commanders organized large winter offensives to defeat Indians by depriving them of dwellings, food, horses, and accoutrements at the most vulnerable time of the year. They experimented with pack mules to better transport supplies in the remote areas and with the heliograph to quickly relay messages in the field. They perfected the art of converging columns to force the Indians into smaller areas, where soldiers could mass for one or two decisive battles, rather than settling for many small and inconclusive skirmishes. They coordinated troop movements so as to control scarce water supplies and important mountain passes and river crossings so as to prevent the free movement of off-reservation Indians.

Finally, as in the case of Gen. George Crook and other innovators, they found ways to enlist sufficient numbers of Indian scouts to turn the tide of battle. Finding small groups of so-called renegades in such an enormous landscape required the kind of local knowledge that only Indians possessed. Sometimes the scouts were enlisted from tribes that had long-standing grievances against other tribes, and they eagerly cooperated with soldiers to manipulate their newfound alliances against old rivals. On other occasions, as Crook proved with his masterful use of Apache scouts, recruits came from within the many bands of Apaches to protect their interests against other bands and individual leaders.[10]

Amid these successful innovations, the army failed in one important way—it too often punished the innocent along with the guilty. Historian Robert Utley captured the irony of an army caught in the midst of unconventional warfare:

> Rather, the frontier army was a conventional military force trying to control, by conventional military methods, a people that did not behave like conventional enemies and, indeed, quite often were not enemies at all. Usually, the situation did not call for warfare, merely for policing. That is, offending individuals needed to be separated from the innocent and punished. But this the conventional force was unable to do. As a result, punishment often fell, when it fell at all, on guilty and innocent alike.[11]

How then does one, in the light of Utley's conclusion, evaluate the overall performance of the U.S. Army between 1865 and 1898? Certainly it was not the purely romantic institution fondly recalled in John Ford's movie trilogy of *Fort Apache* (1948), *She Wore a Yellow Ribbon* (1949), and *Rio Grande* (1950). Nor was it the brutal exterminator of Indians as presented in Ralph Nelson's *Soldier Blue* (1970), Arthur Penn's *Little Big Man* (1970), and Kevin Costner's *Dances with Wolves* (1990). Quite simply put, the army was one institution within a larger assemblage of policy-making bodies, and like the others, it mirrored the strengths and weaknesses of the entire American system. Because most policy makers and average citizens of the late nineteenth century saw their nation as virtually exempt from foreign conflicts, they perceived little need for a large, expensive, and professionalized army. Seemingly safe behind the twin walls offered by the Atlantic and Pacific oceans, they felt that the wisdom of the Founding Fathers was still operable as the century wore to a close. Public opinion still reflected a fear of European-style armies that could so easily impose tyranny on their peoples. Likewise, most Americans still believed that a constabulary of soldiers was adequate to police the frontiers against declining Indian problems. Should the nation ever again face a foreign power on the field of conventional warfare, the citizen-solder would again rise to the occasion and show the superiority of the American fighting man.

When that time came unexpectedly in 1898, the U.S. Army was not prepared for a war that involved combat in Cuba, Puerto Rico, Guam, and the Philippines. Again, the nation called on state volunteer forces to march into battle, and when victory came relatively easily after only three months of fighting, traditionalists felt vindicated for their faith in the traditional method of organizing, outfitting, and leading armies. Yet the sudden victory concealed the central weakness of the frontier army as it tried to meet the unknown challenges of the new century. The difference was that in the future, American troops would no longer face Indian opponents, but rather diverse peoples within the New American Empire. Spain had not offered a true test to the American military system in 1898, but events in Europe would lead the world to disaster in 1914, and Americans would be woefully unprepared for the new demands of a highly technological war. During the darkest days of World War I, veterans of the Old Army could fondly remember their service to the country during the so-called Indian-fighting days. But they would also have to ponder how much the world had changed during their lifetimes and how much the military establishment would have to change to meet the new realities.

NOTES

1. Ulysses S. Grant, *Personal Memoirs of U.S. Grant,* vol. 2 (New York: Charles I. Webster, 1886), 531.

2. Emory Upton, *The Military Policy of the United States from 1775* (Washington, DC: U.S. Government Printing Office, 1904), 23–24, 67, 256–57.

3. Ibid., 67.

4. Ibid., 67, 234, 259–60, 420. Emory Upton, *The Armies of Asia and Europe* (New York: D. Appleton, 1878). Allan R. Millett and Peter Maslowski, *For the Common Defense: A Military History of the United States of America* (New York: Free Press, 1984), 255–58.

5. Upton, *Military Policy,* 67, 245.

6. Ibid., 263, 323.

7. Russell F. Weigley, *Towards an American Army: Military Thought from Washington to Marshall* (New York: Columbia University Press, 1962), 128–29.

8. Ibid., 128–35. John A. Logan, *The Volunteer Soldier of America* (Chicago: R. S. Peale, 1887). Relevant coverage of early militia activities appear in Jim Dan Hill, *The Minute Man in Peace and War: A History of the National Guard* (Harrisburg, PA: Stackpole, 1964), 1–31, 99–137; and Martha Derthick, *The National Guard in Politics* (Cambridge, MA: Harvard University Press, 1965), 15–27.

9. Robert M. Utley, "The Frontier Army: John Ford or Arthur Penn?" In *Indian–White Relations: A Persistent Paradox,* ed. Jane F. Smith and Robert M. Kvasnicka (Washington, DC: Howard University Press, 1976), 135–36.

10. Robert M. Utley, *Frontier Regulars: The United States Army and the Indian, 1866–1891* (New York: Macmillan, 1973), 53–56.

11. Utley, "Frontier Army," 142.

2   FROM GLORY TO AMBIGUITY: RECRUITMENT OF A PEACETIME ARMY

The American Civil War proved to be the defining moment in nineteenth-century American life. In addition to ending slavery, overturning legalistic arguments about the right of secession, and expanding federal powers, the end of the conflict produced a radically redefined role for the U.S. Army. The enlistment of over one and a half million Union soldiers during those 4 tumultuous years contrasted sharply with the previous 70 years of national existence. Between the presidencies of George Washington and James Buchanan, the size of the American army had never exceeded 18,000 authorized troops, and military budgets had remained relatively small throughout the extended period. Most of these men had served in coastal defense units and in the isolated military posts of a rapidly expanding frontier that by 1848 reached from the Mississippi River to the Pacific Ocean. Furthermore, these "peacetime" regiments had rarely operated at their authorized levels, so in many instances, two or more undermanned companies had to be merged into single units to reach operational status.[1]

The Civil War, with its massive recruitment drive and virtually limitless expenditures, lifted the army from virtual obscurity to an institution associated with national honor. Yet when the war ended, the overwhelming majority of veterans sought quick separation from military duty and an immediate return to civilian life. Even more rapidly than it had been mustered into service after the first battle of Bull Run, the army began its transformation into an attenuated force. Unfortunately, it soon became associated with the controversial military occupation of the formerly rebellious South and with the ever-frustrating campaigns against western Indian tribes. In the eyes of many Americans, the army again became virtually invisible or, in some cases, was viewed as an incompetent organization unable to corral relatively small numbers of "savages" on the Plains and in the Southwest. When, in 1885, a cultured society matron was introduced to a colonel of the army, she exclaimed in disbelief, "What, a colonel of the Army? Why, I supposed the Army was all disbanded at the close of the war!"[2] Although her incredulity was extreme, this refined lady articulated some of the same astonishment that vast numbers of Americans felt in the "era of peace" from 1865 to 1898.

A group of soldiers during the American Civil War. Only a tiny fraction of Civil War veterans served in the frontier army. (*Courtesy of the National Archives*)

The quick demobilization of the army was more than an anecdotal perception of events; the trend was indelibly documented in the statistical tables. As of May 1, 1865, barely three weeks after Robert E. Lee's surrender at Appomattox, 1,034,064 soldiers were still in federal service. By mid-November, 800,963 of these men had been paid and mustered out. Within a year, the total number of troops on duty had shrunk to a miniscule 11,043.[3] This trend brought the size of the army back to modest pre–Civil War levels and indicated that government officials were content to turn the hands of the clock back to the time of a small regular army, existing on an even smaller budget.

The return to a philosophy of "less is better" partly owed its existence to intellectual patterns established during the American Revolution. Since the days of British colonial domination, the American public had feared that large standing armies assembled during peacetime represented a threat to democratic institutions and individual freedoms.[4] The Founding Fathers continued this tradition of small armies, a democratized officer corps, and financial dependence on Congress. Periodic efforts to increase the size of the force during the antebellum period accordingly were rebuffed by Congress, the White House, and public opinion.

While the nation lionized the veterans of the Civil War, and groups such as the Grand Army of the Republic gradually increased their lobbying power, soldiers of the peacetime army came to feel that they were taken for granted by an uninformed and uncaring public. An article appearing in a September 1877 issue of *Army and Navy Journal* demanded increased funding for the suffering soldiers. Yet it also pessimistically declared, "The present trouble with the Army is that it is separated from the knowledge and affections of the people who pay the taxes, and is only seen from year to year in the form of heavy appropriations."[5]

This estrangement between citizens and soldiers was echoed time and again by officers who saw the manpower and economic problems firsthand. Speaking before an 1878 congressional committee about the army's need for better public relations, Gen. John Pope concluded that unless the American people could better understand the army's assigned role and its limitations, contentiousness would further undermine military effectiveness.[6] While officers generally stressed the misconceptions that harmed public policy making, enlisted men more often pointed to the fundamental flaw that civilians routinely looked down on soldiers as little better than the dregs of society. One enlisted man wrote in 1877, "Let a regular soldier go into any of the cities of the States and you will see all the citizens stick up their noses." Commenting similarly during the following year, Pvt. Daniel Barrow reported in the New York *Herald,* "There are only two creatures who look upon a soldier here without scorn and contempt, and they are little children and dogs."[7] In describing the accidental drowning of a military mail courier near Ft. Richardson, Texas, an even more frustrated Sgt. Harry H. McConnell sarcastically remarked, "The loss of one soldier, however, more or less, is not of much importance to anybody, as a general thing, and is hardly worth recording."[8]

Even years after completing their service, enlisted men bitterly recalled this pattern of neglect at the hands of the government and the public at large. In a 1924 letter to *Winners of the West,* an advocacy publication for soldiers' pensions, former 12th Infantry Pvt. Charles Birnbaum reminisced about his years of difficult frontier duty. He then concluded with an equally harsh remembrance of how civilians routinely embarrassed Indian war veterans by insinuating that "there must be something wrong with a man who joined the regular army."[9] Likewise, Teresa Griffin Vielé, an officer's wife of the pre–Civil War era, called upon her readers to recognize the bravery and self-sacrifice of the small detachments that stood "like a chain of sentinels" across the enormous frontier lands.[10] But it was a crude inscription carved on a tombstone at Ft. Clark, Texas, that offered the most poignant message to a public that had long ignored its Indian war veterans:

> Oh pray for the soldier,
> You kind-hearted stranger;
> He has roamed the prairie for many a year.
> He has kept the Comanches away from your ranches,
> And followed them over the Texas frontier.[11]

Despite the level of neglect that soon would return to military appropriations, Congress began the post–Civil War era with a generous nod to the army. President Andrew Johnson signed the act during July 1866, which increased the cavalry from 6 to 10 regiments and the infantry from 19 to 45 regiments. The previously authorized five regiments of artillery remained the same in the new legislation. One new entity was also created: up to 1,000 Indian scouts who would serve as irregular forces and could be recruited as needed. Although no specific numbers were stated in this 1866 "Act to Increase and Fix the Military Peace Establishment of the United States," the sums that were calculated from the prescribed size and numbers of troops in each authorized company totaled 54,302 officers and enlisted men.[12]

Fully one-third of these troops were directed to Reconstruction duties in the South for the remainder of the 1860s, but the vast area of the Trans-Mississippi West occupied most of the War Department's attention. It was divided into two military divisions: Division of the Missouri, headquartered at St. Louis, and Division of the Pacific, headquartered at San Francisco. Within these were further divided the seven military departments. Although departmental boundaries would change according to army needs during the following three decades, the basic organizational scheme was maintained.[13]

RESTORING THE BUREAUCRACY

The War Department further resurrected the bureaucratic structures of the antebellum period with 10 administrative units. These ranged from the Quartermaster's Department, which oversaw the construction of buildings, procurement of goods, and transportation of personnel and supplies, to the Inspector General's Department, which made inspection tours of the far-flung posts to report on morale, discipline, living conditions, and possible malfeasance cases. Included in this spectrum of administrative bureaus were the departments of the Adjutant General, Judge Advocate General's Office, Subsistence, Medical, Pay, Ordnance, Signal Corps, and the Corps of Engineers.[14] Unfortunately, tensions were common between the "staff officers" who filled these War Department bureaucracies and the "line officers" who primarily served in the field. Line officers especially resented that their counterparts had undue political influence in the nation's capital and that they frequently promoted policies that served their narrow career interests but that proved unpopular and unrealistic among garrisons on the frontier. Furthermore, staff officers allegedly enjoyed greater privileges and comforts by virtue of their assignments in the larger cities of the nation. Their periodic inspections, heavy-handed regulations, and second-guessing of difficult decisions made under pressure in the field further alienated line officers, who suffered from the oppressive decisions.[15]

Even though the saga of the post–Civil War army most often has been related through the eyes and accomplishments of senior officers, the basic tactical unit that made the army work was at the company level. Enlisted men's first loyalty was always to their particular company, and units were often pitted against each other in both formal and informal competitions by regimental commanders. Some of the competitions were as innocent as a baseball game, but others were based upon important criteria, such as unit citations, battlefield commendations, and even reenlistment rates.

By terms of the 1866 legislation, all infantry and cavalry companies (called "troops" in the cavalry regiments) were set at 64 privates. Twelve years later, cavalry troops were raised to a maximum of 100 privates, though many units remained operationally well below the optimum figure. Whatever the size of the infantry company or cavalry troop, each one functioned as a self-contained social and military entity. Besides forging a group loyalty, the men of a single company also shared a sense of self-sufficiency. Accordingly, many companies and troops included their own tailor, cobbler, and barber. The men bunked together by company units, owed first allegiance to their own sergeants, and shared the collective fame and shame of their unit's performance.[16]

RECRUITING OFFICERS AND MEN

Recruitment of a new army for Reconstruction and frontier duty presented promising prospects as well as a new set of problems. In the former case, a large corps of trained officers stood ready to reenlist in the regular army now that their Civil War duties were completed. Unfortunately, the entire army was authorized to employ no more than 2,835 officers of all ranks. Appropriation bills of 1869 and 1870 made even further cuts in this optimum number.[17] Lt. Gen. William Tecumseh Sherman lamented the speed with which the federal government had mustered out of service virtually all volunteer units, many of whom had served on the Great Plains during the Civil War. To make matters worse, this downsizing occurred just at the moment that the Plains Indian wars were reaching a crescendo. Volunteer officers with Indian-fighting experience were being removed from military service, undermanned garrisons were left without adequate supplies and leadership, and eastern-bred officers could not receive commissions quickly enough to assume frontier commands.[18]

Recruitment of enlisted men presented a bigger problem because even though many experienced veterans existed in the pool of talent, relatively small numbers demonstrated any desire to continue their enlistments. Another flaw within the system was the so-called bounty jumper, who would sign up at an eastern enlistment station to receive a bonus and then disappear from the training depot after a few weeks, only to reenlist under another name at a different location. Sgt. Harry H. McConnell later described these larcenous individuals as "blackguards and criminals of various degrees" who gave the entire army a bad name.[19]

Pvt. C. C. Chrisman recalled that some of the 15 men who enlisted alongside him surely were former residents of a penitentiary, and he believed they should be returned there immediately. Indeed, of the 16 men in his recruit class, 14 deserted before completing their initial term of service.[20] Such unpatriotic behavior compelled the New York *Sun* to refer to the majority of enlisted men as "bummers, loafers and foreign paupers."[21] Yet not until October 1889 did the War Department implement a policy that background checks be performed on all new recruits.[22] The sentiment was a good one, but in an era when many people readily adopted aliases and when identification records were meager and widely dispersed, threats of background checks were unlikely to solve the problem.

Although negative judgments abounded about the possible criminal records of soldiers, some observers took the high road in praising the innate qualities of recruits. John F. Finerty, a journalist for the *Chicago Times* who accompanied General George Crook's command in the 1876 campaign against the Sioux, distinguished the positive characteristics that separated city-born from country-born enlistees. In highly opinionated fashion, he praised the former group for their superior "intelligence, courage and loyalty." The latter group seemed to him to have fewer faults and vices, thus making the country-bred recruits more receptive to discipline and training in the early stages of military life. Both, however, rated about equal in matters of endurance.[23]

Col. George Forsyth recalled many years later the diverse backgrounds of the enlisted men who accompanied him on wagon escort duty in December 1865. The anecdotal list included "a bookkeeper, a farm boy, a dentist, and a blacksmith, a young man of position trying to gain a commission and a salesman ruined by drink, an ivory carver and a Bowery tough."[24] The list seems fairly representative of the saints and sinners who might have been employed by any sizable American institution during the late nineteenth century.

Just as the backgrounds of soldiers were diverse, so were their motivations for joining the army. In the period between 1865 and 1898, economic factors appear to have been the most frequently mentioned reasons. First Cavalryman William Hustede left a 2-dollar-per-week grocery store job to seek the 13-dollar-per-month army pay. Another enlistee from the nation's capital was so dissatisfied with his 16-hour day at a salary of 50 cents per day that he also sought out military employment.[25] Charles Cheek, a black

Pvt. C. C. Chrisman's sketches of six hated duties that soldiers faced—drill, kitchen police, post cleanup, construction detail, guard duty, and guardhouse. (*Courtesy Arizona Historical Society/Tucson/MS0152*)

farm laborer, happily joined the army as a way of avoiding "looking mules in the face from sunrise to sunset" for the rest of his life.[26]

Other recruits viewed military service not as a mere short-term answer to their economic problems, but rather as part of a strategy for fulfilling long-term ambitions. Samuel Harris, an enterprising black man from Washington, D.C., joined the army in hopes that he could attain an impeccable service record so that he someday could petition for a lucrative and comfortable government job.[27] Matthew A. Batson turned to the army after he ran out of money to complete his legal studies. William Bladen Jett followed the same plan when he exhausted his funds for medical school. Both men set about to prove themselves and gain commissions as officers so that they could make careers of soldiering.[28]

Other men joined to escape special pressures in their lives. Pvt. Harry Thayer ran away from home because of his parents' relentless badgering for him to attend college. James Reagles Jr., who had served as a surgeon during the Civil War, reenlisted in 1866 to elude the unhappy remembrances of a failed courtship. Many left home and sought the soldier's life to avoid debts and punishments for crimes. Ironically, some European immigrants left their native countries to avoid harsh military service, only to wind up joining the U.S. Army when better job prospects proved elusive.[29]

The promise of job skills also lured some men into the army. Sgt. Theodore Guy, who aspired to someday become a lawyer, signed the enlistment papers so that he could learn to read and write the English language to overcome his handicap as an illiterate Polish immigrant. Another man, recently made unemployed by the Panic of 1873, joined the military as a way of improving his math, reading, and vocabulary skills. He hoped that these tools would help him land a good job upon completion of his military tenure. He was apparently quite committed to the plan as he studied vocabulary words from a pocket dictionary even during field campaigns.[30]

While many men had very specific reasons for seeking military service, some merely joined out of a general spirit of patriotism and adventure. When he signed the enlistment papers in 1871, British traveler Jacob Howarth did so under the mistaken impression that Indian fighting would bring him thrills and glory. He spent five miserable years at Ft. Griffin, on the west Texas frontier, where he occasionally participated in scouting patrols, mail escort duty, and protecting surveyors. Yet not once did he ever see a hostile Indian, much less engage in combat with one. With great relief, he left the army upon completion of the single term of service and returned to Great Britain.[31]

Equally desirous of the adventurous life, along with an eventual commission into the officers' ranks, was Pvt. William Bladen Jett. Raised in a prominent Virginia family that provided him with social status and a good education, Jett hardly seemed to be a candidate desperate to join the enlisted ranks. Combining his love of horses and his desire for experiencing the exotic western landscape, he was delighted to sign the papers making him a member of the cavalry. On the second day of service, after watching a hot-tempered officer curse a recruit and threaten him with the ball and chain, young Jett was eager to depart the army. He spent the next five years "serving his sentence" until he could legally sever his relationship with Uncle Sam's horse soldiers.[32]

Mixed with the innate appeal to patriotism that abounded at recruiting stations were the persuasive promises made by the recruiting officers. A ditty entitled "The Old Army Guardhouse Song" depicted a recently arrived immigrant who observed the crowds surrounding a New York City recruitment office, complete with flags waving and bands playing. The naïve young man received a full dose of propaganda about glory, camaraderie with other young men, and promises of quick promotion so that he enlisted without further thought. The song's following words served as his revenge against lying recruiters:

> May the devil take the sergeant and his circumventin' crew
> Who seduced me to the rendezvous and dressed me up in blue.[33]

At the heart of so many soldiers' disenchantment with the military was their own gullibility about what constituted typical military life. Most expected discipline, but not of the magnitude that governed virtually every hour of their existence. Savvy officers and noncoms of long service offered the best advice to naïve young men. When Capt. Simon Snyder learned that one of his relatives was contemplating enlistment, he wrote to his own mother to prevent the action at all costs because the boy would "regret such a move as long as he is in the ranks."[34] Capt. John G. Bourke also tried to deflate false patriotic notions in his 1891 classic book *On the Border with Crook.* Even though the autobiographical work was filled with stories of army combat against fierce Apache, Sioux, and Cheyenne warriors, Bourke warned potential enlistees not to expect an exciting life or one that produced honors from a grateful nation.[35]

Of all the warnings issued against the false impressions about military life, the sarcastic words of Sgt. Harry H. McConnell of the 6th Cavalry rang the truest:

> If these sketches should ever meet the eye of some youth who burns for military glory or hankers to go West and lead the "idle and lazy life of a soldier," I would like to give him a "pointer" that if he can find some soft and easy job working on a railroad for ten hours a day with a pick and shovel driving a scraper, or pushing a wheelbarrow, he had better embrace that opening.[36]

"Buyer beware" might well have been the most appropriate sign to display prominently at the recruiting stations because too many young men enlisted under false illusions and groundless promises.

ETHNICITY IN THE RANKS

Since numerous immigrants joined the U.S. Army in the three decades after the Civil War, ethnicity was commonly discussed in the ranks. A recent random sample of 1,040 white enlisted men reveals that 42.3 percent were born in Europe. A second tabulation of those either born in Europe or possessing at least one foreign-born parent raises the total of first- and second-generation immigrant soldiers to 62.1 percent. Among this sample, 71.8 percent of the first-generation immigrants were either Irish or German.[37]

Utilizing a different sample from the 16th Infantry, historian Robert Bluthardt concluded that during the years 1866–1869, foreign-born enlisted men constituted 40 percent of Company F, and between 1880 and 1890, the totals reached 49 percent.[38] Ratios of foreign-born soldiers declined somewhat during the following decade because a new regulation was enacted in 1894, requiring that all new first-time recruits be U.S. citizens, intend to become citizens, or, at least, be able to read, write, and speak the English language. During slim recruiting periods, the regulation was waived, however, so that projected quotas could be attained.[39]

The most concrete numbers assembled by the War Department regarding ethnicity were published in 1876 and were drawn from the enlistment records maintained between January 1, 1865, and December 31, 1876. Although these include men who were mustered into service during the last three months of the Civil War, the figures accurately reflect the ratios that were common to the peacetime army. They include the following countries of nativity: United States (96,066); Ireland (38,649); Germany (23,127); England (9,037); and Canada (4,703). These statistics do not distinguish American-born soldiers who had at least one foreign-born parent. Thus second-generation enlistees are included under the category of the United States.[40]

The lion's share of what was written during the late nineteenth century about ethnicity in the army was matter-of-fact, and only rarely did the discussion exemplify the passionate hatred that governed the broader nativistic trends in American society. British-born journalist and adventurer Henry M. Stanley wrote proudly of the diverse troops he met at Ft. Harker, Kansas, in 1867, pronouncing the post to be a "miniature world, a faithful duplicate of the big world we live in." But unlike in the broader world, where conflict between ethnic groups and nation states was common, he found only harmony in the frontier community.[41]

Despite the infrequency of violence between European ethnic groups, stereotypical affirmations revealed a more subtle form of prejudice just beneath the surface of military life. Gen. James Parker clearly favored the Irish as "more intelligent and resourceful as a rule."[42] Equally flattering was Sgt. Harry H. McConnell, who evidenced his own ethnic preferences when he wrote, "I think I am impartial when I say the Irishman is by far the best soldier in our army." He went on to single out the Irish veterans for their leadership abilities, quick learning skills, obedience to superiors, strong bodies, and cheerfulness in the face of privation and danger. His description of German soldiers was not so kind. In establishing the pecking order for routine duties, McConnell suggested giving the Irishman a pick or shovel, the American an axe, and for the lowly German, his task should be to pull weeds by hand because "it's all the —— fellow is good for."[43] Lt. Col. Alfred A. Woodhull saw things differently when he contrasted the grumbling, laziness, and insubordination of British immigrants with the patience and trustworthiness of German recruits.[44] In short, despite the ethnic stereotypes that abounded, no one view dominated over all the others. Nor did rigid ethnic loyalties divide American troops in any significant way.[45]

RECRUIT DEPOTS AND INITIAL TRAINING

For both native- and foreign-born men, specially created recruit depots were the important transition points from civilian to military life. Future cavalrymen generally passed through Jefferson Barracks, Missouri, and infantrymen went through either David's Island, New York, or Columbus Barracks, Ohio. Until it was closed in the early 1870s, Newport Barracks, Kentucky, also served as an initial assembly point for new infantrymen. In 1894, the army abolished these depots in favor of sending all recruits directly to their assigned regiments for training.[46]

Even before being sent to the appropriate depot, each recruit was subjected to a health inspection by a medical officer. In addition to answering questions about his background, he was examined for deformed limbs, visible tumors or ulcers on the legs, rupture, inadequate hearing or vision, infectious disorders, and organic diseases, such as tuberculosis. The worst cases were rejected, but the doctors were given great latitude in deciding what condition was acceptable and what was not. Since the army had already spent considerable time and money getting these men into the recruitment cycle, the emphasis was on accepting the highest number possible. Those with chronic medical problems could be released from service at some future time if absolutely necessary, but for now, they helped fill the quotas that were deemed so important.[47]

After taking their oaths of allegiance at the depot, all of the men were officially considered soldiers of the regular army. Their training was demanding and unrelenting, both in terms of the physical requirements and the mental strain. Marching and drilling were their constant companions throughout the depot experience, even for men who had some previous military experience. During the first two decades after the Civil War, soldiers were expected to learn all procedures and regulations by observation. Finally, in 1884, the pocket-sized manual *The Soldier's Handbook* was published to help standardize regulations and to make the information more accessible.[48]

The recruit depot experience was the first step in making soldiers out of civilians, and according to the philosophy of the time, it was intended to be a punitive and disorienting transformation. Pvt. William Bladen Jett contended that his stay at Jefferson Barracks was more like a prison environment. Officers ruled in an autocratic fashion, frequently assaulting recruits with vile words and physical attacks. They seemed to have no concern for the welfare of the men or in easing their transition into the soldier's life.[49] Augustus Meyers recalled his own experiences that went back to 1854, when he was recruited as a drummer boy at age 12. Despite his youthful age, he was subjected to the same hazing that the older men were. During his mock "blanket court martial," he was forced to answer numerous charges about bogus crimes and then was subjected to a jerking away of the blanket on which he stood. The "punishment" was "both rough and dangerous," and Meyers was left very sore after the assault.[50] Such incidents of harassment usually continued for awhile, even after the men reached their regiments, and this was considered to be part of the breaking-in process.[51]

The training of troops was a never-ending cycle of monotony, and it was the source of grumbling at every post. In truth, much of the excessive training was aimed not so much at polishing combat skills, but rather at occupying much of the idle time that faced soldiers everywhere. Each military installation followed a regular order of duties from Monday to Saturday. In accordance with honoring the Sabbath and for raising morale, these duties were significantly reduced or eliminated altogether on Sundays.

During the weekdays, rigid schedules set the order of activities. Bugle calls that began with the assembly of trumpeters at 5:20 A.M. and ended with the call for extinguishing lights at 9:30 P.M. alerted men to move from one set of routines to another. Depending on the needs of the post and the special assignments given to specific companies and individual soldiers, drill and fatigue duty dominated each day's activities with monotonous regularity.[52] The latter may have been even more hated than drill because fatigue was associated with nonmartial tasks. These included cleaning stables, hauling water, cutting wood, kitchen work, serving as room orderlies, and attending to whatever needs the officers identified. Andrew Flynn, an enlisted man of the Seventh Cavalry who later served in the 1890 Wounded Knee campaign, noted that troops stationed at Ft. Riley, Kansas, in 1888 were particularly perturbed when a large group

Soldiers with the 6th U.S. Cavalry train horses under rifle fire at Fort Bayard, New Mexico Territory, ca. 1885. (*Courtesy of the National Archives*)

of them were sent to pull up 10-foot-high sunflowers that had taken root on the parade ground. Bristling at the demeaning labor, they declared that they had joined the army to be soldiers, not gardeners.[53]

Even officers complained about the disproportionate amount of fatigue duty that did little to sharpen military skills. In testimony before a subcommittee of the House of Representatives in 1878, Lt. Col. Edmund H. Rice noted that at some of the smaller forts, soldiers went virtually without drill because all their time was devoted to keeping up the buildings and grounds.[54]

MARKSMANSHIP TRAINING AND EQUIPMENT

One occupation that did satisfy virtually all soldiers, while improving a vital martial skill, was marksmanship training. Cavalrymen practiced with revolvers by shooting at hardtack boxes while advancing on horseback first at a walk, then a trot, and then at a gallop. Infantrymen practiced with rifles and carbines by shooting at bull's-eyes ranging from 8 to 36 inches in diameter. They fired from different distances, usually ranging from 100 to 500 yards, and were expected to hit the target at least half the time.[55]

The biggest impediment to regular marksmanship drill was the relatively high cost of ammunition. Because the War Department faced lean budgets throughout the late nineteenth century, it never provided enough ammunition to its soldiers for adequate target practice. Gen. Edward S. Godfrey recalled his years as a lieutenant when he commanded two new Gatling guns that were taken to the 1867 Medicine Lodge treaty conference in southwestern Kansas. He wanted to allow his inexperienced crews to take some target practice and also to impress the Indians with the gun's unmatched firepower. Unfortunately, he did not follow through on the plan after his commanding officer made it clear that Godfrey might have to pay for the ammunition out of his own pocket.[56]

The immediate impact of ammunition shortages was bad marksmanship in units that received little target practice and rifle instruction. Pvt. David L. Spotts wrote in his diary about how soldiers of the 19th Kansas Volunteer Cavalry could not even hit buffalo with regularity, despite the fact that the massive beasts came within 50 feet of them. He explained that in the excitement of the moment, soldiers forgot to follow the basic rule of using their rear gun sites so as to avoid aiming too high.[57] Similarly, when a rattlesnake was discovered in the field camp west of Ft. Riley, Kansas, Lt. Samuel Tillman fired five times at a distance of only 8 or 10 feet and missed every time.[58] Both cases proved that not only was accuracy important, but also that soldiers had to maintain coolness under pressure.

The other result of inadequate training with firearms was the high incidence of accidents—some of them fatal. Government statistics compiled between July 1, 1865, and December 31, 1875, revealed 3,123 gunshot wounds within the army. Some of these occurred during combat or were the results of homicides, suicides, and soldiers trying to maim themselves to get out of the service, but the majority were the result of accidents or pranks. Carelessness with what were thought to be unloaded guns, inexperience with unfamiliar weapons, and inattention to proper storage and transport of firearms were common ingredients for disaster. Ironically, a number of accidents occurred on the ranges when target setters were shot by men who did not cease fire on officers' directions.[59] Artillery accidents were often even more grisly. On three separate occasions, while celebrating Fourth of July festivities at different forts, artillerymen were

Front view of uniformed men, sitting, standing, kneeling, and lying down, some taking aim with rifles for a posed photograph. (*Courtesy of the Library of Congress*)

injured. Severe burns resulted in each case, and in the 1868 Ft. Stevenson, North Dakota, incident, one man had part of his mangled arm amputated. At Ft. Davis, Texas, in 1873, Pvt. Jourdain lost sight in his right eye.[60]

While a few commanding officers worked tirelessly to secure adequate ammunition for training, others simply gave up the budgetary pursuit. Lt. Rodney Glisan (assistant surgeon) suggested that officers encourage hunting parties and target shoots for cash prizes as a way of improving marksmanship and morale at the same time.[61] The commander at Ft. Union, New Mexico, approved a plan for officers to contribute money as prizes for an 1886 St. Patrick's Day shooting contest among enlisted men.[62] During Christmas celebrations at Ft. Bidwell, California, two years earlier, Maj. Andrew Burt presided over a marksmanship competition involving not only soldiers, but also civilians and a few Paiute Indians.[63]

Weaponry improved significantly in the decades after the Civil War as awkward muzzle-loading rifles gradually gave way to breech-loading weapons that utilized metallic cartridges. The attainment of rapid fire was finally possible because soldiers no longer had to load the muzzle with powder and a ball that had to be separated from a paper cartridge. Nor did they have to utilize a percussion cap for igniting the powder. The standard issue army rifle of the day was the Springfield, which underwent several modifications to improve its range and reliability. Also utilized by some units was the Spencer rifle, which fired seven rounds of .50-caliber ammunition in succession. Less adaptable to rapid firepower, but equally reliable, was the single-shot Sharps carbine, which was modified in 1869 to accommodate a .50-caliber metallic cartridge.

Coordinated rifle fire with these weapons gave soldiers a significant advantage over the cumbersome muzzle loaders used by their pre–Civil War colleagues. They could now fire many more rounds per minute and could even reload while riding on horseback. Thus while the average soldier may not always have been deadly accurate with his aim, at least he and his fellows could maintain an effective rate of fire against an enemy, so long as the ammunition held out.[64]

THE SERGEANT AND HIS COMPANY

Two features that the army did not seek to modify during the full extent of the nineteenth century were its faith in a rigid command structure and a belief that authority always ranged from top to bottom. Even in a so-called democratic country, rank always had its privilege, and virtually no one within the system attacked that basic premise. Officers lived in a different social world than enlisted men, and in turn, senior officers dominated the lives of junior officers in every way. No reformist crusade would ever seriously challenge this hierarchy of authority, which drew its organizational schemes from highly systematized European armies.

The entrenched elitism, however, did disguise one important feature of an army command system—the need for excellent noncommissioned officers. Just as individual companies served as the major building blocks of regimental cohesion, so too did the company sergeants determine the efficiency of the hierarchical system. Harry H. McConnell, himself a former first sergeant of the 6th Cavalry, declared that "the First Sergeant is virtually in command of the company." During stressful field operations, his advice was routinely sought by junior commissioned officers, who often had far less combat experience than he. The first sergeant's job was to maintain order and efficiency within the company ranks. While some accomplished this goal with stern discipline that made their men fear them, others developed an affection for their men, which earned them respect. Whichever method they pursued, the first sergeants could hope to have a long and reasonably comfortable career in the army. As McConnell pointed out, this noncommissioned officer was due complete deference from all enlisted men, could live in his own quarters, take his own food, and have his horse cared for if he was a cavalryman, and, within reason, could assign his own duties.[65]

The cumulative experience of army sergeants made them the true veterans of each regiment, with perhaps only the senior officers having an equivalent duration of service. A check of the 1894 "Roster of Non-commissioned Officers of the First United States Cavalry" indicated that virtually all the sergeants in the sample had held that rank for 10–16 years, and most of them had previous service as privates and corporals.[66] In his 1900 laudatory book about life in the frontier army, Col. George A. Forsyth reserved his most glittering praise for these true veterans:

> It was a fine sight to see one of these old men on muster or monthly inspection. Erect and soldierly, with his red face glistening, his white hair cut close, his arms and accouterments shining, not a wrinkle in his neat-fitting uniform, not a speck of dust about him, his corps badge, and it may be a medal, on his breast, he stood in the ranks among the others like an oak tree in a grove of cottonwood saplings.[67]

This characterization seems to be the model that Hollywood director John Ford utilized in his frontier army trilogy *Fort Apache, She Wore a Yellow Ribbon,* and *Rio Grande.* The Irish sergeant, brilliantly acted by Victor McLaglen, personified all the qualities described by Col. Forsyth, but with a more human face and with the spirit of a protective patron overseeing the welfare of his charges.

The iconic depiction of the kindly and dutiful sergeant filled movies, novels, and paintings, but historian Don Rickey Jr. came closer to the truth when he stressed the toughness of noncommissioned officers over their more humane side. Because they were the primary disciplinarians within the army, no sergeant could be viewed as soft or an easy mark among the enlisted men. Better they be regarded as bullies and brawlers than as weak willed and overly sentimental. Rickey noted that although many sergeants found themselves busted back to the rank of private if they physically abused their men, the majority were subsequently restored to the higher rank. This was because they were the only ones capable of handling the hard luck cases within the regiment.[68]

One of the best documentations of this type of abuse appeared in the diary of Pvt. William Earl Smith of the 4th Cavalry, who described Sgt. Major Stephen Walsh as the epitome of the tyrant in uniform. Walsh was prone to drunkenness, violent emotional outbursts, arbitrary enforcement of regulations, and occasional acts of savage violence against his troops. One senses from reading the diary today how difficult it was for enlisted men to petition their superiors for better treatment from Walsh, and how he could make their lives into a living hell if he found out about their petitions. With some sense of poetic justice, punishment eventually caught up with the beastly behavior of this sergeant major. In 1877, owing to some unknown offense, he was busted to the rank of private, never again to reclaim his noncommissioned officer's status. Eight years later, this 20-year veteran of the army was discharged because of his advanced age of 51 years and his failing health. His subsequent marriage to a prostitute and his alcoholic binges further reduced his position in society. He died from an overdose of opium, unmourned by the army that had been his home for so many years, and his wife was denied the right of collecting his pension.[69]

Despite the structural and budgetary problems that afflicted the U.S. Army between 1865 and 1898, the nation was committed to the continuation of this constabulary force. As in the case of the even smaller antebellum army, only one element allowed the post–Civil War military to occasionally emerge from obscurity: a combat record. Sometimes it came in the form of significant victories, such as the 1874–1875 massive operations on the southern plains against the Comanches, Kiowas, and Southern Cheyennes during the fabled Red River War. At other times, fame came from disaster, such as the so-called Fetterman Massacre of 1866 at Ft. Phil Kearny and the better-known debacle at Little Big Horn 10 years later. It seems ironic today that even though the army contributed to the development of the country in a myriad of ways, only its role in the colorful Indian wars garnered much attention from the government, press, and public at large. Personal glory remained an elusive goal and proved almost impossible for soldiers to obtain without the presence of accompanying gunfire and omnipresent danger. Dime novelists, artists, and other purveyors of popular culture learned this truth early, and they capitalized upon the bold cavalier image from the earliest times forward.

NOTES

1. J. G. Randall and David Donald, *The Civil War and Reconstruction,* 2nd ed. (Lexington, MA: D. C. Heath, 1969), 529–31. Robert M. Utley, *Frontiersmen in Blue: The United States Army and the Indian, 1848–1865* (New York: Macmillan, 1967), 18–19. Robert M. Utley, *Frontier Regulars: The United States Army and the Indian, 1866–1891* (New York: Macmillan, 1973), 13–14.

2. "The Button for Retired Officers," *Army and Navy Journal* 23 (July 4, 1885): 999.

3. Maurice Matloff, ed., *American Military History,* Office of the Chief of Military History (Washington, D.C.: U.S. Government Printing Office, 1969), 282.

4. Lester D. Langley, "The Democratic Tradition and Military Reform, 1878–1885," *Southwestern Social Science Quarterly* 48 (September 1967): 192.

5. "Military Reorganization," *Army and Navy Journal* 15 (September 8, 1877): 72–73.

6. U.S. Congress, House, *Reorganization of the Army,* 45th Cong., 2nd sess., 1878, H. Misc. Doc. 56, 34.

7. Both quotations cited in Jack D. Foner, *The United States Soldier between Two Wars: Army Life and Reforms, 1865–1898* (New York: Humanities Press, 1970), 74–75.

8. H. H. McConnell, *Five Years a Cavalryman, or Sketches of Regular Army Life on the Texas Frontier, 1866–1871* (Jacksboro, TX: J. N. Rogers, 1889), 101.

9. Letter of Charles Birnbaum, *Winners of the West,* September 1924, 3.

10. Teresa Griffin Vielé, *Following the Drum: A Glimpse of Frontier Life* (New York: Rudd and Carleton, 1858), 175.

11. Clarence C. Clendenen, *Blood on the Border: The United States Army and the Mexican Irregulars* (New York: Macmillan, 1969), xviii.

12. "Act to Increase and Fix the Military Peace Establishment of the United States," *U.S. Statutes at Large* 14 (July 28, 1866): 332–38.

13. Utley, *Frontier Regulars,* 13–14.

14. Ibid., 11–12. Foner, *United States Soldier,* 2–3.

15. Utley, *Frontier Regulars,* 30–32.

16. Don Rickey Jr., *Forty Miles a Day on Beans and Hay: The Enlisted Soldier Fighting the Indian Wars* (Norman: University of Oklahoma Press, 1963), 48–49, 109–10.

17. Edward M. Coffman, *The Old Army: A Portrait of the American Army in Peacetime, 1784–1898* (New York: Oxford University Press, 1986), 218–20.

18. Report of Lt. Gen. William T. Sherman, 1 October 1867, in *Annual Report of the Secretary of War, 1872,* 30–31.

19. McConnell, *Five Years a Cavalryman,* 13.

20. Rickey, *Forty Miles a Day,* 20.

21. Foner, *United States Soldier,* 74. "Rank and File," New York *Sun* article excerpted in *Army and Navy Journal* 15 (October 20, 1877): 170.

22. Foner, *United States Soldier,* 87.

23. John F. Finerty, *War-Path and Bivouac, or the Conquest of the Sioux: A Narrative of Stirring Personal Experiences and Adventures in the Big Horn and Yellowstone Expedition of 1876, and in the Campaign on the British Border in 1879* (Norman: University of Oklahoma Press, 1961), 306.

24. George A. Forsyth, *The Story of a Soldier* (New York: D. Appleton, 1909), 92. Two equally interesting listings of diverse backgrounds of enlisted men are provided in the memoirs of a former corporal, Thomas T. Smith, ed., *A Dose of Frontier Soldiering: The Memoirs of Corporal E. A. Bode, Frontier Regular Infantry, 1877–1882* (Lincoln: University of Nebraska Press, 1994), 124; and in David K. Strate, *Sentinel to the Cimarron: The Frontier Experience of Fort Dodge, Kansas* (Dodge City, KS: Cultural Heritage and Arts Center, 1970), 56.

25. Rickey, *Forty Miles a Day,* 19.

26. Coffman, *Old Army,* 335.

27. Rickey, *Forty Miles a Day,* 19.

28. Coffman, *Old Army,* 334.

29. John M. Oswald, "History of Fort Elliott," *Panhandle-Plains Historical Review* 32 (1959): 17–18. Jere W. Roberson, ed., "A View from Oklahoma, 1866–1868: The Diary and Letters of Dr. James Reagles, Jr., Assistant Surgeon, U.S. Army," *Red River Valley Historical Review* 3 (Fall 1978): 19. Coffman, *Old Army,* 329, 335.

30. Rickey, *Forty Miles a Day,* 25. Further examples of immigrant soldiers using the army's educational opportunities are found in Marvin E. Fletcher, "The Army and Minority Groups," in *The United States Army in Peacetime,* ed. Robin Higham and Carol Brandt (Manhattan, KS: Military Affairs/Aerospace Historian Publishing, 1975), 107–8.

31. Ty Cashion, "Life on Government Hill: Fort Griffin before the Boom," *West Texas Historical Association Year Book* 70 (1994): 113.

32. Henry P. Walker, ed., "The Reluctant Corporal: The Autobiography of William Bladen Jett," *Journal of Arizona History* 12 (Spring 1971): 1–7.

33. Letter of Col. Albert Fensch, *Winners of the West,* July 30, 1927, 5.

34. Rickey, *Forty Miles a Day,* 28.

35. John G. Bourke, *On the Border with Crook* (New York: Charles Scribner's Sons, 1891), 7.

36. McConnell, *Five Years a Cavalryman,* 104–5.

37. Kevin Adams, "'Pat Has a Small Chance of Showing His Blood Out in the Wilderness': Class and Ethnicity in the Ideas and Institutions of the Frontier Army, 1865–1890," paper presented at the Western History Association Meeting, Las Vegas, 2004. Aspects of the ethnic soldier debate are examined in William Bruce White, "The Military and the Melting Pot: The American Army and Minority Groups, 1865–1924" (PhD diss., University of Wisconsin, 1968), 300–15.

38. Robert F. Bluthardt, "The Men of Company F," *Fort Concho Report* 15 (Summer 1983): 7.

39. Coffman, *Old Army,* 331–32. For an excellent analysis of ethnicity among northern soldiers in the Civil War, see William L. Burton, *Melting Pot Soldiers: The Union's Ethnic Regiments* (Ames: Iowa State University Press, 1988).

40. U.S. Congress, House, 44th Cong., 1st sess., 1876, H. Rep. 354, 228. Statistics on foreign-born members of the officer corps are harder to come by, but in 1874, the *Army Register* tabulated that of the 193 officers commissioned from the ranks, fully 87 were from foreign nations. See Utley, *Frontier Regulars,* 18.

41. Henry M. Stanley, *My Early Travels and Adventures in America* (London: S. Low Marston, 1895), 4–5.

42. James Parker, *The Old Army: Memoirs, 1872–1918* (Philadelphia: Dorrance, 1929), 18.

43. McConnell, *Five Years a Cavalryman,* 80, 106–7. More generous in his stereotyped descriptions of Irish, German, Scandinavian, and black soldiers was Finerty, *War-Path and Bivouac,* 306–7. Typical of the highly stereotyped descriptions of the alleged Irish drinking and fighting is Francis S. Landrum, ed., "From the Sketchbook of 1st Sergeant Michael McCarthy, Troop H, 1st U.S. Cavalry: Excerpts, 1873," *Journal of the Shaw Historical Society* 9 (1995): 9–10.

44. Alfred A. Woodhull, "The Enlisted Soldier," *Journal of the Military Service Institution of the United States* 8 (March 1887): 28–29.

45. Adams, "Pat Has a Small Chance," 10–12. See also Kevin Mulroy, "Wearing of the Blue: The Irish in the United States Army, 1776–1876," in *Myles Keogh: The Life and Legend of an "Irish Dragoon" in the Seventh Cavalry,* ed. John Langellier, Kurt Hamilton Cox, and Brian Pohanka (El Segundo, CA: Upton and Sons, 1991), 29–44.

46. Rickey, *Forty Miles a Day,* 33; Coffman, *Old Army,* 336–37.

47. Rickey, *Forty Miles a Day,* 31–32. Peter D. Olch, "Medicine in the Indian-Fighting Army, 1866–1890," *Journal of the West* 21 (July 1982): 33.

48. Rickey, *Forty Miles a Day,* 38.

49. Walker, "Reluctant Corporal," 7–8.

50. Augustus Meyers, *Ten Years in the Ranks of the United States Army* (New York: Stirling Press, 1914), 11–12.

51. Rickey, *Forty Miles a Day,* 83–85.

52. Listing of the specific bugle calls and their attendant duties at Ft. Stevenson, North Dakota, during 1868 is provided in Ray H. Mattison, "Old Fort Stevenson—A Typical Missouri River Military Post," *North Dakota History* 18 (April–July 1951): 71–72. This description compares favorably to the more detailed list provided in Tom Lindmier, *Drybone: A History of Fort Fetterman, Wyoming* (Glendo, WY: High Plains Press, 2002), 94–95.

53. Andrew M. Flynn, "Looking Back over Forty-Nine Years," *Winners of the West,* November 1939, 4.

54. U.S. Congress, *Reorganization of the Army,* 246.

55. Rickey, *Forty Miles a Day,* 103–4. For a discussion of marksmanship contests and medals during the frontier era, see William K. Emerson, *Marksmanship in the U.S. Army: A History of Medals, Shooting Programs, and Training* (Norman: University of Oklahoma Press, 2004), 3–33.

56. Rickey, *Forty Miles a Day,* 99–100.

57. David L. Spotts, *Campaigning with Custer and the Nineteenth Kansas Volunteer Cavalry on the Washita Campaign, 1868–69,* ed. E. A. Brininstool (Los Angeles: Wetzel, 1928), 53.

58. Dwight L. Smith, ed., "The Kansas Frontier, 1869–1870: Lt. Samuel Tillman's First Tour of Duty," *Kansas History* 12 (Winter 1989–1990): 206.

59. James E. Potter, "'He…Regretted Having to Die That Way': Firearms Accidents in the Frontier Army, 1806–1891," *Nebraska History* 78 (Winter 1997): 175–84. A standard detail manual on weapons and marksmanship training is Edward S. Farrow, *Mountain Scouting: A Hand-Book for Officers and Soldiers on the Frontier* (New York: E. S. Farrow, 1881), 25–40.

60. Ray H. Mattison, ed., "The Diary of Surgeon Washington Matthews, Fort Rice, D.T.," *North Dakota History* 21 (January 1954): 16–17. Barry Scobee, *Fort Davis, Texas, 1583–1960* (El Paso, TX: Hill, 1963), 67. George Ruhlen, "Fort Hancock—Last of the Frontier Forts," *Password* 4 (January 1959): 29.

61. Rodney Glisan, *Journal of Army Life* (San Francisco: A. L. Bancroft, 1874), 54.

62. Dale F. Giese, "Soldiers at Play: A History of Social Life at Fort Union, New Mexico, 1851–1891" (PhD diss., University of New Mexico, 1969), 113.

63. Merrill J. Mattes, *Indians, Infants and Infantry: Andrew and Elizabeth Burt on the Frontier* (Denver: Old West, 1960), 248–49.

64. Utley, *Frontier Regulars,* 69–73.

65. McConnell, *Five Years a Cavalryman,* 86.

66. Rickey, *Forty Miles a Day,* 60.

67. Forsyth, *Story of a Soldier,* 131–32.

68. Rickey, *Forty Miles a Day,* 58–60.

69. Sherry L. Smith, ed., *Sagebrush Soldier: Private William Earl Smith's View of the Sioux War of 1876* (Norman: University of Oklahoma Press, 1989), 26, 28, 30, 33, 38, 135–37.

3 NEW DUTIES: FROM RECONSTRUCTION SOUTH TO OLD WEST

Even as the U.S. Army mustered out its vast throngs of Civil War veterans during the late spring and early summer of 1865, policy makers recognized that military occupation of the defeated Confederate states could not end with the Union victory at Appomattox. Scattered pockets of martial resistance continued in remote areas of the South, especially in Texas and Indian Territory. Official opposition did not end in these places until June 1865, with the surrender of Gen. Stand Watie and his mixed force of white and Cherokee soldiers. Furthermore, on the Great Plains, in the Great Basin, and in the desert Southwest, Indian resistance to American pressures had reached high levels in the wake of government neglect of tribal treaty rights during the Civil War. Especially important for triggering the new rounds of heightened violence were the massacres of Southern Cheyennes at Sand Creek and Shoshones at Bear River as well as the brutal murder of Mimbres Apache leader Mangas Coloradas.

Thus the post–Civil War army found itself engaged in two radically contrasting theaters of conflict that competed for national attention. On the one hand, its officers and men were to serve as a constabulary to protect the lives, property, and legal rights of black freedmen and white Unionists throughout the South. They would have to execute these difficult duties without having a clear legal mandate to arrest civilians or to interfere in the domestic affairs of citizens. In contrast to these new, poorly defined responsibilities, they would also have to return to their prewar frontier assignment of simultaneously protecting and punishing western Indian tribes. This would redirect the army to its oldest of all missions—waging unconventional war against Native Americans—which had always been its greatest source of frustration since the republic had been founded.

By the beginning of 1866, Texas best represented the convergence of both army roles. There Division of the Gulf commander General Philip Sheridan stationed a massive force to deal with the lawlessness directed against Provisional Governor Andrew Jackson Hamilton, who had implemented a moderate form of Reconstruction on the state. Despite his following President Andrew Johnson's nonpunitive plan to speedily restore civil government in the Lone Star State, Hamilton faced tremendous opposition from the planter class that had represented the heart of prewar secessionism.

By August 1866, Hamilton's Unionist Democrats had been voted out of office, and ex-Confederates had virtually restored their political dominance with the election of Governor James W. Throckmorton. In the wake of these changes, violence increased against black freedmen and Unionists who had been viewed as traitors to the Confederacy during the Civil War.[1]

At the same time the U.S. Army had to walk a tightrope in dealing with Texas's political affairs, it had to address two other borderland problems. The primary Indian threat within the state had always been the Comanches, and they had been active throughout the last two years of the war, raiding the isolated ranches and communities of the northwestern counties. Texans, who had long held a problematic relationship with the federal government and its military representatives, placed much of the blame for Comanche depredations on the federal government and the army in 1866–1867. They overstated their case that the line of settlements across northwestern Texas had receded at least a hundred miles eastward during the previous two years. Furthermore, many Texans unfairly blasted the government for protecting Indians on their treaty lands north of the Red River, while simultaneously feeding and arming them. But most venom among Texas frontiersmen was reserved for the U.S. Army, which was accused of being incompetent at best and cowardly at worst.[2]

FRENCH MENACE IN MEXICO

If army officers did not suffer enough from incessant Southern criticism of their Reconstruction policies and western criticism of their Indian-fighting techniques, another crisis briefly garnered significant military attention. The presence of French troops in Mexico to prop up the puppet regime of Emperor Ferdinand Maximilian posed a potential threat all along the international boundary line, and especially in Texas. The problem had simmered since early 1862, when French emperor Napoleon III had sent troops to Mexico, ostensibly to collect international debts. Fighting alongside their Mexican conservative allies, the French were locked in a struggle from which they could not extricate themselves. President Abraham Lincoln had repeatedly protested the continued European occupation of an American sister republic in violation of the Monroe Doctrine, but he lacked the power to do much about the situation. With the end of the American Civil War, President Andrew Johnson could now bring greater weight to solving the dilemma. He made sure that arms shipments reached the republican forces of Benito Juárez and that further European diplomatic pressure was directed against Napoleon III and Maximilian. The American army, stationed in relatively isolated posts extending from south Texas to the California coast, served as the visible evidence of U.S. resolve to evict the French interlopers. Fortunately, no direct confrontations between France and the United States occurred before Juárez's forces defeated the French and their Mexican allies, and on June 19, 1867, the rebels executed Emperor Maximilian.[3]

RECONSTRUCTION DUTY IN THE SOUTH

By the time this international crisis had been resolved, the U.S. Army found itself embroiled in the most frustrating stage of the Reconstruction process. A more radical Reconstruction phase began in the South by 1868, one committed to the greater protection of black rights and to the dismantling of the traditional white leadership that had brought on secession and the Civil War. Because these new state governments were exceedingly unpopular among unreconstructed Southerners, new levels of violence reached out from every urban area to every rural hamlet. Inadequate and often untrustworthy local law officers were unable or unwilling to fully enforce the new laws.

Again, as in the initial moderate stages of Reconstruction, the army was called upon to enforce government policies and constitutional decisions. Most textbooks have written favorably about military officers risking their lives to protect freedmen from lynchings and safeguarding fair elections. Yet less well known were the other mandates with which commanders of the various military districts were entrusted. These included what one historian has summarized as coping with "horse stealing, moonshining, rioting, civil court proceedings, regulatory commercial law, public education, fraud, removing public officials, registering voters, holding elections, and approving of new state constitutions by registered voters."[4] The obligations assigned in the performance of these duties were unprecedented in American history, but the authority to implement the policies remained in a legalistic limbo. Thus the army faced criticism from Southerners for being tyrannical and from Northern reformists for being too weak willed in the enforcement of federal policies. By mid-1867, fully one-third of the army's total manpower was committed to occupation duty in the South. Because many of these units were composed of black enlisted men, racial animosities fomented further white resistance to congressional policies.[5]

Even before Reconstruction entered its most contentious stage of Radical Republicanism, Gen. William Tecumseh Sherman had already sensed the utter futility of unpopular military rule. Commenting in 1865, he declared in a private letter, "No matter what change we may desire in the feelings and thoughts of people [in the] South, we cannot accomplish it by force. Nor can we afford to maintain there an army large enough to hold them in subjugation."[6] Although Sherman had been referring primarily to the intractability of Southern thought and behavior, he might as well have added several other reasons why the various Reconstruction policies would remain unrealized. First, Northern public opinion never would have supported an endless military occupation of the South. Second, budgetary problems would never have provided adequate troops or resources to administer such policies. Third, most Northern whites hoped for national reconciliation, not the creation of large standing armies to suppress the constitutional rights of Southern whites.[7]

In the wake of General Sherman's original bleak forecast for the future of Reconstruction, other officers who had direct experience in the South came to share their leader's pessimism. Some 15 months after assuming command of the Division of the Atlantic in May 1866, Gen. George G. Meade wrote to a fellow officer that military service in Omaha, Nebraska, on the edge of the frontier, would probably be preferable to duty in the South, where "you have not only to be a soldier, but must play the politician."[8] When Gen. Alfred Terry ran afoul of legal technicalities in enforcing Reconstruction policies in Georgia during 1870, he told Gen. Sherman, "The pressure upon me from the contending parties, is very great and I would not again go through with a job of this kind even if it would make me a Marshal of France."[9] Upon being dispatched to New Orleans to take command of the Fifth Military District in 1867, Gen. Winfield Scott Hancock lodged a sarcastic complaint in a letter to his wife, which stated, "I have not been educated to overthrow the civil authorities in time of peace."[10] Predictably, his policies soon drew the ire of Radical Republicans, who pressured his transfer from the most volatile of all military districts.[11]

Although the Reconstruction process continued in various guises for a dozen years, and although it helped promote the civil rights of freedmen in many ways, its accomplishments were mostly lost on the white soldiers who enforced those rights.

Gen. William Tecumseh Sherman became commander-in-chief of the Army in 1869 and inherited the problems associated with Southern Reconstruction and reoccupation of the western forts, all with under-manned and under-funded units. (*Courtesy of Chaiba Media*)

By 1876, the majority of Southern state governments had already returned to control by white citizens who opposed the liberal reordering of their region. The Compromise of 1877—actually an amalgam of tradeoffs between Northern and Southern interest groups—brought an end to the last phases of military occupation of the former Confederate states. White officers and enlisted men alike were relieved that their unpopular and frustrating constabulary duty could now end and that they could turn their full attention to Indian issues in the West. Black soldiers, however, like their black civilian counterparts, had little reason to celebrate the end of Reconstruction, which came to symbolize an unfulfilled promise.

Army Appropriation Problems in 1877

Before the final withdrawal of occupation troops had been completed, American fighting men suffered one final indignity associated with the Reconstruction imbroglio.

The November 1876 elections brought a Democratic majority to the House of Representatives and severely reduced the Republican majority in the Senate. Partisan politics flared into a fight over the Army Appropriations Bill (HR 4692) in 1877. Some sponsors simply argued that the size of the army had to be reduced due to inadequate federal revenue. But the real debate between party extremists was the bill's provision that no part of the appropriation could be used in any state to maintain political power within that state. The provision was aimed at bringing down the Radical Republican government in Louisiana and the alleged carpetbagger officeholders of South Carolina. Vitriol dominated the debate and eliminated any chance for compromise language in the bill. A deadlocked Congress therefore adjourned without approving any army appropriations for the foreseeable future.

The most immediate effect of this political impasse is that all ranks of soldiers went without pay from June 30, 1877, to November 21, 1877. For enlisted men, most of whom had no personal savings, this meant a major financial hardship. Some eastern banks extended credit to officers during the crisis, as did some local merchants who catered to servicemen. The majority of soldiers, however, could only hope that the local post sutler would maintain a tab on each of them until regular pay schedules could be restored.

A secondary problem was created within the massive supply system that could make or break military efficiency. For instance, the Quartermaster Department was left without any funds to purchase necessary goods for the posts. Officers simply negotiated purchases based on their promise that appropriations would soon be restored—though their promises were not legally binding. The Quartermaster Department amassed a $1,200,000 deficit merely for the transportation of supplies, and other administrative departments ran up their own bills. National embarrassment about these results did not immediately produce compromise legislation, and in fact, the fierce debate continued at an even more shrill level until finally settled in November 1877.[12] Two months prior to passage of new legislation, army wife Frances M. A. Roe drafted a family letter that lambasted congressional irresponsibility:

> I wonder what the wise men of Congress, who were too weary to take up the bill before going to their comfortable homes—I wonder what they would do if the Army as a body would say, "We are tired, Uncle, dear, and are going home for the summer to rest. You will have to get along without us and manage the Indians and strikers [railroad strikes of 1877] the best way you can."[13]

ADJUSTMENTS IN WESTERN INDIAN CAMPAIGNS

It is indeed ironic that the twilight years of Reconstruction in the South occurred during the most important years of the fabled American Indian wars of the West. Even though casualties suffered during these undeclared wars were nowhere near the staggering proportions reached during the Civil War, the years that stretched between 1865 and 1898 were anything but a peacetime era. Field campaigns against elusive Native American warriors were grueling, and the lack of conclusive results in the nameless skirmishes produced a high level of frustration for military men of every rank. To be sure, American soldiers had waged war against Indian tribes since the earliest days of colonial militia, but no concrete strategy ever had been devised to counter this unconventional style of guerilla warfare. Continuing with the formation of the continental army during the American Revolution, American soldiers were primarily trained in

European tactics to defeat conventional armies. Assembling large forces on battlefields to outmaneuver and outnumber an opponent bore little relationship to the realities of Indian warfare. Furthermore, the massed formations utilized in the Civil War had developed into a reliance on frontal assaults to break an enemy's lines.

This was not the reality of Indian wars in the West. Elusiveness proved to be the most common element in the battle tactics of western tribes. More often than not, they lived in relatively small villages that could be disassembled and moved with alacrity, or abandoned altogether. If villagers received adequate warning of a hostile force's approach, the noncombatants could flee to relative safety, and the warriors could elect to make a stand or to withdraw and choose another time and place for battle. Likewise, small raiding parties could easily assemble or disperse, depending upon changing conditions. Rarely, however, did they choose to give battle that might result in large numbers of casualties among themselves. Such a massed defense would occur only when no other choice remained, as in the case of the large village of Sioux, Northern Cheyenne, and Arapaho assembled along the banks of the Little Big Horn in June 1876. This greatest of all Plains Indian victories, however, was something of an aberration since the religious fervor of the Sun Dance, not prior military planning, had brought so many Indians together in one place at one time.

Excepting this type of aberration that led to a military disaster, army officers would have preferred to meet large bodies of Indians on a chosen battlefield, where the former could utilize their superiority in numbers and technology. Instead, they fought what seemed to be countless skirmishes that resulted in a tiny number of Indian casualties, if any at all. Edward S. Farrow, an officer in the First Cavalry and author of an important instruction guide for novice soldiers, succinctly stated the problem that faced his fellow soldiers: "Strategy loses its advantages against an enemy who accepts few or none of the conventionalities of civilized warfare. The Indian is present one day and when next heard from is marauding in another state or territory.... He is like the flea 'put your finger on him and he is not there.'"[14]

Capt. John G. Bourke, a man with considerable firsthand knowledge of campaigning both on the plains and in the Southwest, came to understand the art of guerrilla warfare as practiced by the Apaches. In his short history of one such 1883 campaign, he used the same insect metaphor in affirming that "to attempt to catch such a band of Apaches by direct pursuit would be about as hopeless a piece of business as that of catching so many fleas."[15] Bourke, like his mentor Gen. George Crook, came to rely upon Apache scouts to locate and defeat "hostile" Apache bands that soldiers alone could never find. The words and actions of Bourke echoed the sentiments of Gen. Randolph B. Marcy, who wrote in 1866 about his pre–Civil War frontier experiences, especially with the Plains tribes of Texas, New Mexico, and Indian Territory. Like Bourke, Marcy found little value in applying bookish strategy lessons to fighting western Indians, "an enemy who is here to-day and there to-morrow,... who is every where without being any where; who derives his commissariat from the country he operates in;... who comes into action only when it suits his purpose, and never without the advantage of numbers or position."[16]

The "Total War" Concept against Native Americans

Most twentieth-century historians agree that the frontier army faced an exceedingly difficult and frustrating task corralling the western tribes during the three decades after the Civil War. They are less unified, however, in defining the overall strategy that ultimately turned the tide against indigenous peoples. Robert Utley, the most thorough scholar of the subject, argues that the military leadership eventually endorsed a philosophy of "total war," which placed emphasis on destroying everything that might be of use to defiant Indians. Soldiers were frequently ordered to destroy homes, personal accoutrements, weapons, food supplies, livestock, and even water sources that might enable Indians to remain free of the reservation life.[17] A tiny minority of officers carried the scorched-earth concept even further and applied it to human beings. Col. Philippe Régis de Trobriand candidly stated the most extreme position on the subject when he declared, "The confessed aim is to exterminate everyone, for this is the only advantage of making the expedition; if extermination were not achieved, just another burden would be added—prisoners."[18]

Utley did not mean to imply that soldiers campaigned with a sense of blood lust or that they routinely massacred defenseless Indians. Yet he did infer that the theory of total war that was applied in the West drew inspiration from successful Civil War operations, such as Gen. William Tecumseh Sherman's 1864 "March through Georgia." Echoing the same theme in a slightly different fashion, historian Russell Weigley avoided the phrase *total war,* but chose as his chapter title for the 1865–1898 era, "Annihilation of a People: The Indian Fighters." The chapter opened with an unambiguous order from Gen. Philip H. Sheridan to Col. Ranald S. Mackenzie as he crossed the Rio Grande into Mexico during 1873 to attack the villages of Kickapoo and Lipan Apache raiders: "I want you to be bold, enterprising, and at all times full of energy, when you begin, let it be a campaign of annihilation, obliteration and complete destruction."[19]

Historian Robert Wooster has rejected the notion that the frontier army adopted a strategy of total warfare that was modeled on Civil War antecedents. For him, the concept implied too much of a formal policy, one that was constructed over time with considerable thought and one that was administered universally throughout the West.[20] Further examination of the contrasting interpretations reveals, however, that the opposing views are not really that far apart. All three historians identified the same innovative approaches that were used, and they agreed that common sense played the key role in devising these approaches.[21]

First and foremost, virtually all commanding officers came to share the opinion that only offensive tactics could bring an end to the costly wars. The ability to track down recalcitrants in their last refuges and inflict decisive defeats on them was evident in the massive military operations associated with the 1874–1875 Red River War. Five converging columns drove the remaining Comanches and Kiowas into a relatively small area of the Texas panhandle, where they traditionally had been able to seek sanctuary. This time, however, they faced overwhelming numbers of troops working in coordination with each other, well supplied with the necessities of an extended campaign, and armed with precise knowledge of where the last remaining encampments were located. A number of important skirmishes occurred during this operation, but the decisive blow was delivered by Col. Ranald S. Mackenzie beneath the high protective walls of Palo Duro Canyon. Mackenzie was protective of the many prisoners taken that day, but he did employ some techniques of total warfare to assure that these Indians would never again be able to operate freely away from their reservation at Ft. Sill. In addition to destroying all of the useful items within the village, he ordered that the great majority of Indian horses be shot. This would eliminate future mobility and force the Indians to remain on the reservation.[22]

A second adaptation widely utilized by frontier officers was the increased demand for mobility to match that of most Indian tribes. To defeat the enemy was first to catch the enemy. Officers learned that they had to move troops quickly from the far-flung

Col. Ranald S. Mackensie understood well the value of large offensives directed at Indian strongholds, such as operations against Comanches, Kiowas, and Southern Cheyennes in the Texas Panhandle during the Red River War of 1874–1875. (*Courtesy of the National Archives*)

posts, either in the pursuit of small raiding parties or to fashion large campaigns, as in the 1874–1875 Red River War and the 1876–1877 Great Sioux War. The gradual extension of railroads immeasurably aided the deployment of troops and the delivery of supplies, but field campaigns still had to rely on mule pack trains for the latter. Gen. George Crook made efficient use of this system in the Southwest when he waged war against Apache bands in some of the most difficult desert and mountain terrain anywhere in the nation. His initial successes in the borderlands led him to carefully prepare a similar supply system against the Sioux and Northern Cheyennes in 1876.[23]

Mobility rested mostly upon the use of cavalry regiments in the vast open spaces of the West. Infantry could man posts, escort supply wagons, protect mail coaches, defend fixed points, and perform other necessary tasks, but they were not capable of pursuing Indian raiding parties.[24] Col. Philippe Régis de Trobriand articulated a widely held frontier view that while "the infantry is absolutely useless in pursuing Indians on the 'warpath' and must be left in garrison...the cavalry is the only arm that can be used effectively in pursuing Indians." But de Trobriand went on to warn that unless the army attracted better horsemen into service, properly trained them in cavalry tactics,

"General Crook's headquarters in the field at Whitewood. On starvation march, 1876." This closeup scene shows tents improvised from wagon frames during the Yellowstone expedition. (*Courtesy of the National Archives*)

and coordinated them with auxiliary squadrons of experienced white and Indian scouts, they would always remain inferior to their Indian foes.[25]

Paralleling the mobility was a third practical innovation: the use of winter campaigns to press Indians at their most vulnerable time of year. The concept was an old one, again dating back to the colonial era and best exemplified by Gen. John Sullivan's 1779 operations against Iroquois villages in western New York. Soldiers hated this type of operation because it also subjected them to great hardship and possible death from extreme weather changes, but it was difficult to argue against the potential results. Indians might be able to escape direct conflict with the army, but should they lose all of their camp equipment during the flight, they most likely would have to turn themselves in at the agencies. The army's winter campaign of 1876–1877 was particularly brutal for soldiers and northern Plains Indians alike, resulting in what became known as the "starvation march" for Gen. George Crook's troops, who were forced to eat their own horses and mules. Yet in the wake of two of the greatest Indian victories—the battles of Rosebud Creek (June 17, 1876) and Little Big Horn (June 25, 1876)—Lakota and Northern Cheyenne warriors were compelled to surrender to authorities on the Great Sioux Reservation or seek temporary sanctuary in Canada with Sitting Bull.[26] While most of the celebrated winter campaigns were directed against Plains tribes, even the commander of the District of Arizona admitted in 1866 that Apaches could not be easily located and forced to fight in the warm months. Only a midwinter campaign

A horse-drawn stretcher carries a wounded soldier from the Battle of Slim Buttes in the Dakota Territory, September 1876. (*Courtesy of the National Archives*)

aimed at destroying the wickiups and their contents could force the Apaches to negotiate for peace.[27]

Although large campaigns, especially the successful ones, have received the greatest attention in textbooks, army officers of the late nineteenth century learned the value of one other practical innovation: the development of loose-order tactics. Traditional European tactical instructions as well as those that were developed during the Civil War stressed large formations, where infantry, cavalry, and artillery forces acted in concert. But the realities of small patrols engaging in even smaller skirmishes with western Indians returned tactical thinking to the company level. The idea was to restore greater flexibility to a body of troops rather than having them rigidly bound to the movements of a larger formation. Company sergeants were the key to preserving cohesion in these combat situations that sometimes resulted in hand-to-hand fighting. Emphasis on a smaller cadre of soldiers acting together also promoted greater initiative so that one could take advantage of ever-changing battlefield conditions.[28] Col. John Gibbon wrote in 1879 that "the 'elbow touch' of the regular soldier, admirable as they are in ordinary warfare, are utterly thrown away in contests with the Indian."[29] Capt. Charles King likewise paid tribute to a group of dismounted cavalrymen in the 1876 battle of Slim Buttes who climbed a ridge and seized the initiative by reassessing the situation "practically, not tactically."[30]

HARDSHIPS DURING FIELD CAMPAIGNS

While no formal doctrine existed to precisely define military strategy in the Indian wars, all seasoned veterans agreed with two realities. First, field campaigns, and even extended reconnaissances, were generally grueling. Second, weather, more than Indians, dictated life-threatening situations during these operations. Capt. Guy V. Henry, no novice to military privation, described the effects of a sudden "Norther" descending upon his men during a winter 1874 patrol in the Black Hills. The delayed effects of frostbite left Henry with a face that was blackened and swollen as well as rotted flesh peeling from his fingers.[31] When Col. Joseph J. Reynolds returned from the March 1876 campaign on the Powder River, during which temperatures plunged to 39 degrees below zero, he wrote to Gen. Sherman, calling for the suspension of winter campaigns for the foreseeable future. Reynolds concluded with the words "Cruelty is no name for them— the month of March has told on me more than any five years of my life."[32]

But winter offensives were not the only dangerous undertakings in the unmapped regions of the West. During July 1877, Capt. Nicholas Nolan departed Ft. Concho with 63 soldiers of the 10th Cavalry to check reports of small Comanche raiding parties in the southern sections of the Texas panhandle. Unfortunately, 1877 was a drought year in west Texas, and when the column missed its expected water hole and could not locate a nearby party of buffalo hunters for support, it found itself facing desperate conditions. The men were reduced to drinking the blood of their horses and, in some cases, to drinking their own urine. Before the column was finally rescued after 86 hours on the Staked Plains without water, all semblance of order had broken down, and four troopers had died.[33]

On other occasions, direct Indian combat brought on the suffering. To be sure, newspapers and rumor mills often crafted totally fictitious tales of Indian massacres of soldiers. Typical of this genre was an 1867 newspaper story that was widely and uncritically reprinted in the eastern press. It alleged that the entire command at Ft. Buford, Dakota Territory, had been annihilated. In intricate detail, fiendish acts were described about how post commander Capt. William Rankin had been burned at the stake, his wife "mistreated ... in a most uncivilized manner," and the dead soldiers had been chopped up and eaten by the victorious Indians.[34] Such reports were better suited to dime novels, but they also seemed to be common ingredients for sensationalistic journalism aimed at a naïve public.

In real life, the annihilation of large assemblages of troops was uncommon, but terror could be real nonetheless for small groups of soldiers who found themselves engaged in skirmishes. Corp. William Bladen Jett recalled his combat against a concealed Chiricahua Apache enemy in Guadalupe Canyon at the southernmost convergence of Arizona and New Mexico. On the first volley from the hillside, Pvt. Neihause was killed by a bullet to the brain. The camp sentry, who previously had stated his desire to get into an Indian fight, was the second victim as he fell dead in mid-stride. A company sergeant was the next casualty, suffering four severe wounds. The several soldiers who survived the ordeal did so by offering some resistance and then fleeing the camp. At no point in this bloody fight did they ever see their adversaries.[35]

During the 1877 Battle of the Big Hole in Montana Territory, Lt. Charles A. Woodruff of the 7th Infantry experienced the feeling of imminent death when he and his command were almost overrun by determined Nez Percé warriors. The soldiers fought well, but with resignation about their expected fate, some wounded men even covering their heads to await death. When Woodruff summarized the situation from a safer position on the next day, he remained shaken by the incident: "I got my two revolvers, said my prayers ... and determined to kill a few Indians before I died."[36]

One of the most graphic images to emerge from the Indian wars on the plains was an 1867 photograph of Sgt. Frederick Williams of the 7th Cavalry, who was killed in a skirmish with Southern Cheyennes at a stage station near Ft. Wallace, Kansas. His body was stripped of its clothing, pierced with at least five arrows, and gashed with knives.

Capt. Albert Barnitz, who almost lost his life in the same fight, described Sgt. Williams as a gentleman-soldier, always friendly and attentive to duty. The grisly photograph, taken by Dr. William A. Bell of Philadelphia, found its way into many national newspapers and books and became emblematic of the ferocity of Indian warfare. Further delineating the brutality of such events, Capt. Barnitz described how the company bugler was also shot from his horse and speedily descended upon by a lone warrior, who stripped off the soldier's clothes and dashed out his brains with a tomahawk.[37]

Tales of unbelievable Indian atrocities had been a staple of American storytelling since the colonial era, and when merged with credible eyewitness accounts of tortures and mutilations, soldiers came to expect horrible treatment at the hands of their adversaries. Even seasoned military men were conditioned to expect the worst treatment as they traveled in small parties through dangerous Indian country. Martha Summerhayes, wife of an 8th Infantry lieutenant, later recalled how real the fear had been in 1875 when she and her husband traveled with a small patrol while they changed Arizona posts. As they approached a deserted-looking pass, both husband and wife shared the same panicked thought of an imminent Apache attack. Jack Summerhayes instructed his wife to keep her derringer cocked and ready so that if the command was overrun, she should kill her baby and herself. He repeated a horrific warning that she had heard many times before about the cruel treatment that captives received from Indians, including the admonition, "Don't let them get either of you alive." The patrol then moved through the pass without any such ghastly event transpiring.[38]

The hardships endured by frontier soldiers and their families were certainly real, and a relative few among them made the ultimate sacrifice of their lives in the line of duty. Some who died in the larger battles, such as Little Big Horn, had their names preserved in history books, but most remain obscure or anonymous players in the epic story. To better understand the level of hardship experienced by soldiers in the field, one should look more carefully at the monthly reports that were submitted in the regimental returns. They represent the "normal" activities of the army, as opposed to the more aberrational events associated with a few big battles.

Historian Ernest Archambeau excerpted the monthly reports of the Fourth Cavalry during its stationing in west Texas from 1872 to 1874. These years were comparatively busy ones for the regiment, but a perusal of monthly reports indicates more a pattern of monotony than one of battlefield glory. Two types of observations dominate these official summaries of activities. The first type of information lists the lines of march undertaken by each patrol (mostly at full company level) and the precise distances that they traveled. The second category of facts concerns the condition of horses in the field—especially about infectious diseases, accidents, fatigue, and theft by deserters. With the exception of reports on the Red River War offensive, very few entries describe contact with Indians or outlaws.[39]

COURAGE AND COWARDICE IN THE FIELD

Field operations, whether involving the massive numbers of converging columns or small reconnaissances, brought out the best and the worst behaviors in soldiers of all ranks. Stories abound of heroism under fire and of the citations that were bestowed on some of the deserving men. Lt. Powhatan Clarke braved withering Apache gunfire to rescue the badly wounded Cpl. Edward Scott, an event that was highlighted in national news magazines and a memorable illustration by Frederic Remington.[40] In a similar act of valor, Sgt. Bernard Taylor saved the life of Lt. Charles King in the 1874 fight at

Sunset Pass, Arizona, by throwing the wounded officer over his back and descended 300 yards amid an intense Apache crossfire.[41] Likewise, 15 soldiers who manned Reno Hill in the midst of the Little Big Horn disaster volunteered for extremely hazardous duty by leaving their rifle pits while under fire and crawling down to the river banks to secure water for their suffering comrades.[42] During the June 17, 1877, battle of White Bird Canyon, Idaho, two troops of First Cavalry were ambushed by Nez Percé warriors, who vastly outnumbered them. Sgt. Michael McCarthy took charge of six men who were cut off from the main force and organized a resistance to slow the Indian advance. They subsequently fought their way through the Nez Percé, McCarthy having two horses shot out from under him in the melee, before five of the men were able to reach safety.[43] In all of these cases, the heroes were awarded the Medal of Honor for courage under fire.

Honoring soldiers for outstanding displays of courage was not only ethically correct, but also important to promoting good morale. Unfortunately, the system of awarding citations was a haphazard process at best, often requiring that officers witness the event and that details be corroborated by other officers. For instance, 24 enlisted men of the 7th Cavalry received the Medal of Honor out of 35 troopers who were nominated or mentioned for the award. A comparison of the two groups reveals no obvious evidence to separate those who were honored and those who were not. The system of selection was complicated, arcane, and serendipitous, thus denying many men the acknowledgment that they richly deserved.[44]

During 1874, Congress authorized another type of commendation that did not rank as high as the Medal of Honor, but it did recognize acts of extreme bravery in combat. These Certificates of Merit could only be issued to enlisted men who were "in good standing," whose action occurred on the battlefield, and whose commanding officer vouched for the authenticity of the event. Unlike the Medal of Honor, the Certificate of Merit carried with it an extra two dollars per month in army pay. Between 1874 and 1891, only 59 of these parchment certificates were awarded, and they apparently were valued by the few men who received them. Congress finally updated the commendation in 1934 by retroactively allowing all recipients to apply for the Distinguished Service Cross as a supplement to the earlier certificate.[45]

Stories of heroism were what the public wanted to hear about the frontier army, but sometimes the tales dealt with indecision and outright cowardice. Journalist John F. Finerty wrote admiringly about the officers and men he accompanied during Gen. George Crook's 1876 Sioux campaign, but he singled out one unnamed enlisted man for special criticism. Finerty challenged the soldier face-to-face and called him the "only constitutional coward in the whole command." Instead of coming to his own defense, the man responded that he would never again serve in a campaign, even if he had to desert to avoid the duty. He was quite content to be one of the soldiers assigned to protect the wagon camp rather than continue on to expected combat on the Rosebud or Little Big Horn.[46] Pvt. Billy Blake never became a target of journalistic ridicule, but he was much maligned by fellow troopers of the 7th Cavalry for his cowardice at the battle of Little Big Horn. While his comrades fought desperately to maintain their exposed positions along Reno Hill, Pvt. Blake allegedly pretended to be hurt, and he sought a relatively safer position among the wounded to wait out the bloody ordeal.[47]

Cases of cowardice were not limited to enlisted men. Sgt. Perley S. Eaton recalled that at the 1882 battle of Big Dry Wash in Arizona, an unnamed captain pushed a soldier from behind a tree so that he could seek safety there. The exposed soldier was immediately shot dead by Apache marksmen.[48] A more credible account came from Sgt. John B. Charlton,

"Soldiering in the Southwest—the Rescue of Corporal Scott"
by Frederic Remington gave the American public a romanticized view of courage under fire. (*Courtesy of the Library
of Congress*)

who remembered a patrol that was attacked by a group of Indians. The unidentified
lieutenant panicked, leading his men into a disorganized retreat. Charlton caught up
with the fleeing officer and organized an impromptu defense that turned back the Indian
attackers. The shameless officer later begged his sergeant not to report the incident to
his superiors, and Charlton never did.[49]

Despite the anecdotal accounts of courage and cowardice on the battlefield, most
Americans paid more attention to the big picture rather than the smaller, human stories.
National newspapers and politicians provided extended coverage about major campaigns, big battles, and the opinions of senior officers. They also focused on one other
issue of great importance to the public: the cost of military operations against Indians.
Disasters such as Little Big Horn always prompted investigations by Congress, and
in most cases, the cumulative costs were a primary feature of the official inquiries. In
response to a Senate Resolution, the War Department prepared a report on the cost of

the controversial Sioux war of 1876. Total expenses for involvement of the Departments of the Platte and Dakota in the operations amounted to a whopping $2,312,531.[50] Such a staggering sum overwhelmed Americans in an age when federal budgets were relatively small and Indian wars seemed so far away from most people's lives.

An Exciting and Difficult Time for the Army

In categorizing the various eras in American military history, textbooks tend to refer to the long period of 1865–1898 as the "Peacetime Army." It stands like some extended aberration between the monumental Civil War and the one-sided Spanish-American War that moved the United States toward the beginnings of its overseas empire. A modern reassessment of the last three decades of the nineteenth century, however, reveals not an era of peaceful slumber, but rather an exciting and difficult time for the U.S. Army. As early as 1869, Gen. William Tecumseh Sherman articulated what the public did not fully understand: "While the nation at large is at peace, a state of *quasi* war has existed, and continues to exist, over one-half its extent, and the troops therein are exposed to labors, marches, fights, and dangers that amount to war."[51] The words proved prophetic during the next two and a half decades amid the most important years of the fabled Indian wars.

NOTES

1. Maurice Matloff, ed., *American Military History,* Office of the Chief of Military History (Washington, DC: U.S. Government Printing Office, 1969), 281. William L. Richter, *The Army in Texas during Reconstruction, 1865–1870* (College Station: Texas A&M University Press, 1987), 14–27, 62–75. Carl H. Moneyhon, *Texas after the Civil War: The Struggle of Reconstruction* (College Station: Texas A&M University Press, 2004), 38–56.

2. Rupert N. Richardson, *The Frontier of Northwest Texas, 1846 to 1876: Advance and Defense by the Pioneer Settlers of the Cross Timbers and Prairies* (Glendale, CA: Arthur H. Clark, 1963), 245–54, 269–81.

3. Clarence Clendenen, *Blood on the Border: The United States Army and the Mexican Irregulars* (New York: Macmillan, 1969), 57–59. Michael C. Meyer and William L. Sherman, *The Course of Mexican History* (New York: Oxford University Press, 1979), 387–401.

4. Matloff, *American Military History,* 284. Donald W. Whisenhunt, *Fort Richardson: Outpost on the Texas Frontier,* Southwestern Studies Monograph, no. 20 (El Paso: Texas Western Press, 1968), 9, 16.

5. Matloff, *American Military History,* 284. James E. Sefton, *The United States Army and Reconstruction, 1865–1877* (Baton Rouge: Louisiana State University Press, 1967), 94–100.

6. William Tecumseh Sherman to John Sherman, 21 September 1865, in Rachel Sherman Thorndike, ed., *The Sherman Letters: Correspondence between General and Senator Sherman from 1837 to 1891* (New York: Charles Scribner's Sons, 1894), 256.

7. Allan R. Millett and Peter Maslowski, *For the Common Defense: A Military History of the United States of America* (New York: Free Press, 1984), 246.

8. George G. Meade to Col. Philippe Régis de Trobriand, 28 August 1867, in Marie Caroline Post, *The Life and Memoirs of Comte Régis de Trobriand* (New York: E. P. Dutton, 1910), 347.

9. Sefton, *United States Army,* 203–4.

10. Almira R. Hancock, *Reminiscences of Winfield Scott Hancock* (New York: Charles L. Webster, 1887), 120–32.

11. Sefton, *United States Army,* 174–76.

12. Henry P. Walker, "Bugler! No Pay Call Today! The Year the Army Went Payless," *Montana, Magazine of Western History* 21 (Summer 1971): 34–43. Robert M. Utley, *Frontier Regulars: The United States Army and the Indian, 1866–1891* (New York: Macmillan, 1973), 60–64.

13. Frances M. A. Roe, *Army Letters from an Officer's Wife, 1871–1888* (New York: D. Appleton, 1909), 159.

14. Edward S. Farrow, *Mountain Scouting: A Hand-Book for Officers and Soldiers on the Frontiers* (New York: E. S. Farrow, 1881), 239.

15. John G. Bourke, *An Apache Campaign in the Sierra Madre: An Account of the Expedition in Pursuit of the Hostile Chiricahua Apaches in the Spring of 1883* (New York: Charles Scribner's Sons, 1886), 27–28. A brief overview of the tactical problems associated with counterguerrilla warfare is found in John M. Gates, "Indians and Insurrectos: The U.S. Army's Experience with Insurgency," *Parameters: The Journal of the U.S. Army War College* 13 (March 1983): 59–68.

16. Randolph B. Marcy, *Thirty Years of Army Life on the Border* (New York: Harper and Brothers, 1866), 47–48.

17. Utley, *Frontier Regulars,* 50–52.

18. Philippe Régis de Trobriand, *Military Life in Dakota: The Journal of Philippe Régis de Trobriand,* ed. Lucile M. Kane (Saint Paul, MN: Alvord Memorial Commission, 1951), 64.

19. Russell F. Weigley, *The American Way of War: A History of United States Military Strategy and Policy* (New York: Macmillan, 1973), 153. Also endorsing the total warfare theme is Paul Hutton, who agrees with Weigley that the antecedents are found in the colonial Indian wars, not in the Civil War. See Paul Andrew Hutton, ed., *Soldiers West: Biographies from the Military Frontier* (Lincoln: University of Nebraska Press, 1987), 6–7.

20. Robert Wooster, *The Military and United States Indian Policy, 1865–1903* (New Haven, CT: Yale University Press, 1988), 140–43.

21. An excellent discussion of these interpretive similarities and differences is found in Perry D. Jamieson, *Crossing the Deadly Ground: United States Army Tactics, 1865–1899* (Tuscaloosa: University of Alabama Press, 1994), 48–53.

22. William H. Leckie, *The Military Conquest of the Southern Plains* (Norman: University of Oklahoma Press, 1963), 187–235. William H. Leckie, ed., "Special Issue on the Red River War, 1874–1875," *Red River Valley Historical Review* 3 (Spring 1978): 143–276. Wilbur S. Nye, *Carbine and Lance: The Story of Old Fort Sill* (Norman: University of Oklahoma Press, 1942), 213–35.

23. Charles M. Robinson III, *General Crook and the Western Frontier* (Norman: University of Oklahoma Press, 2001), 116–17, 190, 203, 257. Emmett M. Essin III, "Mules, Packs, and Pack-trains," *Southwestern Historical Quarterly* 74 (July 1970): 52–63. Archibald A. Cabaniss, "Troop and Company Pack-Trains," *Journal of the U.S. Cavalry Association* 3 (September 1890): 248–52.

24. A brief but interesting assessment about the limited fighting ability of cavalry is found in James S. Hutchins, "Mounted Riflemen: The Real Role of Cavalry in the Indian Wars," in *Probing the American West,* ed. K. Ross Toole et al. (Santa Fe: Museum of New Mexico Press, 1962), 79–85.

25. De Trobriand, *Military Life in Dakota,* 64–65.

26. Paul Andrew Hutton, *Phil Sheridan and His Army* (Lincoln: University of Nebraska Press, 1985), 54–55. Robert M. Utley, *The Lance and the Shield: The Life and Times of Sitting Bull* (New York: Henry Holt, 1993), 174–82. John Stands In Timber and Margot Liberty, *Cheyenne Memories* (New Haven, CT: Yale University Press, 1967), 212–25.

27. Jamieson, *Crossing the Deadly Ground,* 38.

28. Jamieson, *Crossing the Deadly Ground,* 44–45. Don Rickey Jr., *Forty Miles a Day on Beans and Hay: The Enlisted Soldier Fighting the Indian Wars* (Norman: University of Oklahoma Press, 1963), 289–94.

29. John Gibbon, "Arms to Fight Indians," *United Service* 1 (April 1879): 240.

30. Charles King, *Campaigning with Crook: The Fifth Cavalry in the Sioux War of 1876* (Norman: University of Oklahoma Press, 1964), 121–23.

31. Jamieson, *Crossing the Deadly Ground,* 28.

32. Ibid., 28.

33. The detailed story of this suffering is well told in Paul H. Carlson, *The Buffalo Soldier Tragedy of 1877* (College Station: Texas A&M University Press, 2003).

34. Robert Athearn, "The Fort Buford 'Massacre,'" *Mississippi Valley Historical Review* 41 (March 1955): 675–84.

35. Henry P. Walker, ed., "The Reluctant Corporal: The Autobiography of William Bladen Jett," *Journal of Arizona History* 12 (Spring 1971): 33–35.

36. Lt. C. A. Woodruff, "Letters from the Big Hole," *Montana, Magazine of Western History* 2 (October 1952): 55–56.

37. Robert M. Utley, ed., *Life in Custer's Cavalry: Diaries and Letters of Albert and Jennie Barnitz, 1867–1867* (New Haven, CT: Yale University Press, 1977), 70–73. The photograph of Sgt. Williams's mangled body is found on page 67 of the same book.

38. Martha Summerhayes, *Vanished Arizona: Recollections of the Army Life of a New England Woman,* 2nd ed. (Salem, MA: Salem Press, 1911), 110–11.

39. Ernest R. Archambeau, ed., "Monthly Reports of the Fourth Cavalry 1872–1874," *Panhandle-Plains Historical Review* 38 (1965): 95–154. A chronological list of all official military actions undertaken by the U.S. Army during the nineteenth century appears in Francis B. Heitman, *Historical Register and Dictionary of the United States Army, from Its Organization, September 29, 1789, to March 2, 1903,* vol. 2 (Washington, DC: U.S. Government Printing Office, 1903), 391–474. It should be closely compared to a similarly conceived reference source: George W. Webb, *Chronological List of Engagements between the Regular Army of the United States and Various Tribes of Hostile Indians during the Years 1790 to 1898, Inclusive* (St. Joseph, MO: Wing, 1939).

40. Letters of Powhatan Clarke, 4 and 10 May 1886, in Frank N. Schubert, *Voices of the Buffalo Soldier: Records, Reports, and Recollections of Military Life and Service in the West* (Albuquerque: University of New Mexico Press, 2003), 139–40. Peggy Samuels and Harold Samuels, *Frederic Remington: A Biography* (Austin: University of Texas Press, 1982), 70–73.

41. Don Russell, *Campaigning with King: Charles King, Chronicler of the Old Army,* ed. Paul L. Hedren (Lincoln: University of Nebraska Press, 1991), 50–53.

42. Larry Sklenar, "Medals for Custer's Men," *Montana, Magazine of Western History* 50 (Winter 2000): 55–65.

43. Jerome A. Greene, *Nez Perce Summer, 1877: The U.S. Army and the Nee-Me-Poo Crisis* (Helena: Montana Historical Society Press, 2000), 39–43.

44. Sklenar, "Medals," 64–65.

45. Rickey, *Forty Miles a Day,* 309–11. James Robert Moriarity III, "The Congressional Medal of Honor during the Indian Wars," in Ray Brandes, ed., *Troopers West: Military and Indian Affairs on the American Frontier* (San Diego, CA: Frontier Heritage Press, 1970), 149–67.

46. John F. Finerty, *War-Path and Bivouac, or the Conquest of the Sioux: A Narrative of Stirring Personal Experiences and Adventures in the Big Horn and Yellowstone Expedition of 1876, and in the Campaign on the British Border in 1879* (Norman: University of Oklahoma Press, 1961), 74–75.

47. Rickey, *Forty Miles a Day,* 303.

48. Ibid., 304.

49. Robert G. Carter, ed., *The Old Sergeant's Story: Winning the West from the Indians and Bad Men in 1870 to 1876* (New York: Frederick H. Hitchcock, 1926), 92.

50. U.S. Congress, Senate, *Message from the President of the United States,* 45th Cong., 2nd sess., 1877, S. Exec. Doc. 33, 1–4.

51. Jamieson, *Crossing the Deadly Ground,* 23.

4 ARMED LABORERS: BUILDING AND MAINTAINING A NETWORK OF POSTS

As the U.S. Army sought to muster out the majority of its Civil War veterans and to reconstitute units for Reconstruction and frontier duties, it also had to deal with the question of permanent stations for its troops. This was especially difficult in the western regions stretching from the Great Plains to the Pacific coast. Most of the pre–Civil War posts had been abandoned between April 1861 and April 1865, as the Union reassigned most of its soldiers to the eastern theater of combat. During those years, volunteer regiments from midwestern states and local militia units raised in the territories tried to protect the frontier from increased lawlessness and Indian attacks, but their understrength forces were no match for the violent times. These new realities, plus the reluctance of Congress to vote larger budgets for again garrisoning the western territories, therefore posed difficult choices for the War Department in 1866.

Rather than simply reoccupying forts that had been abandoned during the Civil War, military leaders had to prioritize their expenditures and create new posts that were better situated to deal with new threats. To the casual observer, these decisions often seemed to be arbitrary and unjustifiable. One frequently repeated story captured the essence of this public perception and was picked up later by journalist John Finerty. Writing 10 years after the actual events, this *Chicago Times* columnist claimed that the site selected for the construction of Ft. Phil Kearny, Wyoming, owed its origins not to careful consideration by military planners, but to the whims of the wife of commanding officer Col. Henry Carrington. According to the story, Margaret Carrington decided that she did not want to travel any farther up the difficult Bozeman Trail, and she pronounced to her husband, "You may march all you please...but here I will remain. This is as good a place for your fort as any other."[1] Finerty went on to remind his readers that the chosen site was a poor one, with its surrounding hillsides allowing easy approach by hostile Indians. It had also become the cemetery for 80 troopers under Capt. William Fetterman, who were killed by Lakota warriors on December 21, 1866.

NEW LINES OF DEFENSE—FORTS IN THE WEST

Despite the seeming plausibility of Finerty's tale, it was probably apocryphal. In truth, the War Department conducted methodical and purposeful surveys for potential post sites, but it rarely found perfect locations for construction. Every fortification suffered from at least one liability—it was too remote, too difficult to supply, lacked reliable water, had no resources for building materials, was vulnerable to attack, or faced other inadequacies. Yet in spite of the list of liabilities, the army did maintain a cogent strategy for the placement of installations that went well beyond mere guesswork.

For instance, military planners effectively updated a logistical arrangement that had existed in Texas before the Civil War. By the end of the 1860s, the army had largely abandoned the line of forts that extended from Ft. Belknap in the north, through Ft. Mason in the center, to Ft. Hudson near the Rio Grande. In place of these obsolete fortifications that served only as picket stations for small patrols after 1869, soldiers built Ft. Griffin in the north, Ft. Concho in the center, and Ft. Stockton in the west. These installations reflected a bold move by the army to expand farther onto the plains of Texas, where they could deal more effectively with Comanche, Kiowa, Mescalero, and Lipan Apache raids. All of these posts and their companion fortifications in the Texas defense line were deemed hard duty assignments because many of them lacked basic amenities and were also located in some of the driest and hottest environs of the nation.[2]

At the opposite end of the Great Plains, the War Department demonstrated its accommodation to a different set of environmental conditions. In 1866, it began the reoccupation of forts stretching along the Missouri River across Dakota Territory. Among the criteria used in selecting specific sites were the availability of good drinking water, timber for construction material and fuel, grass for livestock, adequate flat land upon which to erect the structures, and a good spot for a steamboat landing. Like a vast highway stretching across the northern plains, the Missouri River provided the logical pathway for an integrated system of installations that could be readily supplied and reinforced. Flooding proved to be a problem at some locations, such as the Cheyenne River Agency, but soldiers usually rebuilt the structures on higher ground within close proximity to the original riverside posts.[3]

An examination of the Military Department of Dakota reveals that 31 forts were built throughout the Dakotas and Montana between 1866 and 1891—first along the Missouri River axis, and then in more remote areas. Historical geographer Gary Freedom divided these into three categories, noting that the earliest tier of Missouri River posts constituted those in "advance of civilian settlement." Only four of the forts in the Military Department of Dakota were established "concurrent with civilian settlement": Ft. Seward (Jamestown), Ft. Abraham Lincoln (Bismarck), Ft. Meade (Sturgis), and Ft. Keogh (Miles City). The two former posts were built to protect construction crews of the Northern Pacific Railroad, so adjacent towns developed quickly alongside them. The final category described by Freedom is forts built in "response to settlement." These primarily included the Montana installations built after 1874 that were associated with the large campaigns against the Sioux and Northern Cheyennes.[4] Thus strategies for constructing military posts may have developed somewhat differently in each section of the West and may have changed with the passage of time as new strategies became necessary, but the U.S. Army evidenced considerable planning in its construction program. Personal whims of commanding officers' wives, or any other personnel for that matter, certainly did not dominate the selection process.

Fort Meade in South Dakota was built to protect miners in the Black Hills, 1888. (*Courtesy of the Library of Congress*)

As army defense plans evolved over the course of the late nineteenth century, debates occasionally flared in Congress about rising expenditures to build so many new forts. By official count in 1869, the army occupied 255 forts throughout the entire nation, though admittedly, many of these were only subposts or picket stations, housing no more than a dozen soldiers each.[5] The high number of posts, however, generated considerable rhetoric against the allegedly "spendthrift" War Department. Generals William T. Sherman, Philip Sheridan, and Edward O. C. Ord rebutted that dispersal of troops was the only way to deal with highly mobile Indian populations. To amass the bulk of the frontier army at two score installations might save considerable construction and supply costs, but it would not settle the vexatious so-called Indian problem.[6]

Once a site had been chosen for a post, the army had to concern itself with ownership rights. If the land designated for a military reservation was exclusively federal property, officers could begin immediate construction of buildings and other improvements. If, on the other hand, any of the coveted land was owned by private parties, legal terms had to be established through contractual arrangements. Leasing was the preferred method for exchanging rights of use because the army built few installations to last very long. At sites that were considered to have a more certain future, outright purchase was the preferred choice. For instance, when surveyors arrived at Ft. Concho, Texas, in 1870 to carve out 1,640 acres as a military reservation, they found that most of the land had already been claimed around the welcome waters of the Concho River. During the delicate financial negotiations over the sale of these lands, owners inflated the asking price beyond reason. Government representations finally accepted a more complicated set of yearly lease payments, some of which extended all the way to the fort's closing in 1889.[7]

The issue was even more complex at Ft. Griffin, which was established in 1867 to block Comanche and Kiowa raiding parties from entering northwestern Texas from Indian Territory reservations. Savvy landowners at this pivotal post realized that they held the bargaining advantage since the government was unlikely to move such a vital fort to another location. Multiple claimants held out until 1873, when lease contracts were finally signed by all interested parties. Ironically, the Red River War of 1874–1875 eliminated most Indian threats to the northwestern counties of Texas, and Ft. Griffin was deactivated seven years later.[8]

In isolated regions, especially those where adequate drinking water was available in only a few places, the War Department was forced to pay dearly for ownership and leasing rights to military reservations. There simply were no other tenable sites that could be utilized at a cheaper price. But in larger communities, where land could be bid on a more competitive basis, the subject of leasing drew considerable public attention. When Col. Edmund Schriver arrived in San Antonio in late 1872 as representative of the Inspector General's Office, he declared the leases for the San Antonio Quartermaster Depot (forerunner of Ft. Sam Houston) to be a travesty. The army owned no buildings at this most important supply depot, and over the span of 16 years, it had simply rented storage structures wherever it could find them in the town. Schriver noted that the army was paying 27,000 dollars in annual lease fees, including 7,000 dollars for a headquarters building whose basement was used only for the storage of clothes. The rent paid in this case was far greater than that paid for the headquarters of the Division of the Atlantic, located in the center of Philadelphia.[9]

CONSTRUCTION OF POSTS

Once a site had been selected for a military post, budgetary limitations dictated its initial size, available building materials decided its architectural pattern, and its specific mission determined whether or not it would be expanded within the first few years. One thing is certain in this regard: The post–Civil War military installations of the West were not the expansive fortifications, surrounded by wooden palisades and reinforced with imposing guard towers, that Hollywood later made famous. The shortage of timber and other building materials, plus the inadequate funding for grandiose edifices, precluded such improbable construction projects. Fortunately, commanding officers were allowed to take the initiative in deciding the layout of their own posts and in assigning buildings for specific functions. Commanders also understood that installations would need to change over time based on the exigencies of Indian campaigns and other governmental concerns. Forts therefore evolved not according to any grand plan, but rather by the short-term need to expand or retrench their facilities. Parade grounds may have looked the same from place to place, but the pattern of each fortification was unique to its needs and evolution over time.[10]

The actual construction of military posts was also a point of contention, especially in cases where soldiers were the primary laborers. As early as November 12, 1867, the Adjutant General's Office directed that troops routinely would be employed to build fortifications, maintain the structures, cut hay, chop wood for fuel, and perform other construction duties that the presiding officer would designate. In cases where soldiers were involved in extensive field campaigns or were acutely under strength, the department commander could establish short-term contracts with civilian builders.

Soldier-prisoners working off their punishments by chopping and sawing firewood at Ft. Grant, Arizona, 1885. (*Courtesy Arizona Historical Society/Tuscon/19902*)

Furthermore, soldiers who were utilized in this capacity for 10 or more successive days were guaranteed an extra 20 cents per day in their monthly army pay.[11] In some cases, the supplementary compensation was extended to as much as 35 cents a day for experienced carpenters, stonemasons, and mechanics—a sizeable amount considering that the average regular pay for a private was 13 dollars per month during these decades.[12]

Building Instead of Drilling and Patrolling

Officers all across the West were quick to point out the adverse effects of soldiers spending so much time on building projects and too little on drill and patrol. In 1870, Col. Joseph J. Reynolds protested to Gen. William T. Sherman that the high incidence of desertion in Texas was due to the unending labor demands made on enlisted men. Many had joined the army to escape this kind of life, and now their full day was consumed by some of the hardest physical labor imaginable. Reynolds further argued that contracting with civilian companies to build and maintain forts had already proven itself to be economical and efficient. Soldiers were better prepared for combat, and the structures built by civilians were generally superior to those built by indifferent troops.[13] Sherman reiterated the conclusions of Reynolds and other officers in his 1870 annual report, which affirmed that "to build permanent works or roads in which they have but a partial interest, is a kind of labor that ought not to be imposed on our reduced establishment."[14]

Sherman's criticism was leveled at the inadequate budgets that Congress imposed upon the army, forcing it to perform too many tasks simultaneously. Writing 15 years later about the same issue that had not yet been resolved, Gen. Oliver Otis Howard noted that the commander at Coeur d'Alene, Idaho, was instructed to erect a 150,000 dollar set of military buildings on a total budget of 25,000 dollars. This commander's fate would be the same as so many officers—to exclusively rely upon soldiers as laborers and to construct the quarters as cheaply as possible.[15] Most officers kept their grievances within military channels, but Capt. George Frederic Price at Ft. Union, New Mexico, lodged his complaint in the civilian newspapers at nearby Las Vegas, New Mexico, a year

Three men construct a crude building at Fort Keogh, Montana, ca. 1889. (*Courtesy of the National Archives*)

earlier. He fanned the flames of discontent among local civilians, who were unhappy that they could not receive contracts to build structures at the post. He also emphasized that his soldiers were so busy with forced construction projects that less than half of the cavalrymen could be counted on for service against Indian raiders.[16]

Amid all the complaints, however, the loudest responses came from enlisted men. One private stationed at Camp Ruhlen, Dakota Territory (renamed Ft. Meade), wrote to the New York *Herald* in 1878, "Drill has been suspended because there are cellers [*sic*] to dig, bridges to be built, mason and carpenter work to be done; all because the government cannot or will not afford to employ men who are ready and willing to do that work."[17] Equally perturbed were men of the 5th Infantry, stationed at Ft. Stevenson, Dakota Territory. They informed a group of visiting 7th Cavalrymen that their lives were spent laboring in the "poorhouse" because they worked endlessly for so little public gratitude.[18]

Even in their retirement years, veterans recalled the continuous construction demands as their greatest disappointment about military life. Sgt. Harry H. McConnell, one of the most eloquent spokesmen from the enlisted ranks, contrasted his idealism about joining the army to serve his country with the grim realities of the laborer's life. In the end, he sarcastically concluded, the army had proven that the "spade is mightier than the sword."[19] Another former private of the 5th Cavalry lamented that he had given up a good job as a clothing clerk to join the frontier army. Whatever good might have come from his army years, he mainly remembered digging trenches for a water system, shoveling coal from railroad cars to heat the enlisted men's drafty barracks, hauling sand to build new stables, and dealing with blistered hands that were the inevitable result of his manual labor.[20]

Soldiers' complaints occasionally found a receptive ear among civilians. A correspondent for the Omaha *Herald* was especially moved by the plight of a soldier-laborer at Ft. McKinney, Wyoming, who worked on building projects from sunrise to sunset, in rain or shine, and perpetually moved from one finished structure to immediately prepare foundations for another. In an indignant tone, the correspondent concluded that the soldier "is no more nor less than a beast of burden, and what is still worse, he is treated as such." The journalist further noted that when civilians saw these soldiers at work, they inevitably mistook them for convicts since their labor was so difficult and the discipline so strict.[21] Perhaps some of the discontent could have been alleviated if these men had automatically received the mandated supplementary pay for their efforts. Unfortunately, the provisions for the 20–35 cents daily bonus often went unmet because budgets would not cover the higher amounts. Commanding officers sometimes avoided awarding of the bonuses by purposely interrupting the 10 days of continuous labor that were required for extra pay by military law. Such purposeful deceit could only worsen an already deflated morale among the men.[22]

While knowledgeable civilians generally were sympathetic toward the soldiers on these counts, some demonstrated utter contempt for their suffering. At Ft. Fetterman, Wyoming, R. L. DeLay, the civilian operator of the post sawmill, was known to harbor superiority feelings toward the enlisted men. He evidenced a callous attitude when some of the men warned that the civilian workers had neglected the maintenance of equipment and that it was dangerous to operate. DeLay allegedly responded with the flippant remark, "Oh, if it kills anyone it will only be a soldier." On that same day, Pvt. Louis Bauer was killed when the poorly maintained blade broke and hit him in the face. Enraged friends of the dead soldier threatened to kill DeLay and on the following day forced him to flee the area. Inscribed on Pvt. Bauer's tombstone were the piercing words "Killed through Criminal Negligence."[23]

ROAD AND BRIDGE BUILDING

If soldiers deeply resented their forced labor in the construction of posts, a second type of labor angered them even more—road and bridge building. They complained vociferously about this type of nonmartial duty because they had to perform so much of it, had to live in tents while engaged in it, and seemingly received so few direct benefits from the completed projects. Government representatives justified these assignments on the grounds that good roads enabled easier transit and resupply of frontier troops. The assessment was an accurate one, but most of the beneficiaries of these transportation improvements were civilians, especially commercial interests who needed more reliable ways to effectively move passengers and merchandise.

Some of the projects were extensive because geographical peculiarities necessitated special engineering features. For instance, the government spent 25,000 dollars to lay out a road between Sioux City, Iowa, and Ft. Randall, Dakota Territory, a distance of only 140 miles. Much of the funding for this road went into the erection of sizeable bridges across the Big Sioux, Vermillion, and James rivers. Even though Ft. Randall was located on the bluffs overlooking the Missouri River, and the area had been supplied by boats in the pre–Civil War era, this was no longer deemed adequate after the war. Because the river surface froze during the winter, a more reliable system needed to be established. This became even more evident by the 1870s as additional posts were built west of the Missouri River in Dakota and Montana territories. A dependable east–west axis of transportation was now more necessary than ever before. Civilians rushing toward the mining camps of Idaho and western Montana were probably the greatest beneficiaries of this new overland network, which was built almost entirely by soldiers.[24]

Despite being designated as official roads and clearly marked on maps, under no circumstances can these primitive trails be thought of in the context of a modern highway system. The army's primarily construction responsibility was to mark the roads, lower steep grades, remove large obstacles, erect bridges over rivers, and protect civilian traffic from threatening actions of Indians and bandits. Some stretches showed careful work and marked improvement, but for most of the long distances across the West, the roads were virtually indistinguishable from the surrounding countryside. Rudimentary though they may have been, these improvements were widely cheered by the civilians who utilized them. These same civilians also celebrated the fact that so-called military roads helped eliminate some of the outrageously expensive toll roads and toll bridges at key junctures.[25]

Two specific examples of army transportation projects shed light on the contemporary expectations and limitations of these improvements. The Pecos River was one such case as it meandered across the desert wasteland of far western Texas, serving as a welcome landmark and sometime-source of drinkable water among travelers bound for New Mexico, Arizona, and California. Though not a particularly wide or deep river, except during the spring and early summer, or following a cloudburst, the Pecos was nonetheless a difficult crossing point. First contemplated as an army project early in the 1850s, the Pecos River bridge was not built until the early 1870s, about 20 miles downstream from the treacherous Horsehead Crossing. It was a pontoon structure that swung by iron chains attached at both banks. Movable platforms standing on each side could be raised or lowered to accommodate the changing depth of the water. Like other army bridges built in the seeming middle of nowhere, this one was very narrow and could not support the weight of a fully loaded freight wagon. Frustrated teamsters often had to unload and reload their cargoes on opposite sides of the river. When army wife Emily K. Andrews encountered the swaying structure in 1874, she noted that it was "not very safe," but she traveled across it anyway. Three years later, military doctor Ezra Woodruff articulated a more positive feeling and called it "a good pontoon bridge." During much of the bridge's history, it was operated and protected by a small squad of soldiers from Ft. Stockton, serving military and civilian traffic alike.[26]

West of the Pecos River pontoon bridge was a second, more extensive road-building project that bore the personal imprint of 10th Cavalry Commander Col. Benjamin Grierson. While headquartered at picturesque Ft. Davis, he oversaw the construction of a well-integrated road system that linked the valuable regional water holes as well as serving the preexistent Lower Road of the San Antonio–El Paso Trail that bisected the deserts of western Texas. Although the improvements were justifiable in meeting army needs, Grierson wanted the surrounding Davis Mountains region to quickly entice ranchers, farmers, and town builders. He invested his own money in lands and cattle herds, hoping to remain in the area as a well-heeled founding father after his retirement. Furthermore, during the early 1880s, he improved the water supplies at Barilla Springs northeast of Ft. Davis, Barrel Springs west of the post, and Eagle Springs to the northwest and intermittently stationed squads of soldiers at each place. Grierson defended this action on the grounds that soldiers could deprive scarce water sources to small bands of Apache raiders who swept down from New Mexico. Whatever the primary justification, the roads and improved water holes speeded travel and hastened settlement of the Trans-Pecos River country by 1885.[27]

Sometimes soldiers did share in the financial rewards associated with their construction projects, but only with approval from the post commander and only in indirect ways. In 1868, rather than build an expensive bridge across the North Platte River, soldiers at Ft. Fetterman, Wyoming, established a two-boat ferry that operated along a rope securely fastened on both banks. Under the exclusive management of the post quartermaster, and operated by three enlisted men, the ferry provided free passage for military men and supplies but charged civilians for the crossing. Fees ranged from 25 cents per individual to a dollar and a half for a loaded wagon. Profits went into the post treasury and were used exclusively to benefit the men of the garrison. Not until 11 years later was a permanent bridge built to replace the earlier innovation.[28]

For all the energy that soldiers expended in the construction of forts, roads, and bridges, the maintenance schedule on all three must have seemed endless. No project could ever be brought to completion before further extensions were demanded, or previously built structures had to be repaired. On visiting Ft. Kearny in 1867, *New York Herald* correspondent Henry Stanley expressed incredulity over how far the outpost had fallen into disrepair during the Civil War years. When garrison strength had been severely reduced, the complex hardly resembled its celebrated legacy as primary guardian of the Oregon and California trails through which so many overlanders had passed during the 1840s and 1850s. Stanley observed that "it has now become little better than a habitation for owls and prairie dogs. The lovely parade ground that once re-echoed with the tread of many companies of soldiers is now silent. Grass grows on the walks and entangles the wheels of the howitzers." With troop strength of only 12 soldiers and an assortment of musicians under the command of a lone lieutenant, Ft. Kearny certainly seemed destined for oblivion soon after Stanley wrote his bleak description.[29] But the War Department kept it open four additional years, despite the inadequate facilities that were further taxed by the increased number of soldiers that were subsequently transferred there. Troopers were kept constantly at work in repairing the infrastructure, which acting assistant surgeon W. A. Bradley had reported in 1869 was mostly in a dilapidated state.[30]

MAINTENANCE OF ARMY FARMS

One other facet of garrison life that had to be directly addressed by soldiers' labor was the planting, tending, and harvesting of crops. This was one of the more contentious issues among officers because it drew such large numbers of men from their required drill. It had been a common problem for the military ever since it began to construct fortifications in the more isolated areas of the Trans-Mississippi West. Fort Atkinson, spiked in along the western bank of the Missouri River in 1819, was the nation's westernmost installation during the following decade, and by necessity, it had to provide much of the food to a garrison that numbered over 900 men.

During the first year, 160 men succumbed to death by scurvy, a dietary problem that could best be treated with adequate supplies of vitamin C contained in fresh fruits and vegetables. Since congressional budgets could not adequately fund the purchase and transportation of food stocks to this distant post, Col. Henry Atkinson ordered his troops to create extensive farms along the rich bottomland. This agricultural experiment in present eastern Nebraska was a complete success, and it conformed to army regulations established in 1818 to allow local commanders discretion on the issue.[31] The Ft. Atkinson success story became an important precedent for frontier garrisons all across the West even to the end of the nineteenth century.

The 1818 directive was filled with irony because the army was mandated to turn civilians into polished soldiers and to utilize them primarily for martial duties. The reality of life on the frontier, however, dictated that forts be as self-sufficient as possible so that the War Department could save money while supplying them with food and durable goods. In case after case, the twin missions could not be reconciled, and policy shifts were initiated. Thus in 1833, the War Department issued a new directive to override the 1818 general orders that mandated extensive farming activity. For the next 18 years, military experiments with agriculture supposedly declined, but partial evidence indicates that the most isolated posts tended to maintain their gardens, despite the new orders. Then, in 1851, the policy shifted again as the need to cut supply costs and to improve soldiers' health through a better diet forced a broadening of the self-sufficiency approach. Three years later, this revised policy was likewise overturned. So it was that the strategic ball bounced back and forth during the next four decades, and the debate between military preparedness and self-sufficiency continued unabated.[32]

Several examples from the post–Civil War era suffice to explain the extensiveness of the agricultural operations and their overall significance within the supply system. As early as 1866, Maj. Gen. Irvin McDowell, commanding the Department of California, which included present-day Arizona, remarked in his annual report that the military reoccupation of Arizona would be virtually impossible without the initiation of government farms to feed soldiers. Because most of Arizona's forts were so far removed from the pivotal supply depots on the California coast and at San Antonio, Texas, they would have to be more self-reliant than most. McDowell further observed that a large-scale farm had already been established at Ft. McDowell in the valley of the Verde River and was producing abundant crops. Thus at many of the anticipated sites for future posts, soldiers could produce adequate fresh foods to supplement their army supplies if given ample time and tools to do so.[33]

Output varied greatly from installation to installation, depending on length of growing season, preferred crops, ready availability of water, and dedication of the post commander and his men. Ft. Ellis, Montana, was representative of one of the largest and highest-yield farms. The plowed area eventually extended over 26 acres, requiring the labor of many soldiers. In 1879 alone, it yielded 172 bushels carrots, 3,865 bushels potatoes, 336 bushels onions, 785 bushels turnips, 105 bushels beets, 75 bushels parsnips, and 12,500 heads of cabbage. The total market value of this vitamin-rich yield was estimated to be 7,182 dollars.[34]

More typical in size and output was the garden at Ft. Laramie, which in 1868 had only two and a half acres in cultivation. But under the careful attention of the post chaplain, the small acreage was packed with 6,000 strawberry, 250 raspberry, 250 blackberry, 50 rhubarb, 100 currant, and 600 asparagus plants. By 1878, the Ft. Laramie garden had only expanded to five acres, but the well-watered location seemed to produce adequate sources of ascorbic acid to alleviate scurvy and other dietary diseases.[35]

Dependable sources of water were key to successful farming in the arid regions of the West. Lt. Col. Zenas Bliss noted in 1879 that Fort Stockton, Texas, "was the best garden I have ever seen at a military post." Under careful administration by men of the 9th Cavalry and 25th Infantry, and amply served by the huge volume of water from Comanche Spring, the garden produced more vegetables than were required at the fort. Surpluses of sweet corn, melon, and grapes were routinely sold on the open market to appreciative civilians.[36] At Ft. Fetterman, Wyoming, soldiers dammed La Prele Creek to conserve its precious water for irrigating their crops. Likewise, at Sidney Barracks, in the southern part of the Nebraska panhandle, soldiers dammed the somewhat reliable Lodgepole Creek, a tributary of the South Platte River, and irrigated their three and a half acre plot with its waters.[37]

Over time, some of the forts evidenced fairly sophisticated improvements in their water-delivery systems. At Fort Supply in northwestern Indian Territory, adequate surface water proved to be an elusive prize as soldiers watched healthy crops wither on the vine during repeated July and August dry spells. After several disasters, they finally erected windmills to draw subterranean water up to fill their irrigation system.[38] In the same year, a Halladay windmill was placed over a preexisting well and alongside a 33,000-gallon tank at Ft. Niobrara, Nebraska, to create a reservoir of drinking water as well as for irrigating purposes.[39] To the south, at Ft. Wallace, Kansas, the garrison was fortunate to draw water from the Smoky Hill River without having to rely on well-drilling equipment. Their extensive irrigation system provided ample water for the post's four-acre vegetable garden and for grass lawns at some of the officers' quarters.[40]

Farming Benefits to Soldiers and Future Settlements

Soldiers frequently groused about being assigned to agricultural duties, but most sensed that this was one form of labor that could directly enhance their quality of life. This was especially true at installations where commanding officers approved several types of agricultural experiments operating simultaneously. At Ft. Wadsworth, Dakota Territory, three varieties of farms existed in the mid-1860s to provide fresh fruits and vegetables to a garrison that normally drew its supplies from over 200 miles away, in Minnesota. One plot belonged to the hospital, a second plot to the officers, and a third to the individual companies stationed at the post. This arrangement provided extra incentive for men to be attentive to their duties, especially in the third case, where some of the food that showed up on company mess tables came directly from their own efforts. Each company chose the crops it wished to plant and decided when these items would be harvested for their dinner table.[41] At other posts, soldiers were allowed to sell any surplus produced in their company gardens and use the proceeds to purchase other "luxuries" for the use of the entire company.[42]

In addition to growing fresh fruits and vegetables, many forts supplemented their diets by maintaining small livestock herds. At Ft. Fetterman, Wyoming, in 1875, officers introduced cattle and chickens to the post. During the same era, soldiers at Ft. Buford, Dakota Territory, tended a successful beef herd to supplement the heavily salted and tasteless dry beef that was delivered by distant contractors. Milk cows were also introduced at Ft. Fetterman in 1875, and a few years later at Ft. Elliott in the Texas panhandle. Fresh milk was highly prized and more avidly sought than the canned milk that sometimes made its way into sutlers' stores.[43]

Despite the numerous agricultural experiments undertaken by the army, not all were successful. Soldiers found their efforts confronted by the same grim realities that overwhelmed homesteaders in the arid regions of the West. Bumper crops were harvested during some years, only to be followed by utter devastation during the following year. At Ft. Stevenson, in the center of present North Dakota, Col. Philippe Régis de Trobriand recalled how a grasshopper infestation suddenly appeared on the heels of a powerful summer thunderstorm. For six solid hours, the insects passed like low-level clouds over the post, many of them descending into the garden and others affixing themselves to the wooden windows, doors, and porches of the buildings. Then, like a miracle, a second blast of wind passed through the area in the late afternoon and blew away the millions of uninvited guests. Fortunately, the soldiers were able to salvage much of the garden because the grasshoppers inexplicably did not attack the potatoes or corn.[44]

Not all forts were so lucky because drought, heat, floods, plant diseases, and insect infestations were common. As at Ft. Stevenson, soldiers merely salvaged what they could, relied upon food shipments through the normal supply system, and hoped for better agricultural results during the following year. They hoped that dietary deficiencies associated with lack of fresh fruit and vegetables would not produce major health problems in the interim.[45]

While Mother Nature decided the fate of more post gardens than any single cause, one other factor could interfere with agricultural pursuits: competition from civilian contractors. The pressure exerted at Ft. Concho, Texas, was especially noteworthy because the civilian-owned Bismarck Farm lobbied effectively and won its claim. This enterprise had originally leased the acres to the army to produce lettuce, beans, corn, squash, melons, okra, peas, and potatoes. But over time, the soldiers produced a surplus of these items and began selling them on the local market at San Angelo. The owner of Bismarck Farm succeeded in his case, canceled the 10-acre lease, and effectively ended the competition.[46]

Despite periodic complaints from the War Department and senior commanders in the field about too much time being expended on agricultural pursuits, the farms and gardens were clearly justified. They saved considerable money for the supply system, provided a healthier diet, and enhanced soldier morale in most cases. They also contributed in small ways to the body of scientific knowledge that helped promote eventual civilian farming in the areas of the arid West. Noteworthy among regional newspapers was Montana's *Helena Weekly Herald*, which praised the dryland farming experimentation at Ft. Assiniboine. It claimed that continued success would assure Montana an agricultural future that someday would equal the value of its mining wealth.[47]

Historical geographer Gary Freedom affirmed this trend by describing the evolution of forts in the Dakota Territory and Montana. Among these northern plains installations, he found a clear pattern of army agriculture preceding civilian farmers into most of the areas. Furthermore, he discovered that army writings about trial-and-error planting and harvesting techniques found their way into the agricultural and scientific literature of the day. They provided extensive observations on soil content, weather patterns, insects, preferred crops, and watering methods that were reproduced in academic journals and booster newspapers alike.[48]

Despite these long-term positive effects for broader society, the monotonous tasks assigned to soldiers differed little during the entire extent of the nineteenth century. During the 1850s and 1860s, soldiers at Fort Ridgely, Minnesota, referred to themselves as "brevet architects," rather than as bona fide soldiers. The description mirrored the sentiments of an 1838 comment by an unidentified enlisted man who described his demoralized peers as "armed laborers."[49] After all, they were the primary workforce for constructing and maintaining posts, establishing and improving roads and bridges, and implementing military farms and gardens throughout the West. These assignments emanated from practical concerns, not from military theory. For all of its desire to minimize these nonmartial responsibilities, the U.S. Army had few options other than to confront reality and try to become as self-sufficient as possible.

The price paid along the way was a high one. Soldier morale rose and fell according to these duty assignments, as did soldiers' perceptions about their own worth to society. Such endless tasks faced by the real frontier army found little mention in the romanticized images offered by artists, novelists, and movie makers. Yet these were essential endeavors to an institution that could not count on inadequate Congressional budgets to refine the army's infrastructure throughout the entire West. As historian Francis Paul Prucha accurately noted, these guardians of the nation simultaneously became wielders of the broadaxe and the bayonet, and the two roles of laborer and warrior remained closely entwined for almost a full century.

NOTES

1. John F. Finerty, *War-Path and Bivouac, or the Conquest of the Sioux: A Narrative of Stirring Personal Experiences and Adventures in the Big Horn and Yellowstone Expedition of 1876, and in the Campaign on the British Border in 1879* (Norman: University of Oklahoma Press, 1961), 53. The officer's wife in question, Margaret Irvin Carrington, makes no mention of this story in her *Absaraka, Home of the Crows: Being the Experience of an Officer's Wife on the Plains* (Philadelphia: J. B. Lippincott, 1868).

2. Loyd M. Uglow, *Standing in the Gap: Army Outposts, Picket Stations, and the Pacification of the Texas Frontier, 1866–1886* (Fort Worth: Texas Christian University Press, 2001), 8–13.

3. Ray H. Mattison, "The Army Post on the Northern Plains, 1865–1885," *Nebraska History* 35 (March 1954): 19–20.

4. Gary S. Freedom, "The Role of the Military and the Spread of Settlement in the Northern Great Plains, 1866–1891," *Midwest Review* 9 (Spring 1987): 1–11. Two other articles by Freedom also deal with the issue of selecting fort sites: "Military Forts and Logistical Self-Sufficiency on the Northern Great Plains, 1866–1891," *North Dakota History* 50 (Spring 1983): 4–11; and "Moving Men and Supplies: Military Transportation on the Northern Great Plains, 1866–1891," *South Dakota History* 14 (Summer 1984): 114–33.

5. Jack D. Foner, *The United States Soldier between Two Wars: Army Life and Reforms, 1865–1898* (New York: Humanities Press, 1970), 2.

6. Robert M. Utley, *Frontier Regulars: The United States Army and the Indian, 1866–1891* (New York: Macmillan, 1973), 46–48.

7. Bill Green, *The Dancing Was Lively: Fort Concho, Texas, a Social History, 1867 to 1882* (San Angelo, TX: Fort Concho Sketches, 1974), 8.

8. Eula Haskew, "Stribling and Kirkland of Fort Griffin," *West Texas Historical Association Year Book* 32 (October 1956): 61–69.

9. Walter C. Conway, ed., "Colonel Edmund Schriver's Inspector-General Report on Military Posts in Texas, November 1872–January 1873," *Southwestern Historical Quarterly* 67 (April 1964): 571. Two additional Texas posts deserve attention because of the special problems that developed from the surveys that were done prior to the leasing process. See James M. Oswald, "History of Fort Elliott," *Panhandle-Plains Historical Review* 32 (1959): 43–47; and George Ruhlen, "Quitman's Owners: A Sidelight on Frontier Reality," *Password* 5 (April 1960): 54–62.

10. Alison K. Hoagland, *Army Architecture in the West: Forts Laramie, Bridger, and D. A. Russell, 1849–1912* (Norman: University of Oklahoma Press, 2004), 3–10. Two additional sources provide detailed plans of structures and their purposes. See Roy Eugene Graham, "Federal Fort Architecture in Texas during the Nineteenth Century," *Southwestern Historical Quarterly* 74 (October 1970): 165–88; and Willard B. Robinson, *American Forts: Architectural Form and Function* (Urbana: University of Illinois Press, 1977).

11. Raymond L. Welty, "The Daily Life of the Frontier Soldier," *Cavalry Journal* 36 (1927): 585.

12. Don Rickey Jr., *Forty Miles a Day on Beans and Hay: The Enlisted Soldier Fighting the Indian Wars* (Norman: University of Oklahoma Press, 1963), 95, 126.

13. Welty, "Daily Life," 585.

14. Report of William T. Sherman, 10 November 1870, in *Annual Report of the Secretary of War for 1870*, 5.

15. Foner, *United States Soldier*, 14–15.

16. Dale F. Giese, "Soldiers at Play: A History of Social Life at Fort Union, New Mexico, 1851–1891" (PhD diss., University of New Mexico, 1969), 167.

17. Foner, *United States Soldier*, 15.

18. Ami Frank Mulford, *Fighting Indians in the 7th United States Cavalry* (Corning, NY: Paul Lindsley Mulford, 1879), 72. See similar outrages in Giese, "Soldiers at Play," 167–68; and Rickey, *Forty Miles a Day*, 93.

19. H. H. McConnell, *Five Years a Cavalryman, or Sketches of Regular Army Life on the Texas Frontier, 1866–1871* (Jacksboro, TX: J. N. Rogers, 1889), 53.

20. Letter of E. A. Selander, *Winners of the West*, October 1925, 7.

21. "A Correspondent of the Omaha *Herald*," *Army and Navy Journal* (August 30, 1879), 63.

22. Foner, *United States Soldier*, 17.

23. David P. Robrock, "A History of Fort Fetterman, Wyoming, 1867–1882," *Annals of Wyoming* 48 (Spring 1976): 71.

24. Freedom, "Moving Men and Supplies," 116–20.

25. Merrill G. Burlingame, "The Influence of the Military in the Building of Montana," *Pacific Northwest Quarterly* 29 (April 1938): 144–45. The more famous Bozeman Trail linking Ft. Laramie with the same mining camps of Idaho and western Montana led to the army establishing Forts Reno, Phil Kearny, and C. F. Smith as protection of this road through the heart of the Powder River country. Red Cloud's War on the Bozeman (1866–1867) resulted in a major army defeat and abandonment of the three posts under terms of the Ft. Laramie Treaty of 1868. See Ralph K. Andrist, *The Long Death: The Last Days of the Plains Indians* (New York: Collier Books, 1964), 97–134.

26. Clayton Williams, *Texas' Last Frontier: Fort Stockton and the Trans-Pecos, 1861–1895,* ed. Ernest Wallace (College Station: Texas A&M University Press, 1982), 126–27, 159. Sandra L. Myres, ed., "A Woman's View of the Texas Frontier, 1874: The Diary of Emily K. Andrews," *Southwestern Historical Quarterly* 86 (July 1982): 72. Elvis Joe Ballew, "Supply Problems of Fort Davis, Texas, 1867–1880" (MA thesis, Sul Ross University, 1971), 19.

27. Ballew, "Supply Problems," 13–15. Mary L. Williams, "Empire Building: Colonel Benjamin H. Grierson at Fort Davis, 1882–1885," *West Texas Historical Association Year Book* 61 (1985): 65–67. During the late 1870s, Grierson had developed similar road and water projects while commanding Ft. Concho, Texas, the place where he originally staked his investments for the future. See Frank M. Temple, "Colonel B. H. Grierson's Administration of the District of the Pecos," *West Texas Historical Association Year Book* 38 (1962): 85–93. Mary Sutton, "Glimpses of Fort Concho through the Military Telegraph," *West Texas Historical Association Year Book* 32 (1956): 129–30.

28. Tom Lindmier, *Drybone: A History of Fort Fetterman, Wyoming* (Glendo, WY: High Plains Press, 2002), 43–44.

29. Henry M. Stanley, *My Early Travels and Adventures in America* (London: S. Low Marston, 1895), 108–9.

30. D. Ray Wilson, *Fort Kearny on the Platte* (Dundee, IL: Crossroads Communications, 1980), 180–82.

31. Roger L. Nichols, "Soldiers As Farmers: Army Agriculture in the Missouri Valley, 1818–1827," *Nebraska History* 52 (Fall 1971), 242–43. Virgil Ney, *Fort on the Prairie: Fort Atkinson on the Council Bluff, 1819–1827* (Washington, DC: Command, 1978), 133–49.

32. *Annual Report of the Secretary of War for 1851,* 164–65. Miller J. Stewart, "To Plow, to Sow, to Reap, to Mow: The U.S. Army Agriculture Program," *Nebraska History* 63 (Summer 1982): 194–95. Edward E. Coffman, *The Old Army: A Portrait of the American Army in Peacetime, 1784–1898* (New York: Oxford University Press, 1986), 168, 171.

33. Report of Irvin McDowell, 18 October 1866, in *Annual Report of the Secretary of War for 1866,* 36.

34. Merrill Burlingame, *The Montana Frontier* (Helena, MT: State, 1942), 340.

35. Mattison, "Army Post," 27.

36. Williams, *Texas' Last Frontier,* 158.

37. Lindmier, *Drybone,* 97. R. Eli Paul, ed., "Battle of Ash Hollow: The 1909–1910 Recollections of General N.A.M. Dudley," *Nebraska History* 62 (Fall 1981): 384.

38. Robert C. Carriker, *Fort Supply, Indian Territory: Frontier Outpost on the Plains* (Norman: University of Oklahoma Press, 1970), 139–40.

39. Thomas R. Buecker, "Fort Niobrara, 1880–1906: Guardian of the Rosebud Sioux," *Nebraska History* 65 (Fall 1984): 305.

40. A. Bowen Sageser, "Windmill and Pump Irrigation on the Great Plains 1890–1910," *Nebraska History* 48 (Summer 1967): 107.

41. Paul M. Edwards, "Fort Wadsworth and the Friendly Santee Sioux, 1864–1892," *South Dakota Department of History Report and Historical Collections* 31 (1962): 93.

42. Raymond L. Welty, "Supplying the Frontier Military Posts," *Kansas Historical Quarterly* 7 (May 1938): 165. Mildred Wertenberger, comp., "Fort Totten, Dakota Territory, 1867," *North Dakota History* 34 (Spring 1967): 134. Henry Hale, "The Soldier, the Advance Guard of Civilization," *Mississippi Valley Historical Association Proceedings* 7 (1913–1914): 96–97.

43. Stewart, "To Plow," 213. Mark Harvey, "Securing the Confluence: A Portrait of Fort Buford, 1866 to 1895," composite issue, *North Dakota History* 69, nos. 2–4 (2003): 38–39. John M. Oswald, "History of Fort Elliott," *Panhandle-Plains Historical Review* 32 (1959): 20–21.

44. Philippe Régis de Trobriand, *Military Life in Dakota: The Journal of Philippe Régis de Trobriand,* ed. Lucile M. Kane (Saint Paul, MN: Alvord Memorial Commission, 1951), 314–16.

45. William D. Thomson, "History of Fort Pembina: 1870–1895," *North Dakota History* 36 (Winter 1969): 33. David K. Strate, *Sentinel to the Cimarron: The Frontier Experience of Fort Dodge, Kansas* (Dodge City, KS: Cultural Heritage and Arts Center, 1970), 52–53. George Ruhlen, "Quitman: The Worst Post at Which I Ever Served," *Password* 12 (Fall 1966): 119.

46. Green, *Dancing Was Lively,* 34–36, 50. James T. Matthews, "Using the Diety's Name in Reverence: The Chaplains at Fort Concho," *Panhandle-Plains Historical Review* 68 (1995): 39–40. Stewart, "To Plow," 210.

47. "Off for Assinaboine," *Helena Weekly Herald,* October 1881, 7.

48. Freedom, "Military Forts," 7–11.

49. Paul Hedren, "On Duty at Fort Ridgely, Minnesota: 1853–1867," *South Dakota History* 7 (Spring 1977): 185. "Desertions from the Army," *Army and Navy Chronicle* 6 (May 17, 1838): 314–15.

5 THE REGIMENTAL FAMILY: PATRONAGE, POWER, AND SOCIAL DYNAMICS

Long-time veterans of the frontier army took station at many widely scattered posts during their careers. Although individual officers and enlisted men differed in their perceptions about what constituted a "good luck" assignment, their real loyalties were never to a specific fort or region of the country. Their strongest bonds were always to the regiment, or, for enlisted men, even to the individual companies within a regiment. While it is an overdrawn cliché to speak today of the "army family," that is precisely the way that many observers viewed military life in the late nineteenth century. The regiment was their family—especially as seen through the eyes of commissioned officers, their wives, and even noncommissioned officers. Perhaps only veterans who had extensive service records could fully appreciate this group identity, but those who completed brief military careers could also understand this reality, even when they sometimes were victims of its exclusivity.

In her three autobiographical accounts of army life, Elizabeth Custer reflected upon problems associated with the transfer of 7th Cavalrymen from one Great Plains fort to another during the late 1860s and early 1870s. Saying farewell to familiar surroundings, civilian friends, and even to some companies of the 7th which were detached for duty elsewhere were indeed sad affairs. Yet the one constant in each move was the sense of regimental unity, whereby every member of the 7th was theoretically bonded to his fellows, and the sense of brotherhood remained intact wherever the regimental and company guidons flew.[1] Furthermore, the sense of belonging to a regiment followed each man even into his retirement years and into the following generations of soldiers who would venerate the proud martial traditions of their particular regiments.

COMPETITION AMONG OFFICERS' FAMILIES

On a more finite level, another form of social organization also governed loyalties at military posts: the clique of officers' families who dominated all phases of fort life. The commander of the regiment and the senior officers at each post possessed considerable power over military matters and in deciding who would be influential and who would not.

Although this practice was far from democratic, it was endemic to American and European military systems of the nineteenth century. Officers' careers often depended upon their family connections, their marriage partners, and the web of helpful alliances that they carefully groomed. In some cases, the interventions reached well beyond the local level and into national policy making. Martha Summerhayes, no shrinking violet when it came to promoting her husband's career, took advantage of a social occasion to speak to President Grover Cleveland about how the opinions of field officers were frequently countered by bureaucratic minds in the War Department. When a vacancy subsequently occurred in the Quartermaster's Department, President Cleveland pressured the highly prized appointment for Lieutenant Summerhayes, followed by a promotion to captain.[2]

In a similar situation, Yuma's *Arizona Sentinel* reported that during the spring of 1875, while attending a reception in the nation's capital, Mary Crook interceded with President Ulysses S. Grant in behalf of her husband, George. Arguing that the desert conditions of Arizona had adversely affected her spouse's health, she personally requested that he be reassigned as commander of the Department of the Platte, the administrative area covering the northern Great Plains. According to the newspaper, when President Grant responded that General Crook was too important an officer to be transferred from the troubled Southwest, Mrs. Crook pushed the issue further, even to the point of embarrassing the president. While the *Arizona Sentinel* may have published an apocryphal story in this case, the fact that senior officers' wives could pursue such pressure tactics would not have surprised military insiders. General Crook was indeed reassigned to the Department of the Platte in 1875, but this was due to more complex command reasons that his spouse's heavy-handed tactics.[3]

Resentments between line officers, who were most often stationed on the frontier, and staff officers, who were routinely in or near Washington, D.C., sometimes boiled over, and entire families were brought into the controversies. Officers serving on the Indian frontier resented the close associations that their Washington-based colleagues formulated with powerful politicians to attain promotions and comfortable assignments. Lobbying efforts for these prizes became so widespread during Secretary of War William W. Belknap's administration that he issued an order in the spring of 1873 that army officers could no longer approach congressmen about military matters without his prior approval. The well-intentioned directive was entirely ineffective.[4]

Even Commanding Gen. William Tecumseh Sherman, who was supposed to represent the interests of line officers in the nation's capital, found himself caught up in the political intrigue. Repeatedly, he tried to block the promotion of Col. Nelson A. Miles to a generalship because of the man's alleged vanity and unbridled ambition. Mary Miles broke the deadlock on her husband's possible promotion by appealing to her uncle John Sherman, who was then serving as secretary of treasury under President Rutherford B. Hayes. Just before Hayes left office, he forced Gen. Edward O. C. Ord to retire so as to make it possible for Miles to receive the artificially created vacancy. Gen. Sherman was livid about the highly politicized maneuver, especially since it had been initiated by Mary, who was his niece as well, but there was little he could do about it.[5]

Junior officers could also receive favorable treatment based upon their family connections. Lt. Charles Throckmorton's socially prominent mother avoided approaching Gen. Sherman for help in shaping her son's military career because she knew that he would rebuff her efforts. Instead, she went directly to her close friend, President Grant, with a proposal for a comfortable staff appointment for her son. The assignment was not possible, but the young officer did avoid deployment to distant Alaska, and he was given a more desirable post in the East.[6]

Brig. Gen. Nelson A. Miles (second from left) and Buffalo Bill (far left) viewing an Indian camp near the Pine Ridge Indian Reservation in South Dakota following the Wounded Knee Massacre, January 16, 1891. (*Courtesy of the National Archives*)

More direct were the efforts of medal of honor winner Thomas Cruse, who after six and a half years of meritorious service had not yet advanced beyond second lieutenant. He traveled to the nation's capital in 1886 to urge that Charles Gordon be retired early so as to make a space available for his promotion to first lieutenant. The congressman from his Kentucky district helped promote the cause, but the aggrieved Gordon enlisted the aid of two senators to beat back the clumsy attempt. Cruse returned to the Arizona frontier and was not promoted until a year later, and he did not attain the rank of captain until 1896.[7]

Officer cliques within each regiment also played significant roles in the promotion process, especially in cases where senior officers refused to support the efforts of some of their junior officers. More important, commanders so thoroughly dominated duty assignments at each post that they could reward favored officers while leaving drudgery tasks for the unfavored. Under Lt. Col. George Armstrong Custer's tutelage, the 7th Cavalry stood as one of the most obvious examples of regimental cliquishness and patronage. The Custer "family"—including brothers Capt. Tom and Boston, nephew Harry Armstrong Reed, and brother-in-law Lt. James Calhoun as well as close friends Capt. George Yates and Myles Keogh—dominated all phases of policy making and social life within the regiment. Not so fortunate were Maj. Marcus Reno and Capt. Frederick Benteen, who both frequently suffered the invectives and social ostracism of their commander. The alienation followed them all the way to Little Big Horn during that fateful confrontation with Lakota and Northern Cheyenne warriors on June 25, 1876. The debacle resulted in the deaths of all the above-mentioned "Custer family" members and initiated the strong but unsubstantiated contention from some Custer defenders that Reno and Benteen had purposely failed to rescue Custer and his command.[8]

The whimsical nature of family alliances had been evident in the 7th Cavalry almost from the time Custer had taken command. Capt. Albert Barnitz had served with Custer in the Third Division of the Second Ohio Cavalry during the Civil War, and upon his reenlistment in the regular army in November 1866, he happily took station with Custer's new regiment. The two men who shared so much in common became friends, and their wives also developed positive relationships with each other. Yet before the friendship had matured into something deep and lasting, Barnitz turned against his mentor, holding Custer personally responsible for abusing the enlisted men and playing favorites among his officers. While camped near Ft. Hays, Kansas, in May 1867, Capt. Barnitz wrote to his wife Jennie about the imperious behavior of his former friend in punishing soldiers for the slightest indiscretions, and he contemplated resigning his prized commission if the barbarism continued. The following day, Barnitz wrote a second letter to wife Jennie, instructing her not to join him so long as Custer occupied the post. Bluntly, he explained to her that "I have become so thoroughly disgusted with Genl. Custer, that I will not ask even the *slightest* favor of him, and if you were here, I should be in a measure dependent on him for many little indulgences!"[9] Barnitz remained in service throughout the Washita campaign against Southern Cheyennes, but following more alleged abuses by his superior and suffering with a battlefield wound, he left military service for good in mid-1870. Even though Capt. Barnitz and his wife became victims of cliquishness within the army, they never lost their fondness for the 7th Cavalry and its subsequent activities. Both were deeply saddened by the regiment's fate at Little Big Horn and the loss of so many of their former friends and acquaintances—officers and enlisted men alike.[10]

CASTE AND SNOBBERY IN THE ARMY FAMILY

Despite the injustices that resulted from the factionalism within the officer corps, the sense of a regimental family was best evidenced in the activities of army wives who accompanied their husbands to far-flung posts. It is true that the prevailing social caste system shaped their lives too since tradition required that officers' wives only rarely associate with their enlisted rank counterparts. This snobbery, complete with its notion of a self-anointed aristocracy dominating and directing an inferior class of workers, even produced clear distinctions *within* the officer ranks. Especially targeted by this snobbery were the wives of officers who had been promoted from the enlisted ranks. Like their "lesser officer" husbands, these so-called halfway ladies were socially suspect. While stationed at Ft. Sedgwick, Colorado, well-bred Ada Vogdes complained that most of the women on officer's row were "westerners" and not equal to her refinement and social standing. One lieutenant stationed at Ft. Arbuckle in Indian Territory perceived that his wife's "western" origins would make her unacceptable to the proper ladies of the regiment, and so he sent her east to receive a finishing school education that would improve her social graces.[11] Sometimes the elitist bias even made commanding officers' wives into targets of derision. May Banks Stacey especially took offense at the lack of social skills shown by the wife of Ft. Grant, Arizona's, commander. She labeled the woman as ugly and uninteresting and wrote in 1879, "When I see such women in high [positions] I determine more and more to be intelligent and accomplished."[12] Equally judgmental was Eveline Alexander, who found the wife of Capt. Joseph H. Van Derslice to be "a very plain woman but perfectly unobjectionable. We exchange visits occasionally [at Ft. McDowell, Arizona] in which we talk of chickens (not to take too high a flight for her)."[13]

On other occasions, domestic spats within families of senior officers proved to be both amusing and embarrassing. Especially notable was the confrontational style of Hattie Hatch, wife of Col. Edward O. C. Hatch, who commanded the 9th Cavalry. Lt. William Paulding later recalled the frequent tiffs between the couple, tiffs that were quite loud and quite public. Paulding described Mrs. Hatch as a "terror" who sometimes let her strong personal views interfere with official military policies. When she joined several officers and their families to initiate a social reform campaign within the regiment, she directly confronted her husband about the need to outlaw all forms of gambling. The highly agitated colonel allegedly responded, "My God, Hattie, I wish you would mind your own business and let me run the post."[14]

At Ft. Sill, a similar incident occurred about the same time when Clara Davidson, wife of commander John W. "Black Jack" Davidson, challenged a military command given by her husband. By the order of the day, Davidson had directed the arrest of anyone—soldier or civilian—who walked across the parade ground. Officer of the day Lt. Henry O. Flipper carried out the order to the letter, even arresting his commander's teenaged son. Col. Davidson, hoping to teach his son a lesson about responsibility, backed up his junior officer's action, but was soon involved in a loud exchange with his own wife about the "arrest." According to Lt. Flipper, Col. Davidson shouted at his wife, "Madam, I'll have you to know I'm the Commanding Officer of this post." To which she retorted just as loudly, "And, I'll have you to understand I'm your commanding officer." Clara Davidson's will prevailed, and the teenager was soon released from confinement.[15]

These confrontational episodes may have led to jokes and gossip about who truly ran these particular households, but they did reflect a broader reality of military existence. Officers' wives did exercise considerable influence at military posts, and even though their power was frequently indirect and understated, they shaped some important decisions within garrison life. The great irony in this power-brokering relationship is found buried in military regulations, for at no time in the nineteenth century did Congress or the War Department ever authorize the presence of army wives at any of its military posts. Only laundresses were approved to live in military quarters, and these were supposed to be unmarried young women or widows. Rather than enforce these unrealistic rules, officials simply ignored them and allowed commanding officers at each fort to decide which women could reside in military housing. To do otherwise would have forced married couples within officer and enlisted ranks alike to be separated for most of the husband's career. Morale would have plummeted, and few soldiers would have remained in service for an extended period.

"Ranking Out": Losing Your Quarters

Despite the absence of clear authority for allowing women to reside on military reservations, a common custom was virtually institutionalized among the officer corps. The practice of "ranking out" occurred any time a higher-ranking officer was transferred to a post and given the choice of quarters over any other officers he outranked. In a system built on a hierarchical command structure, this made some sense, but it also was guaranteed to produce bad feelings, especially among junior officers and their families. Most vulnerable were women such as Frances M. A. Roe, who was twice ranked out of her quarters at Camp Supply, Indian Territory, and Ft. Shaw, Montana, because her husband was only a second lieutenant. As she contemplated the possible promotion of her husband to first lieutenant—an otherwise joyous occasion—all she could think about was transfer to another fort and beginning the "homeless cycle" all over again. She wrote in a family letter, "I am tired and cross; anyone would be under such uncomfortable conditions."[16]

Even the rumor of being ranked out of quarters was enough to create panic. When Caroline Winne, wife of the army surgeon at Ft. Washakie, Wyoming, heard about

"Officers quarters at Fort Rawlins, Wyoming, May 7, 1877." Two men and a woman holding a baby sit in front of the crude structure. (*Courtesy of the National Archives*)

the possible transfer of two senior captains to the post, she fatalistically accepted the demotion in housing since she and her husband occupied one of the newest and largest quarters on the post.[17] More distraught was Josephine Buell, a young army bride who, with her surgeon husband, took station at Ft. Concho, Texas, in 1877. She was elated when after an arduous wagon trip from San Antonio, they were welcomed and given comfortable quarters. They immediately set about cleaning, whitewashing, and painting the interior, putting all their efforts into an anticipated long domicile there. Within days of their completion of the tasks, however, they were confronted with the rumor that they would have to vacate the premises to make room for a superior.[18]

Many officers' wives commented in letters and journals that ranking out was one of the cruelest features of army regulations, but the practice was so well entrenched after the Civil War that no one seriously challenged it on an official level. One unidentified poet, however, described the nation's inattention to adequate housing for officers and their families in a lament published in an 1874 issue of *Army and Navy Journal:*

> I know "Uncle Sam"
> Must be an old bachelor
> For he made no provision for an officer's wife;
> And the very worst fate
> That I ever can wish him,
> Is one room and a kitchen
> The rest of his life.[19]

POST HOUSING AND AMENITIES

Indeed, at most forts, living quarters were small, even for senior officers, and thus men with superior rank exercised their proprietary rights regardless of whose feelings might be hurt. Because so many posts were built and rebuilt in the decade after the Civil War, this period reflected the greatest frequency of complaints about officer housing. Elizabeth Custer recalled her dismay upon arrival at newly constructed Ft. Wallace, Kansas, in 1867, where she found only a "poor little group of log huts and mud cabins ... and dugouts that served for the habitation of officers and men." Most appalling was the so-called guardhouse, which consisted of a large hole in the ground whose only entry and exit was a rickety ladder.[20] General William Tecumseh Sherman was even more blunt when in 1866, he visited Ft. Sedgwick, in the northeastern corner of present-day Colorado. He reported that the sod structures were an embarrassment to the army and that former slaves of the South would even have refused to live in them. In fact, he asserted, if abolitionists had taken the structures on a tour of New England before the Civil War to mobilize public opinion against the Southern planter elite, they could have gained many converts to their cause by the ploy.[21]

Whatever inadequacies existed among the quarters occupied by commissioned officers, conditions were generally worse for noncommissioned officers who lived with their wives and children. Ft. Robinson, Nebraska, an installation that hosted more units than it could accommodate during the height of the Indian wars, was particularly lacking when it came to matters of housing. Twelve families shared a single building, which was sectioned off into 12 by 35 foot apartments for each of the families. Despite the acute overcrowding, their quarters were better than those of the corporal and his family, who lived in a dilapidated and windowless shack, or the families who lived in tents beyond the parade ground. At another Nebraska post of the same era, Ft. Niobrara, several families lived in the old cavalry stables, where a bad odor of horse excrement continued to arise from the ground.[22]

The quality of furnishings also varied from fort to fort and over the passage of time. Elizabeth Custer described the spartan conditions of her tent-home near Ft. Hays as including "a rude bunk for a bed, a stool, with tin wash-basin, a bucket for water,

By the 1880s, Fort Davis, Texas was a picturesque and expansive installation. Modern refinements made it a welcome assignment during its last decade of service. (*Western History Collection, University of Oklahoma Library*)

and a little shaving-glass for a mirror." Additionally, a carpenter nailed together some benches and a table, which were exceedingly uncomfortable to occupy for more than a short period.[23] At another Kansas post, she observed that the contents of the permanent structures were preferable to those of tents, but officers had to be creative to make life better for themselves. "One," she later wrote, "had a box for a dressing table, and covering it with a gunny sack, such as the grain came in, fringed all around as a cover. For his wash-stand he had driven a pole into the ground of the proper height, and nailed to this a board to hold his tin basin."[24]

Descriptions of housing varied greatly throughout the nineteenth century, but three patterns were obvious. First, small camps and outposts that were never intended as permanent fortifications generally had the worst facilities. Unfortunately, many of these temporary camps remained in service well beyond the period that was envisioned for them. They routinely hosted a few adobe or wooden administrative buildings, surrounded by rows of tents that served as the only quarters for officers and enlisted men alike. Second, huge improvements were undertaken at virtually all of the remaining forts that were still in operation after 1885. As the Indian wars wound down, the War Department closed scores of posts and consolidated all of its troops at fewer locations. This allowed for budgetary savings to be channeled into the improvement of fewer installations, and, for the first time at many of these forts, facilities actually reached a level of true comfort. Third, the expansion of dependable roads and railroads throughout the West made many of the remaining forts more accessible than they had ever been in the past. Over these new transportation arteries came the building materials to improve the infrastructure of the posts and the widely coveted furnishings that easily could be shipped from eastern factories directly to military families. Veterans of the pre–Civil War frontier were amazed at how relatively comfortable and sophisticated army posts had become by the end of the century and at how much of the routine hardship had disappeared.

THE "CULT OF TRUE WOMANHOOD" IN THE ARMY

But modernization of structures was not the most important factor in improving the quality of life at military posts. Rather, the collective efforts of men and women to provide entertainment and social improvement defined the chief morale boosters on any post. Officers may well have had the final authority in deciding what was acceptable on military reservations, but their wives strongly affected those decisions and firmly shaped the entire arrangement of activities. Historians Shirley Leckie and Sandra Myres have well argued that most officers' wives embraced the prevailing values of the nineteenth century's "Cult of True Womanhood." They honored the virtues of piety, purity, domesticity, and submissiveness, but conditions at most forts allowed them freedoms that stretched beyond these overly confining "virtues." In analyzing the lives of Frances Roe, Martha Summerhayes, and Alice Kirk Grierson, Leckie concluded that "their goal was not to escape middle-class domesticity but rather to maintain their homes and care for their families in the face of a primitive [and male-dominated]...environment....In this all three, representing different versions of nineteenth-century 'true womanhood,' succeeded in upholding their values, enduring and 'functioning in that male-defined world *on their own terms.*'"[25]

Although not all women viewed their army lives through this prism, the majority of officers' wives who left written records seem to fit this model of not only successfully adjusting to the military lifestyle, but also helping shape it through their own initiatives.

Most were well educated by the standards of the day, having attended female seminaries and academies, and they had been raised in middle- or upper-middle-class families.[26] Despite their selective acceptance of Cult of True Womanhood values, they were hardly passive creatures when it came to promoting their cherished causes.

As early as 1866, General Sherman acknowledged the benefits of having wives and children at the western posts. and he especially encouraged officers to take their families with them. Not only would this improve morale, it would also establish a more refined and socially invigorated environment for everyone.[27] Newspaper correspondent John F. Finerty, writing a decade later, confirmed the positive effects of women at the Great Plains posts, especially for their civilizing and reformist impulses within the community.[28]

Apparently, the practicality of this philosophy overcame the lack of a formal regulation allowing family residences on military reservations. Scattered surviving reports provide a partial glimpse at the statistics, and they indicate how diverse were the gender and age representations at various times. The surgeon general assembled a reliable count in 1891 that identified 14,450 civilians living on posts, or approximately 60 percent of the army's total strength of 24,234 soldiers. In addition to the total of adult civilian males that were employed by the army, this included 5,456 women and 6,163 children, though no distinction was made between wives and children of officers, enlisted men, and civilian employees. A relatively small number of unmarried laundresses would likewise have been included in these totals.[29]

In order to improve the quality of life around them, officers and their wives frequently put aside their petty bickering and cliquishness to perform as a true regimental family. They may not have always agreed on the details of what they wanted to accomplish or on the methods for reaching their objectives, but they came together to promote civic responsibility. Likewise, they took great pride in the notion that their particular regiment had surpassed other regiments in attaining those lofty civilizing goals. Typical was the accomplishment of Cornelia Black, daughter of the commanding officer at Ft. Union, New Mexico, who in 1884 organized a Japanese tea party to raise money for a new pipe organ for the post chapel. She sent invitations two weeks ahead of time to officers, enlisted men, and their families so that the entire community could feel that it had a vested interest in the project. The festivities not only lifted the spirits of the entire post, the organizers also raised 400 dollars for purchase of the organ, which gave continued pleasure to the regiment for years to come.[30]

WOMEN'S SOCIAL ACTIVITIES

Within the Cult of True Womanhood, two arenas of life beyond the home were partially delegated to the "feminine sphere"—church and school. Not too surprisingly, officers' wives were major participants in both, and in cases where male chaplains and teachers were unavailable, women often took the lead. Sometimes wives informally administered the Eucharist to themselves, their families, and to a small circle of friends. Elizabeth Burt recalled her dismay upon arrival at Ft. Bridger, Wyoming, in 1866 because no chaplain had been assigned to the remote post. She immediately organized regular Sunday religious instruction for all children, including those of the civilian employees of the fort. Years later, she met in Omaha, Nebraska, a grown man who had years before been one of her catechism students. He still carried the Bible she had given him so long ago, and he remarked how important the religious classes had been throughout his adult life.[31]

Even in cases where chaplains were available to perform religious services, officers' wives still took the lead in other aspects of chapel activities. For instance, Frances Roe headed the music program for the chapel at Ft. Shaw, Montana, in 1885. In addition to selecting all the religious music and overseeing practices, she was allowed to recruit the choir and a small string orchestra from the musically gifted soldiers. Although the enlisted men were not required to render these services, they willingly did so, and one sergeant even undertook the laborious task of writing out the musical arrangements for each instrument and for each piece of music. Roe returned the favor to her loyal cadre of musicians by providing them with a cake and a dozen eggs after each Sunday service.[32]

Educational facilities were also important, especially to officers' families who hoped to begin their children's primary education at post schools and subsequently send them to eastern boarding schools, or to live with eastern relatives so that they could secure a proper high school education. Martha Gray Wales, daughter of surgeon Maj. Charles Carroll Gray, recalled that while her father was stationed at Ft. Sully, Dakota Territory, in 1868, she and the other children attended a morning school organized by the wife of the commanding officer. Prior to that, while her father was serving at Ft. Stevenson, Dakota Territory, she attended a school established by her own mother. Upon the family's rotation to far distant Ft. Clark, Texas, Wales found a different type of environment awaiting her educational endeavors. Instead of a small installation inhabited by a few children, she found a sprawling military reservation with too many soldiers for its meager facilities and too many children for maintaining easy control. A school was in operation at the adjoining town of Bracketville, under the tutelage of a Vermont schoolmarm, but the teacher fled the turbulent situation after only a year. Martha's mother gave up on the idea of educating her daughter at the post because there was virtually no attempt to discipline the unruly students. The young girl was therefore sent to live with her New England aunt so that she could have adequate schooling.[33]

Within the realm of adult education, officers' wives also assumed leading roles in organizing literary societies, nature clubs, and theatrical ensembles open to both genders. Elizabeth Custer took special pride in the fact that the "ladies" of Ft. Abraham Lincoln, Dakota Territory, hosted weekly meetings of a reading club to discuss books and ideas. One unidentified wife who had helped create the group kept up on the latest reading lists in the East, and she maintained a constant order for new titles.[34] Other women at Ft. Union, New Mexico, participated in the local chapter of the Louis Agassiz Association, which encouraged children to become budding scientists by examining the animal and plant life around them.[35] At Ft. Keogh, Montana, in 1880, Lt. J.M.T. Partillo and his wife were frequent players in the post dramas and comedies, sometimes participating in two productions during a single evening. At Ft. Niobrara, Nebraska, Fannie Kautz, wife of the commanding officer, managed the theatrical group and encouraged the participation of male and female members.[36] At Ft. Abraham Lincoln, Elizabeth Custer, her brother-in-law Tom, and her sister-in-law Maggie Custer Calhoun were featured in plays such as *Flora McFlimsey with Nothing to Wear*, and in another presentation, George and Elizabeth were featured as Quaker Peace Commissioners to the Indian tribes.[37]

Army weddings also fell under the purview of officers' wives, who recognized the importance of marriage as a way of expanding the regimental family. Because these wives often had a sister, cousin, daughter, or other relative living with them for extended periods of time, they played matchmaker to assure proper matrimonial links. Especially successful in performing this task was Alice Kirk Grierson, wife of 10th Cavalry commander Col. Benjamin H. Grierson, who successfully joined two bright young officers of the 10th with two of her husband's nieces. The husbands—Lt. William Davis Jr. and Lt. Mason M. Maxon—became full-fledged members of the Grierson family, and they shared fully in the lucrative economic enterprises of their relatives, which ranged from cattle and sheep ranching to railroad and land speculation. Equally energetic in her matchmaking skills was Agnes Kislingbury, wife of an 11th Infantry lieutenant, who brought her sister Alice Bullock from the East and immediately began the matrimonial cycle. Seventeen days after meeting Maj. George W. Schofield of the 10th Cavalry, Alice married him.[38]

Officer weddings were major social functions at even the smallest and most remote of forts. In 1882, assistant surgeon Joseph H. Collins married Genevieve La Tourrette, daughter of the chaplain at Ft. Union, New Mexico. Officers turned out in full dress uniform, and civilian friends attended from the nearby towns of Watrous and Las Vegas. After spending two weeks honeymooning in the latter town, the couple returned to the post, where they found that the officers and their wives had decorated the dance room to welcome them home.[39]

On at least one occasion, Ft. Concho officers participated in the wedding of a favored noncommissioned officer, in this case Ordnance Sergeant Robert F. Joyce. He married a servant girl who had only recently arrived to work for the new post surgeon. They were wed only three weeks after the girl's arrival, and Mrs. Grierson could not help but be judgmental when she wrote in private correspondence, "They have married in haste and whether they repent at leisure remains to be seen."[40] Still, she enjoyed the festive occasion, and she noted how well members of the post band serenaded the couple. Her reservations, however, reflected the earlier sentiments of Lt. Rodney Glisan, who had observed several hasty and ill-advised marriages among fellow officers. He warned against marriage to "one of those gay butterflies of fashion, who love so well to flutter and flirt as ball-room belles" but who, under the rigors of frontier life, soon lose their romantic underpinnings.[41]

Although most enlisted men shared a sense of loyalty to their regiment and to their assigned company, military tradition made it impossible for them to feel as if they were full partners in the regimental family. The chasm between officer corps and the enlisted ranks was a deep one, bridgeable only in rare circumstances, and the notion of elitism was maintained even during off-duty hours.

In keeping with this tradition, officers' wives rarely wrote much descriptive detail about enlisted men and their families, and when they did, the words generally reflected a caste bias. Frances Roe complained that common soldiers "are not nearly as nice as one would suppose them to be, when one sees them dressed up in their blue uniforms with bright brass buttons."[42] She further disparaged their lack of formal education and their debased behavior. More often than not, the only enlisted men that these women discussed in their memoirs were strikers, who were paid servants to the officers. Some, such as Elizabeth Custer, developed a genuine affection for her husband's long-term orderly, John Burkman, but she always maintained the wall of class distinction between them, even into their twilight years.[43]

The most severe critique of the army's caste system and its pompous assumptions appeared in 1880, when Lt. Duane M. Greene published *Ladies and Officers of the United States Army; or, American Aristocracy, A Sketch of the Social Life and Character of the Army.* Greene held up the entire social arrangement to ridicule and demonstrated how sharply it contrasted with the republican ideals professed by the American people. In exceedingly florid language, he spelled out the hypocrisies of officers and their ladies who preached temperance to the "vice-ridden" enlisted men, while simultaneously imbibing in alcohol behind closed doors. He also doubted the superiority of many of the officers and their fitness to command in the field or hold social dominance at the post. Although Greene raised some honest questions about the inequities of the caste system, his vituperative book was not read by many people, nor did it generate the kind of fierce public debate that he hoped. His own checkered military career—complete with charges of adultery and lying to gain promotion—also brought into question his veracity and his fitness to lead any kind of army reform movement. Thus a legitimate issue for debate became buried amid the personal failures of one man.[44]

LAUNDRESSES, SERVANTS, AND HOSPITAL MATRONS

Laundresses

Owing to the elitist social structure within the army, only three types of enlisted men's wives received much attention in official reports and personal memoirs—laundresses, personal servants, and hospital matrons—all of whom occupied the bottom rung of the regimental family. While a small number of laundresses were, in fact, prostitutes, the vast majority of them were not. Not until 1802 did Congress recognize the legal status of laundresses on military posts, even though many had served in an unofficial capacity since the outbreak of the American Revolution. The 1802 act established a ratio of four washerwomen per company, later modified to one per every 19.5 enlisted men. In addition to receiving pay from the soldiers for whom they worked, these women were entitled to one daily ration of food. Less certain were their living quarters, which could be on the military reservation, but which otherwise remained unspecified in size and quality.[45] Most forts therefore produced a unique area colloquially known as soapsuds row, and these areas continued to house laundresses, their children, and often their soldier-husbands throughout most of the nineteenth century.

The quality of soapsuds row differed from place to place, but generally, the structures were made from the cheapest materials, were confined to a cramped space, and contained relatively few conveniences. Post surgeons often filled reports with harsh condemnation of these dilapidated quarters and their tendency to serve as breeding grounds for communicable diseases. Captain C. S. Black noted the extent of Ft. Sidney, Nebraska's, unhealthy quarters for laundresses and their families in 1889. Not only were they overcrowded and exposed to the elements, they were also filthy and harbored dangerous maladies, such as diphtheria. Yet surgeon Black's efforts to move the families to a better spot fell on deaf ears, and the alarming situation remained until the fort's closing five years later.[46]

As with all other major decisions, rank had its privilege, and fort commanders exercised the final word on who could be hired as a laundress and her pay scale, living quarters, and working conditions. To prevent problems between these women and their clients, most commanding officers dictated that on payday, each soldier's laundry bill had to be settled before any of his salary could be received. Troopers who tried to underpay laundresses were sometimes shunned by their peers, but they were rarely punished in any significant way. By contrast, any washerwoman who was perceived to be a troublemaker was quickly dealt with by military authorities. At Ft. Concho, Texas, post surgeon W. F. Buchanan speedily punished a laundress who allegedly had stolen property, lied to him, and acted with general imprudence. He removed her from the post and made sure that she did not work within the regiment ever again. A few weeks later, at the same location, Capt. Nicholas Nolan fired three laundresses for their "utter worthlessness, drunkness [sic] and lewdness."[47] Maj. William Dye, commander at Ft. Fetterman in

1867, wrote that he had to send a disreputable laundress to Omaha because she had been dealing whiskey to the soldiers and causing other forms of mischief. In these cases and others, there appeared to be no official hearings or any appeals process to counter the officers' hasty decisions.[48]

Although most of the cases involving dismissal of washerwomen were of a serious nature, soldiers and enlisted men occasionally turned a minor disturbance into a joke. When two laundresses at Ft. Keogh, Montana, got into a row because one of them had burned her trash too close to the other woman's clothes hanging on a line, one of them threatened the other with a baseball bat. The officer of the day, Lt. Foy, saw great humor in the dispute, and he assigned a private to march back and forth between the two women's houses as if he were preventing the outbreak of a war. The two women took umbrage, allied their efforts, and threatened revenge on a company sergeant whom they thought was the fomenter of their humiliation.[49]

One of the best examples of class distinctions and snobbery between officers' wives and laundresses played out in the 7th Cavalry as an equally amusing incident. Pvt. Ami F. Mulford described the utter silence that fell between two women as they passed each other near the parade ground. Both were dressed in their finest clothes, each was intent on not recognizing the presence of the other, and they passed each other "with eyes front and noses up as if each thought she owned the whole reservation, with the troops thrown in." When the officer's wife looked back to inspect the laundress's fancy clothing, she ran headlong into a wheelbarrow. The personal embarrassment had to hurt far more than any physical pain rendered in the collision.[50]

Perhaps this mortified officer's wife would have taken comfort from the fact that all laundresses found themselves under attack during the mid-1870s, and the ultimate goal of this federal investigation was the complete elimination of these laboring women from all military reservations. As early as 1875, Inspector General Randolph B. Marcy noted that 1,316 laundresses were currently authorized and that they were receiving rations worth $100,000 per year. Their moving costs between posts exceeded $200,000 per year, and the additional costs of quarters and fuel reached a similar total. Despite his rather bleak picture of the future for these washerwomen, Marcy argued that laundresses who were already married to soldiers could remain employed until their husband's current enlistment ended. Then, except for extreme cases that were to be decided by commanding officers, married soldiers would be released from service, and no other married men would be allowed into the army.[51]

Marcy's honest attempt to save money for a financially strapped War Department led to a formal set of congressional hearings known as the Banning Committee during the following year. Some of the nation's highest-ranking officers spoke to the issue and its ramifications that stretched beyond the cost-cutting strategy. Gen. Edward O.C. Ord argued that laundresses "make the men more cheerful, honest and comfortable" and that their husbands tended to be the best soldiers. He further warned that if these women were removed from the western forts, their husbands would soon resign from service or, at least, not seek reenlistment. Likewise, Lt. Col. J.C. Kelton strongly advised against this drastic action that would destroy regimental morale and, as Kelton remarked, would produce "immorality, dishonor and dishonesty" throughout the western garrisons.[52]

Despite these and other warnings, General Order No. 37, issued June 19, 1878, ended the employment of all laundresses, except those who still had husbands in the service. Their jobs would be continued so long as their spouses remained on active duty through future enlistments. Like so many other regulations within the nineteenth-century army, this one retained a great deal of ambiguity, and it allowed local commanders to circumvent the law by delaying its local implementation. After the summer of 1883, however, far fewer army laundresses remained in the West because their rations were completely eliminated. After that date, enlisted men's wives who wished to continue their jobs and to remain on the posts had to pay for their own food or work out a deal with the post commander and his commissary officer.[53]

No reliable statistics have survived to indicate how much General Order No. 37 may have affected the total numbers of enlisted men's wives and children residing at western garrisons, nor how it might have affected marriage and desertion rates. Yet one thing is certain: The enlisted family never came close to disappearing from the frontier army. Unknown numbers of these women and their teenaged daughters hired out their labor as cooks, maids, and servants to officers' families both before and after the execution of this War Department directive.

Servants

The employment of this type of domestic help was a further wedge of separation between the officer corps and the enlisted ranks. In the latter case, men were expected to clean their own barracks, military equipment, and personal property as part of the discipline process. Except for the occasional case where an individual company was allowed to employ a female cook or maid on a short-term basis, the system was exclusively reserved for officers. Two or three junior officers sometimes shared the services of a cook or maid as a way of splitting the costs. Senior officers, however, routinely employed their own personal domestic help, which not only eliminated some of the drudgery of daily tasks, but also further confirmed their status at the apex of the fort's social pyramid.

Ironically, most of the domestic help that was hired by officers was from within the ranks. These soldier-servants were motivated to gain extra pay from their employer during off-duty hours. Those who worked for a single family over a long period of time sometimes became closely attached to their benefactors, and this led to cases of favored treatment by superior officers. These men supposedly were given easy assignments or were dismissed from drill early so that they could attend to their other duties. The term *striker* came to have a negative connotation in some quarters because of the double standards applied to them and because soldiers who were not employed in this capacity were extremely jealous of those who were.[54] Misuses of this labor system became so scandalous that Congress passed an act in 1870 preventing continuation of the striker system. Officers largely ignored the directive, partly of their own volition and partly at the urging of their wives. Ada Vogdes echoed the sentiment of other officers' spouses when she wrote a letter to her mother at the time the bill was being debated. She declared that if the system were abolished, "I should not live six months to have everything to do myself, as it is, I am tired to death all the time . . . I was never made to do hard work, as soon as I do, I fade, wilt and die and look like a prairie flower."[55]

On posts where the order was enforced, officers hired more female and male civilians to assume the cooking and cleaning duties. In the later case, blacks, Chinese, Hispanics, and even Indians seemed to be the usual male employees.[56] Most, however, were white women. Some were hired from the local populations, and others were carefully recruited from eastern cities. For instance, Elizabeth Burt employed the 12-year-old daughter of an apostate Mormon family while on her way to Ft. Sanders, Wyoming. The arrangement had a promising beginning, but the Burt family soon tired of the girl's incompetence, and they returned her to her parents in Omaha. Elizabeth Burt wrote in her recollections, "I had become convinced that the responsibility of training so young a girl to be a capable servant was not compensated by her services. She was really only another child on my hands."[57]

Efforts to hire experienced servant women from the East were plagued by a different type of problem: an inability to retain the services of these women. Frances Anne Boyd, wife of Lt. Orsemus B. Boyd, recalled how she and her husband hired a promising housekeeper before departing New York for Ft. Union, New Mexico. They followed military logic that it was best to hire an ugly woman so that she would not quickly find a husband and terminate her work agreement. Within three days after arrival at the post, however, the woman had received a proposal of marriage. Though she rejected the offer because of the man's alleged intemperance, she soon married another soldier.[58] Likewise, Katherine Gibson Fougera noted that the 7th Cavalry rarely was able to retain unmarried servant women from the East, even those who were hired through employment agencies. Within an average of two months, all of these women found soldier-husbands, despite being described by Fougera as the "homeliest females obtainable . . . an army of knock-kneed, cross-eyed, crooked-teethed cooks and bottlewashers." She saw further irony in the fact that the "homeliest of them all acquired a sergeant."[59]

Hospital Matrons

One final category of civilian women also took residence at far-flung military posts: the hospital matron. Despite the exalted nature of the title, this was really a position that lacked status. Some modern observers have misinterpreted these women to have been professionally trained nurses, but nothing could be further from the truth. No formal nursing schools existed within the United States prior to 1873, and even with the burgeoning of volunteer nurses during the Civil War, very few had any real medical instruction. As a result, the army employed no nurses between the Civil War and the Spanish-American War, even though a long-forgotten regulation permitted their hiring at 40 cents a day.[60]

Instead, military doctors relied on male hospital stewards, who were drawn from the ranks of the enlisted men. Although most of these men also lacked formal medical training, they assisted in tasks that ranged from simple record keeping to actually assisting in surgery. They learned by observation, and some became proficient enough that they were entrusted with the more tedious health care tasks. By terms of new legislation in 1878, hospital stewards were divided into three categories, depending upon their duration of service and their special skills. Their salaries ranged from 20 to 30 dollars a month, about the same as for a first sergeant or even higher.[61] Because of the availability of these men and their guaranteed legal status within military law, the army found little need to hire women for medical positions.

Hospital matrons therefore were little more than laundresses and maids who cleaned the post hospital and surgeon's quarters. Their positions were sanctioned within military law, yet they were guaranteed a monthly salary of no more than 10 dollars. No reliable records survive to indicate the average tenures of these women, but as of September 1887, only 169 hospital matrons were employed, and these were mainly at the larger posts and recruitment depots. Perhaps many of these matrons were similar to Ellen Ryan, "a mere child of fifteen," who, in 1870, was married to a sergeant at Ft. Fetterman, Wyoming.[62]

The strangest of all tales regarding the civilian women who resided on various military reservations was that of a Mrs. Nash, who worked as a laundress for the 7th

Cavalry. Elizabeth Custer wrote fondly of "Old Nash," who had many friends at Ft. Abraham Lincoln and who had a reputation as a hard worker and consummate midwife who aided in the birth of several babies. Despite two failed marriages to soldiers who absconded with her savings, Mrs. Nash maintained her friendly and helpful demeanor. In 1878, while married to her third soldier-husband at Ft. Meade, Dakota Territory, she fell desperately ill and begged the women of the post to bury her as soon as she died. The promise was not fulfilled, however, because her friends did not think that such hasty action would be respectful enough. As they prepared her body for burial, Mrs. Nash's female companions discovered the long kept secret. She was a man, and she had lived her difficult life as a woman even before notions of transgendering had become widely recognized.[63]

The ambiguity of Old Nash's true gender paralleled the complexity of the army's social structure during the late nineteenth century. Officers and enlisted men experienced

Elizabeth Custer, whose three books celebrated frontier army life and lionized her husband's reputation among the American public. (*Courtesy of the Library of Congress*)

three levels of identity in their daily lives. First, they saw themselves as members of the larger entity known as the U.S. Army, and most took personal pride in that patriotic association. Elizabeth Custer emphasized the point to her dear friend Katherine Gibson Fougera when she explained that all army women should be honored for their service record, which was performed alongside their dutiful husbands and amid great danger and privation. She viewed the entire institution of the army as providing real heroes, male and female, who "will open up the country to civilization."[64]

Libbie Custer also recognized the second level of army identity: the regiment. Her widely read trilogy of frontier army life was dedicated first to her husband, "Dear Autie," and secondarily to the 7th Cavalry. The regimental song "Garryowen" was recognized nationwide, and the 7th's guidons always received national attention, especially in the decades after the calamitous events at Little Big Horn. Libbie Custer devoted the remainder of her long life to keeping her husband's heroic reputation alive and to creating a literary image for the spirited 7th that would long outlive the frontier era.[65]

Finally, the notion of one's military identity was found at the lowest level, within the individual families. The social chasm between officers and men was indeed a wide one, as it was among their wives and children, but frontier army posts did serve as places where resourceful people made comparatively good lives for themselves. Their living conditions were often spartan, and their long periods of separation from eastern friends and relatives were difficult, but they learned to be self-sufficient and enterprising. Enlisted men and their families certainly left the service with greater frequency than did the officers and their ladies, and the lower echelons of soldiers were certainly frequent victims of class snobbery. Yet in retirement, the multitudes of former soldiers who wrote to service publications such as *Army and Navy Journal* and *Winners of the West* proudly recounted their military records and expressed their continued loyalty to the regimental family that had defined their existences for so many years of their lives.

NOTES

1. Elizabeth B. Custer, *Boots and Saddles, or, Life in Dakota with General Custer* (Norman: University of Oklahoma Press, 1961), 4–7. Other scattered references to regimental loyalty are found in Elizabeth Custer's *Tenting on the Plains, or General Custer in Kansas and Texas* (New York: C. L. Webster, 1887); and *Following the Guidon* (New York: Harper and Brothers, 1890).

2. Martha Summerhayes, *Vanished Arizona: Recollections of the Army Life of a New England Woman,* 2nd ed. (Salem, MA: Salem Press, 1911), 254–56.

3. Patricia Y. Stallard, *Glittering Misery: Dependents of the Indian Fighting Army* (Fort Collins, CO: Old Army Press, 1978), 104, 144.

4. Ibid., 104.

5. Edward M. Coffman, *The Old Army: A Portrait of the American Army in Peacetime, 1784–1898* (New York: Oxford University Press, 1986), 269.

6. Ibid. Sgt. Harry H. McConnell provided a harsh but entertaining criticism of officers who found their way into military service solely through family and friends. See H. H. McConnell, *Five Years a Cavalryman, or Sketches of Regular Army Life on the Texas Frontier, 1866–1871* (Jacksboro, TX: J. N. Rogers, 1889), 127–28.

7. Thomas Cruse, *Apache Days and After* (Caldwell, ID: Caxton, 1941), 215–17. Francis B. Heitman, *Historical Register and Dictionary of the United States Army, From Its Organization, September 29, 1789, to March 7, 1903,* vol. 1 (Washington, D.C.: U.S. Government Printing Office, 1903), 342.

8. Robert M. Utley, *Cavalier in Buckskin: George Armstrong Custer and the Western Military Frontier* (Norman: University of Oklahoma Press, 1988), 115. Michael L. Tate, "The Girl He Left Behind: Elizabeth Custer and the Making of a Legend," *Red River Valley Historical Review* 5 (Winter 1980): 7. Edgar I. Stewart, *Custer's Luck* (Norman: University of Oklahoma Press, 1955), 168–69, 493–95. An excellent example of how a network of highly placed relatives

and friends aided the military career of Andrew Alexander is summarized in Sandra L. Myres, "Frontier Historians, Women, and the 'New' Military History," *Military History of the Southwest* 19 (Spring 1989): 35–36.

9. Robert M. Utley, ed., *Life in Custer's Cavalry: Diaries and Letters of Albert and Jennie Barnitz, 1867–1868* (New Haven, CT: Yale University Press, 1977), 5–10, 59–52.

10. Ibid., 230–46. Further discussion of problems within the army's promotion system is well related in Robert M. Utley, *Frontier Regulars: The United States Army and the Indian, 1866–1891* (New York: Macmillan, 1973), 19–22.

11. Sandra L. Myres, "Army Women's Narratives as Documents of Social History: Some Examples from the Western Frontier, 1840–1900," *New Mexico Historical Review* 65 (April 1990): 195–96.

12. Sandra L. Myres, ed., "An Arizona Camping Trip: May Banks Stacey's Account of an Outing to Mount Graham in 1879," *Arizona and the West* 23 (Spring 1981): 62–63. An excellent example of snobbery and back biting by officers' wives who plotted against each other is found in an 1876 letter of Alice Kirk Grierson: Shirley A. Leckie, ed., *The Colonel's Lady on the Western Frontier: The Correspondence of Alice Kirk Grierson* (Lincoln: University of Nebraska Press, 1989), 84.

13. Sandra L. Myres, "Evy Alexander: The Colonel's Lady at McDowell," *Montana, Magazine of Western History* 24 (July 1974): 31.

14. Mary L. Williams, "Ladies of the Regiment: Their Influence on the Frontier Army," *Nebraska History* 78 (Winter 1997): 161.

15. Theodore E. Harris, ed., *Negro Frontiersman: The Western Memoirs of Henry O. Flipper* (El Paso: Texas Western College Press, 1963), 3–4.

16. Frances M. A. Roe, *Army Letters from an Officer's Wife, 1871–1888* (New York: D. Appleton, 1909), 305, 310, 314.

17. Thomas R. Buecker, ed., "Letters from a Post Surgeon's Wife: The Fort Washakie Correspondence of Caroline Winne, May 1879–May 1880," *Annals of Wyoming* 53 (Fall 1981): 51.

18. Susan Miles, ed., "Mrs. Buell's Journal, 1877," *Edwards Plateau Historian* 2 (1966): 40–42. One particularly ingenious officer at Ft. Sill, Indian Territory, found a way to repeatedly keep from being ranked out of his comfortable quarters. See Wilbur S. Nye, *Carbine and Lance: The Story of Old Fort Sill* (Norman: University of Oklahoma Press, 1942), 283.

19. "'One Room and a Kitchen,'" *Army and Navy Journal* (December 26, 1874): 318.

20. Custer, *Tenting on the Plains,* 387–95.

21. Report of Gen. William T. Sherman, October 1, 1867, in *Annual Report of the Secretary of War for 1868,* 34–35.

22. Coffman, *Old Army,* 309.

23. Custer, *Following the Guidon,* 73–74.

24. Ibid., 255–56.

25. Shirley A. Leckie, "Reading between the Lines: Another Look at Officers' Wives in the Post–Civil War Frontier Army," *Military History of the Southwest* 19 (Fall 1989): 160. Myres, "Army Women's Narratives," 175–98. Barbara Welter, "The Cult of True Womanhood, 1820–1860," *American Quarterly* 18 (Summer 1966): 151–74.

26. Sandra L. Myres, "Romance and Reality on the American Frontier: Views of Army Wives," *Western Historical Quarterly* 13 (October 1982): 417–18, 427. A notable exception was Alice Blackwood Baldwin, who wrote about how some of her most cherished ambitions were stifled by her husband Frank and by military traditions. See Robert H. Steinbach, *A Long March: The Lives of Frank and Alice Baldwin* (Austin: University of Texas Press, 1940), xiii–xiv, 47–50, 147, 189–92. Two accounts of wives who were abused by their officer husbands and fought against the abuse are Teresa Griffin Vielé, *Following the Drum: A Glimpse of Frontier Life* (New York: Rudd and Carleton, 1858), 8–9; and Cheryl J. Foote, "'My Husband Was a Madman and a Murderer': Josephine Clifford McCrackin, Army Wife, Writer, and Conservationist," *New Mexico Historical Review* 65 (April 1990): 199–24.

27. Frances C. Carrington, *My Army Life and the Fort Phil Kearney* [sic] *Massacre* (Philadelphia: J. B. Lippincott, 1910), 61–62.

28. John F. Finerty, *War-Path and Bivouac, or the Conquest of the Sioux: A Narrative of Stirring Personal Experiences and Adventures in the Big Horn and Yellowstone Expedition of 1876, and in the Campaign on the British Border in 1879* (Norman: University of Oklahoma Press, 1961), 302.

29. Coffman, *Old Army,* 308.

30. Dale F. Giese, "Soldiers at Play: A History of Social Life at Fort Union, New Mexico, 1851–1891" (PhD diss., University of New Mexico, 1969), 86–87.

31. David H. Stratton, "The Army and the Gospel in the West," *Western Humanities Review* 8 (Spring 1954): 261. Merrill J. Mattes, *Indians, Infants and Infantry: Andrew and Elizabeth Burt on the Frontier* (Denver: Old West, 1960), 82.

32. Roe, *Army Letters from an Officer's Wife,* 338–40.

33. Martha Gray Wales, "When I Was a Little Girl: Things I Remember from Living at Frontier Military Posts," *North Dakota History* 50 (Spring 1983): 12–22.

34. Custer, *Boots and Saddles,* 79.

35. Giese, "Soldiers at Play," 42.

36. Stephen Ralph Buss, "The Military Theatre: Soldier-Actor Theatricals on the Frontier Plains" (PhD diss., Washington State University, 1982), 49. Summerhayes, *Vanished Arizona,* 251–52.

37. Buss, "Military Theatre," 39–40. Lawrence A. Frost, *General Custer's Libbie* (Seattle: Superior, 1976), 179.

38. Williams, "Ladies of the Regiment," 159–60. Alice Grierson described the Schofield-Bullock wedding in a personal letter reproduced in Leckie, *Colonel's Lady,* 80–81.

39. Giese, "Soldiers at Play," 67–68.

40. Leckie, *Colonel's Lady,* 97.

41. Rodney Glisan, *Journal of Army Life* (San Francisco: A. L. Bancroft, 1874), 52–53.

42. Roe, *Army Letters from an Officer's Wife,* 5–6.

43. The story of eccentric orderly John Burkman and his lifelong attachment to the Custer family is chronicled in Glendolin Damon Wagner, *Old Neutriment* (Boston: R. Hill, 1934).

44. Duane N. Greene, *Ladies and Officers of the United States Army; or, American Aristocracy, A Sketch of the Social Life and Character of the Army* (Chicago: Central, 1880). Coffman, *Old Army,* 284–85.

45. John F. Callan, *The Military Laws of the United States* (Baltimore: John Murphy, 1858), 102.

46. Miller J. Stewart, "Army Laundresses: Ladies of the 'Soap Suds Row,'" *Nebraska History* 61 (Winter 1980): 422.

47. John M. Carroll, ed., *The Black Military Experience in the American West* (New York: Liveright, 1973), 311–12.

48. Marion M. Huseas, "'Tuched Nothing to Drink…': Frontier Army Leisure," *Periodical: Journal of the Council on America's Military Past* 12 (January 1981): 12.

49. Maurice Frink and Casey E. Barthelmess, *Photographer on an Army Mule* (Norman: University of Oklahoma Press, 1965), 94.

50. Ami Mulford, *Fighting Indians in the 7th U.S. Cavalry* (Corning, NY: Paul Lindsley Mulford, 1879), 52.

51. Report of Inspector General Randolph B. Marcy, October 11, 1875, in *Annual Report of the Secretary of War for 1875,* 175.

52. U.S. Congress, House, *Reduction of Army Officers' Pay, Reorganization of the Army and Transfer of the Indian Bureau,* 44th Cong., 1st sess., 1876, H. Rep. 354, 46, 130–31.

53. Tom Lindmier, *Drybone: A History of Fort Fetterman, Wyoming* (Glendo, WY: High Plains Press, 2002), 98. Douglas C. McChristian, "The Commissary Sergeant: His Life at Fort Davis," *Military History of Texas and the Southwest* 14, no. 1 (1978): 27. Stewart, "Army Laundresses," 434.

54. Finerty, *War-Path and Bivouac,* 304–5. Myres, "Army Women's Narratives," 191–92.

55. Coffman, *Old Army,* 306.

56. Ibid., 301–4. Myres, "Army Women's Narratives," 184–85. Summerhayes, *Vanished Arizona,* 224–27. Myres, "Evy Alexander," 32–33. These sources also discuss the paternalism that surrounded the hiring of racial minorities as personal servants.

57. Mattes, *Indians, Infants and Infantry,* 97, 179.

58. Mrs. Orsemus Bronson Boyd, *Cavalry Life in Tent and Field* (New York: J. S. Tait, 1894), 192–94.

59. Katherine Gibson Fougera, *With Custer's Cavalry* (Caldwell, ID: Caxton, 1940), 96.

60. Mary C. Gillett, *The Army Medical Department, 1865–1917* (Washington, D.C.: Center for Military History, United States Army, 1995), 18.

61. Ibid., 19. Coffman, *Old Army,* 383. McConnell, *Five Years a Cavalryman,* 166.

62. Lindmier, *Drybone,* 99.

63. Custer, *Boots and Saddles,* 165–67.

64. Fougera, *With Custer's Cavalry,* 137. For further discussion of officers' wives who viewed themselves as integral parts of the military culture of the regiment, see Anni P. Baker, "Daughters of Mars: Army Officers' Wives and Military Culture on the American Frontier," *Historian* 67 (Spring 2005): 20–42; and Michele J. Nacy, *Members of the Regiment: Army Officers' Wives on the Western Frontier, 1865–1890* (Westport, CT: Greenwood Press, 2000).

65. Stories of several officers and their wives who became involved in scandal, were subjected to double standards, and were forced out of their regiments appear in Bruce J. Dinges, "Scandal in the Tenth Cavalry: A Fort Sill Case History," *Arizona and the West* 28 (Summer 1986): 125–40; and Darlis A. Miller, "Foragers, Army Women, and Prostitutes," in *New Mexico Women: Intercultural Perspectives,* ed. Joan M. Jensen and Darlis A. Miller (Albuquerque: University of New Mexico Press, 1986), 151–55.

6 OFF DUTY, ON POST: THE SEARCH FOR RECREATION AND ENTERTAINMENT

Although hardship and self-sacrifice were regular components of frontier military life during the late nineteenth century, officers, enlisted men, and their families enriched their off-duty hours with parties, competitive games, and cultural events that imitated the social norms of eastern society. Never at any time were they attempting to escape mainstream America, for in truth, they sought ways to emulate and perpetuate those very customs within their own environments.[1] Especially important to the more erudite members of these garrisons was the perceived need to maintain their connections to the icons of "civilization," including lyceums, debating organizations, musical ensembles, dramatic clubs, and literary societies. Like the broader American population, military people desired relief from tedium and enrichment of the soul through their various forms of entertainment. In both regards, recreational pursuits improved morale and strengthened personal relationships between individuals who otherwise would have interacted with each other only in official duty capacities.

HOLIDAY CELEBRATIONS

Despite the hierarchical nature of the army and the automatic deference to rank in all matters, entertainment events that produced the greatest social leveling were those associated with formal holidays. Beyond all other celebratory affairs, Christmas and the Fourth of July symbolized the purest essence of shared experiences that included both genders and all ranks of military men. Every person shared in the unity of the human spirit that abounded at Christmastime, and all identified with the patriotic excitement of Independence Day. These were occasions when even the commanding officer of the post could readily be seen participating in the off-duty activities of the soldiers and when the wives of officers and enlisted men could make common cause in arranging the banquets, picnics, and parties that accompanied these grand holidays. To be sure, these fleeting excursions into egalitarianism were brief, but they were eagerly awaited and enjoyed by all members of the garrison.

Christmas

Christmas season was the most festive time of the year. Yet unlike present circumstances, when the holiday extends for over a month of shopping days, the festival date was limited to Christmas Eve and Christmas Day. In this limited time frame, religious services and elaborate dinners were the most commonly shared experiences. At posts where chaplains were stationed, these religious men took charge of informal duties to make sure that the spiritual meaning of the holiday was not lost among the revelers. One such chaplain at New Mexico's Ft. Union happily noted that the joy of the season always brought out a larger crowd of worshippers than normal, including those who never attended any other services during the year.[2]

Elaborate dinners among the officers and their families were eagerly anticipated, even in the most abject of circumstances. People ordered canned foods from the East throughout the summer and fall so that they could provide the rare delicacies that satisfied even the most discriminating of palates. At Ft. Phil Kearny, Wyoming, in 1866, while Sioux warriors threatened even the largest of military escorts along the Bozeman Trail, officers and their wives enjoyed a meal fit for a king. The menu included canned lobster, cove oysters, salmon, jellies, tomatoes, sweet corn, puddings, pies, doughnuts, plum cake, gingerbread coffee, liquor, and for the men, cigars and smoking tobacco. Even in their isolated and precarious locale, these innovative families were determined to make Christmas Day a memorable event that would allow them to temporarily escape from grim realities. Only four days earlier, 80 soldiers under the command of Capt. William Fetterman had been killed while pursuing Sioux warriors across the nearby Lodge Trail Ridge. The contrast between their silent graves and the customary holiday merriment symbolized the dualities within military life.[3]

The magic of Christmas always resonated most among children, and therefore garrisons went out of their way to make their sons and daughters the focal point of the holiday. At Ft. Keogh, Montana, during the early 1880s, children were regularly written into the featured plays that were presented on Christmas Eve. Officers' wives sewed the special costumes, and a captain directed each of the productions in what became known as Children's Night.[4]

Even more widespread was the practice of officers and enlisted men contributing funds to the purchase of gifts for all children on the post. Although no formal military order dictated this activity, the spirit of the season moved people to this act of generosity. In places as dispersed as Ft. Fetterman, Wyoming, Ft. Logan, Montana, and Ft. Union, New Mexico, presents were made available not only to the progeny of officers and men, but also the children of civilian employees.[5] This tendency seemed to be widespread throughout the late nineteenth century, and it prompted one anonymous officer's wife to write a letter to the *Army and Navy Register.* Appealing to the virtue of brotherly love, the letter called upon all garrisons to provide a Christmas tree for the enjoyment of the entire population of each fort if possible. It likewise beseeched individuals and the regimental companies to contribute money so that every child could have a gift, even if some of these presents were previously used items from the toy boxes of their own sons and daughters.[6]

Efforts to see that all children enjoyed a merry Christmas often evolved into shared activities between the adults of a garrison and the civilians of nearby towns. Some were low-key affairs, such as when army surgeon Charles K. Winne and his wife Caroline accepted the Christmas invitation of the Rumsey family to dine with them in their private residence a few blocks from the Ft. Sidney, Nebraska, military reservation.[7] Other events that joined together military and civilian families were more grandly conceived. At Ft. Arbuckle, in south central Indian Territory, the commander officiated over an 1866 Christmas Day complete with a fox hunt and Indian dances. Eleven years later, the officer in charge of troops at Cheyenne River Agency arranged an elaborate Christmas Eve celebration for soldiers and Indian agency personnel alike. Also attending the festivities were the daughters of the Indian scouts who were employed at the camp. These young women, dressed in their finest clothing and ornaments, took some time to master the dance steps, but they quickly became the "belles of the ball."[8]

Although published records have dealt predominantly with officers and their families at Christmastime, reliable glimpses of enlisted men's celebrations have also survived. Not only was this a day when most regular duties were suspended, but also, men of the ranks had ample opportunity to celebrate within their barracks, in the mess hall, and in other activities that they shared with the officers. Like their superiors, the various companies had been long assembling special foods for the noon feast and had outfitted appropriate buildings with their improvised decorations. At Ft. Rice in Dakota Territory, the German Society of enlisted men presented choral entertainment on Christmas Eve and Christmas Day of 1868. Their homemade beer proved to be a special treat, including among the officers whom they invited to their celebration. Unfortunately, some of these same enlisted men had been stockpiling illicit whiskey supplies throughout the autumn, and this resulted in some heavy drinking that went beyond the weak beer that had been approved for the evening.[9]

Some soldiers were not as fortunate as those who celebrated Christmas within the confines of their forts. A smaller number spent the day on routine patrol or on detached service escorting mail coaches, guarding river crossings, and occupying small encampments between major posts. Often assigned to these duties in groups of no more than two to four men, these soldiers faced solitary Christmas with few amenities and virtually no sense of the special day being different from any other. Typical of the melancholy feeling associated with separation from family and friends during the holiday were the words of Corp. Emil A. Bode of the 16th Infantry. While camped at one of the water holes west of Ft. Concho, Texas, amid a light snow and frigid winds, Bode thought about his own boyhood and standing around a decorated Christmas tree admiring the presents. The pleasant recollection contrasted sharply with his sadness over the death of a black soldier of the 10th Cavalry who had been killed at the spring by one of his comrades on that very day. The man had been buried with military ceremony, but now, on Christmas Eve, howling wolves prowled across his grave. The usual uplifting spirit of the season proved quickly fleeting amid such a tragic scene.[10]

Even more trying were the conditions faced by officers and men who conducted the famous winter campaign against Sioux and Northern Cheyennes during 1876–1877, in the aftermath of the debacle at Little Big Horn. Normally, the army avoided massive operations during the dead of winter, but national pressure was so intense to punish the warriors who had defeated Custer that a delay until the spring was virtually impossible. Pvt. William E. Smith wrote in his journal not only about the foul weather of eastern Wyoming, but also about the shortage of supplies. With sarcastic tone, he described the "reglar Old Crismas Dinner" that his company was served, consisting of nothing more than a piece of bacon fat, hardtack, and a half cup of coffee. Although Smith conjured up warm feelings about many earlier Christmases spent among family, the only tangible reminder of the holiday that he experienced that day was the sharing of some rock candy with a fellow soldier.[11]

Capt. John G. Bourke, accompanying the same column that contained Pvt. Smith, remarked about the suffering of the men and animals on that memorable Christmas Day as they marched near Pumpkin Butte:

> Beards, moustaches, eye-lashes and eye-brows were frozen masses of ice. The keen air was filled with minute crystals, each cutting the tender skin like a razor, while feet and hands ached as if beaten with clubs. Horses and mules shivered while they stood in column, their flanks white with crystals of perspiration congealed on their bodies, and their nostrils bristling with icicles.[12]

Independence Day

When the harsh winter months gave way to spring and then summer, opportunities for outdoor amusement and entertainment multiplied. These diverse activities culminated in Independence Day celebrations at forts throughout the nation. As with Christmas and the lesser holidays, culinary delights abounded at get-togethers that ranged from small private dinners to heavily attended banquets and picnics. Not only did officers and men order delicacies from the East, they usually had ample fresh vegetables from their post gardens and fresh game brought in by hunters.[13]

Food was only one component of Fourth of July activities; competitive games were the highlight of the day in most cases. Fort Yates, one of the larger Dakota posts in 1879, well represented the broad array of contests that could be found around the nation. The day's events included a marksmanship match between enlisted men and officers, a baseball game pitting soldiers against officers, a hundred yard dash, horse races, wheelbarrow races by blindfolded men, and a greased pig chase. The afternoon of sports was followed by fireworks, a patriotic medley performed by the regimental band, and a Grand Ball for the officers and their wives.[14]

Fraternization between soldiers and civilians of nearby communities was especially encouraged on the Fourth of July. In 1882, the city fathers of Las Vegas, New Mexico, invited all soldiers from Ft. Union to attend an unprecedented extravaganza. Businessmen, ever hopeful that military men would spend considerable sums while in town, decorated a few of the buildings and brought evergreens from the mountain slopes to line the parade route. They also arranged for the post commander to supply the cannons that were fired in celebration that day. The friendly exchange between fort and town was apparently repeated annually until 1891, when Ft. Union was finally abandoned.[15]

Equally successful was the string of Independence Day celebrations that connected the populations of Ft. Robinson and Crawford, Nebraska. The 1897 celebrations attracted 1,500 onlookers, many of them arriving by special trains provided by the Burlington and Fremont, Elkhorn and Missouri Valley railroads. Close cooperation between post commander Col. David Perry and members of the village board virtually assured a full range of activities that included a military parade headed by several hundred soldiers, the 9th Cavalry Band and the Gate City Cornet Band, and several baseball games between soldiers and civilians. Local merchants, who were almost totally dependent on the military economy, happily provided cash prizes for both men and women who won the horse races and other team sports. Most unique were the chariot races, which imitated the Roman style by utilizing four horses per team. The day ended with the post band playing the strains of "Annie Laurie" to a cheering throng of well-wishers comprising black soldiers of the Ninth Cavalry and white civilians. Patriotism, not race, appeared to be the focal point of the day's activities.[16]

July 4, 1876, seemed to be a special event among all Independence Day celebrations since it marked the Centennial of the nation. The celebration that linked the citizens of Gillespie County, Texas, with the soldiers at Ft. McKavett was relatively small in terms of the numbers of officers and enlisted men who were authorized to attend the festivities, but the diverse activities paralleled those at larger posts throughout the country. Marksmanship contests, horse racing sweepstakes, and baseball games were the main features of the day, and prizes of 5–15 dollars per winner attracted considerable talent from the military ranks.[17]

Likewise, Centennial Day was celebrated at Ft. Rice, Dakota Territory, not only with the usual competitive games, but also with a mock dress parade and participation by Indians, who raced their horses in the events.[18] At Topeka, Kansas, the 5th Cavalry Band performed in the city park during its layover on the way to join the full regiment for Gen. George Crook's operations against the Sioux and Northern Cheyennes. Despite bad weather that limited the audience size, the *Topeka Daily Commonwealth* reported it to be "one of the finest performances of the kind ever given in Topeka." The newspaper extended hopes for a return of the army musicians and promised them a full house in the future.[19]

Official holidays, such as Christmas and Independence Day, were always major occasions for celebration among soldiers and civilians, who joined together in the best spirit of the two seasons, but the rest of the days of the year were not without their recreational pursuits, too. Even the worst of winter conditions did not eliminate officers' and enlisted men's incessant desire to escape drudgery. Typical of the indoor activities were the billiard tables that attracted paying customers to the sutler's store or, in rarer cases, to those owned by officers or regimental companies who placed them in recreational buildings. Because gambling frequently occurred in these facilities, women either stayed away entirely or played only on special occasions. Julia Gilliss wrote home from Camp Warner, Oregon, in 1868, explaining how pleased she was that the officers had a billiard table, and she was encouraged to play by her officer-husband, who was something of an expert.[20] Less happy was the situation at Ft. Union, New Mexico, where the sutler provided two tables. Officers held exclusive rights to the high-quality one, while enlisted men were restricted to an old, worn, and decidedly unlevel table that required masterful "uphill" shots.[21]

GAMBLING

Card and dice games may have been the most ubiquitous pastimes for all seasons at military posts. Nothing more was required than a deck of cards or pair of dice, a willing group of players, and in most cases, cash or valuable objects that could be wagered on the game. Most participants entered these games as gambling ventures, and not because they were stimulated by the mental and social aspects of the venture. Officers played among themselves exclusively, or occasionally with civilians who were employed at the fort. Likewise, enlisted men played only among their peers because nothing would have caused more command problems than to have officers and enlisted men in debt to each other or carrying a grudge about an ill-fated bet. A variety of card games abounded at military posts, but the favorites tended to be poker, euchre, blackjack, pinochle, whist, and cribbage. Dominoes and chess were also welcome recreational pursuits, but neither was suited for wagering and hence never achieved the widespread devotion that card playing did.[22]

Although periodic efforts to stem some of the worst effects of gambling were well intended, rarely were they successful in the long run. The commander at Ft. Niobrara,

Nebraska, issued orders in 1883 to remove all unauthorized civilians from the vicinity of the enlisted men's barracks. These denizens showed up on each payday and engaged soldiers in betting to the point that they were adversely affecting morale. These card sharks merely resumed their nefarious games at a "hog ranch" about two miles east of the fort. There, at Casterline's Ranch, they carried on a rousing business that combined cards, liquor, and women. Even though soldiers constantly complained about being cheated at the establishment, their frequent visits never slackened.[23]

Some gambling ventures found acceptance among senior officers, who saw them as forms of controlled wagering that could help improve morale. At Ft. Union in 1881, soldiers were allowed to hold a raffle in which paying participants threw dice for a highest and lowest roll. The former winner took away a gold watch, and the latter was rewarded with a nice pistol.[24] Three years earlier, soldiers at the same post received permission to build a five-mile track that was used frequently for sanctioned horse races. One such contest boasted a remarkable purse of 400 dollars.[25]

Whenever the stakes were high enough, the chance for manipulation of outcomes was also high, even to the point of senior officers engaging in illicit activities. According to his orderly John Burkman, Col. George Custer attempted to settle a big gambling debt accrued in a card game by fixing a subsequent horse race. Custer rode his own horse Vic and narrowly nosed out the competitor to earn an alleged purse of 500 dollars.[26]

OUTDOOR RECREATIONS AND SPORTS

Outdoor Recreational Activities

Other military personnel eschewed the gambling pursuits and devoted themselves to family activities. Ada Vogdes described a crisp February day at Ft. Laramie when the Laramie River froze over and practically the entire garrison—officers, soldiers, ladies, and children—turned out for skating. Those who did not participate watched from seats brought out from the fort. Others who could not skate were pushed around in chairs and improvised conveyances that produced a winter scene similar to those in New York City's Central Park.[27]

Julia Gillis recorded a similar February day at Ft. Dalles, when a warming trend helped break the feeling of isolation that had accompanied midwinter. With her officer-husband and other residents of the small Oregon post, she not only enjoyed the pleasures of skating, but also undertook an exciting sleigh ride through the surrounding country.[28] At Ft. Fred Steele, Wyoming, officers and men joined together to build a multiple-passenger ice boat that ran up and down the frozen North Platte River, providing hours of diversion from winter's monotony.[29]

Spring hastened the return of good weather to most areas of the West and ushered in a range of outdoor activities not available during the winter months. Fort Concho, one of the larger Texas outposts during most of its 1867–1889 tenure, offered a full range of activities, all of which could be found at other frontier forts. Picnics were common events, especially when undertaken in celebration of birthdays, holidays, and on the Sabbath. These were especially well organized among officers and their families, who often took along their servants to help with food preparation and management of the children. Picnics were also organized around specific themes, such as swimming parties, horseback riding, fishing, hunting, and collecting pecans along the banks of the Concho River. During Benjamin Grierson's tenure as commander of the post, lawn croquet also became a popular recreational pursuit among officers and their wives.[30]

Military officers picnic with their wives and children under giant cactus near Fort Thomas, Arizona Territory, February 18, 1886. (*Courtesy of the National Archives*)

During their heydays, other large military garrisons sported these same activities, but they also created unique recreational opportunities that suited the particular environment and the predilections of the individual officers. For instance, at Ft. Bennett, Dakota Territory, during the mid-1870s, soldiers built special boats to challenge the civilian employees at the Cheyenne River Agency to rowing regattas.[31] A decade later, officers and their wives formed a bicycling club at Ft. Union, New Mexico, and they also constructed lawn tennis and handball courts.[32] By the 1890s, Ft. Robinson hosted a polo field upon which many equestrian contests were held during the weekends. This and other improvements at the sprawling Nebraska installation during the early twentieth century led to it being dubbed the "Country Club of the Army."[33]

Most of the above-mentioned recreational activities were easy to duplicate elsewhere because they could be enjoyed in small groups, with a minimum of planning, and at only slight cost to participants. As with other social activities, officers and enlisted men rarely joined together in these pursuits. Each had his own sphere, and the dividing lines were scrupulously maintained, unless the post commander gave permission for temporary integration of all ranks in special activities.

Competitive Team Sports

Yet there was another type of recreational endeavor that invited the participation of all men in military services: competitive team sports. Chief among these was baseball, the fastest-rising American professional and amateur team sport during the late nineteenth century. The game was well suited to far-flung army installations because, unlike today, the equipment was meager and inexpensive—little more than a few balls, bats, and simple gloves—and the sport could be enjoyed even by novice players. Facilities varied widely. At many posts, the baseball diamond was little more than a cleared spot at the fringes of the buildings. Larger posts, where the game was played regularly, were often equipped with a backstop, permanent bases, and improved infields. Ft. Mackinac, Michigan, which was located well east of the frontier territories, proudly hosted a regular field and a grandstand for spectators, who paid admissions of 15 and 25 cents. Many army teams also purchased their own uniforms, such as the men at Jefferson Barracks, Missouri, "whose uniforms were as sharp as those for a dress parade." Less fortunate were members of the highly polished Ft. Washakie, Wyoming, team, whose prized uniforms were stolen by a deserting sergeant.[34]

Even the most isolated of installations seemed to support regular teams as well as promote the game among unseasoned players, occasionally including women of the garrison. Maj. Andrew Burt inaugurated or expanded baseball at every post where he served during a long career. His initial efforts were to play more for fun than for ultimate victory, and he was content merely to pit "youngsters" against "oldsters." At Ft. Union, during the 1880s, the commanding officer strongly supported the formation of teams along company lines. He viewed this as a healthy competition that greatly improved morale, and he even encouraged that officers play on the teams alongside their noncoms and enlisted men.[35]

One of the most celebrated semiprofessional teams was Capt. Frederick Benteen's Company H of the 7th Cavalry, familiarly known as the Benteen Baseball and Gymnasium Club. Organized in March 1873, it had a reputation for invincibility, and it achieved many lopsided victories when it played against teams from other posts. For instance, the June 3, 1875, contest with Ft. Randall's premier team resulted in a Benteen Club victory margin of 54 to 5. Always desirous of competition, even among the most adverse of circumstances, Company H. challenged and defeated a team of civilian teamsters while on duty removing illegal prospectors from the Black Hills. A year later, this same unit accompanied Lt. Col. George Armstrong Custer to Little Big Horn. Although Capt. Benteen survived the battle, the starting nine-man team lost one of its players, and four others were wounded.[36]

More fortunate was Capt. Charles King, who participated in the same 1876 operations under the command of Gen. George Crook. King was a baseball enthusiast, and seven years earlier, while on military recruiting duty in Cincinnati, he had played for the city's Red Stockings team. This was one of the first professional baseball teams in the nation, one that paid its players directly rather than maintaining the fiction of "amateur" athletes who were compensated by indirect means. King's return to his regiment ended what might have been a promising baseball career but began a laudable military career.[37]

Competitive games between teams at a single post gave way to traveling squads that played against teams from other forts in the region. The friendly rivalries were mostly limited to special occasions when the "nines" were able to secure leaves last-ing several days and when they were able to travel between posts that were connected by dependable rail service. Such was the case during the late 1880s, when teams from Ft. Robinson and Ft. Niobrara, Nebraska, traded several matches between each other by traveling comfortably on the Fremont, Elkhorn, and Missouri Valley Railroad.[38] Over a decade earlier, a similar friendly rivalry had developed between the army teams at Ft. Fetterman and Ft. Laramie, Wyoming. Following a particularly spirited two-game series in August 1872, special orders were issued that all future matches would have to be played outside the garrison enclosure because so many windows had been broken by batted balls and errant throws.[39]

The most memorable baseball games appeared to be the ones that pitted soldiers against civilians from the surrounding communities. Some of these were merely infre-quent events, such as those involving the "Government Stockings" team, recruited from the 3rd Cavalrymen temporarily stationed at Bear Butte and Camp Devin on the north-eastern fringes of the Black Hills. They visited back and forth on several weekends to play the teams of miners at Crook City and Deadwood.[40] Others were long established rivalries whose outcomes were vitally important to players and spectators alike. The Fort Union Nine made a series of summer tours during the mid-1880s, challenging the best civilian teams of Mora, Wagon Mound, Las Vegas, Santa Fe, and Albuquerque. Rematches were routinely scheduled, and on several occasions, the 23rd Infantry Band went along to entertain the crowds of spectators. The September 1890 series pitting the Ft. Union Nine against the Las Vegas Blue Stockings offered prize money of 50 dollars and a share of the gate receipts to the winning team. Unfortunately for the army boys, the Las Vegas players were too strong, and they won by a score of 24 to 5.[41]

Although extended summer tours for the army baseball teams took men away from drill and other soldierly duties, senior officers encouraged the competitions wherever and whenever they were feasible. Col. John C. Kelton, commander of the Military Di-vision of the Pacific, favored the expansion of athletic events not only because they improved morale and health, but also because they established better rapport between the soldiers and the civilians whom they were entrusted to serve.[42]

DANCES, PARTIES, AND CONCERTS

Organized sports were not the only escapist activities at frontier posts. Dances and formal military balls were commonplace, and any holiday, birthday, or visit by prominent guests was reason enough to organize these festive occasions. Some were even impro-vised on the spur of the moment simply because members of the garrison wanted to host a party. For instance, when Col. Nelson A. Miles arrived at Camp Supply in December 1874 with two troops of cavalry fresh from victory in the Red River War, junior officers of the camp's 19th Infantry hosted a party and dance that extended into the "weesmall hours" of the evening. This was only one of four such hops that were held within a brief period of time, and some of the activities included enlisted men. Pvt. S. S. Peters complimented the excellent management of the events and the beauty of the post library that had been transformed into a gala ball room tastefully decorated with American flags.[43]

Dances for enlisted men were certainly less numerous than those devoted to of-ficers, but companies frequently petitioned their commander for the right to host these events. Pvt. H. Harbers later recalled that at Camp Supply, companies hosted bimonthly hops that were closely supervised by officers, so closely supervised that the strongest drink allowed was lemonade. The biggest problem facing the majority of enlisted men, however, was what Pvt. Louis Ebert curtly referred to as "too few ladies." Similarly, when soldiers at Ft. Ellis, Montana, sent invitations to the unmarried girls of Bozeman to attend an 1876 dance, they found no takers. The men had to content themselves by dancing with the post laundresses, but there were too few of these unattached young women to go around the dancing circle.[44]

In the confines of their own barracks, enlisted men improvised another type of entertainment: the stags. Here men danced with men, made their own music, and cavorted beyond the watchful eyes of their superiors. 7th Cavalry veteran Ami Frank Mulford fondly recalled the enthusiasm of joining in all the popular dances and taking turns posing as women. Civilian teamster Sam Hotchkiss remembered the routine by which gender distinctions were made in these madcap frolics. "Ladies" wore a handkerchief or white cloth on the upper arm, the transfer of which could be easily made to the next designated "lady" as the evening progressed.[45] Frustrated that these stags lacked the proper romantic spirit, some soldiers took dancing lessons in hopes of improving their social skills and marriageability potential. At Ft. Union, a civilian opened a studio in 1883 that attracted a sizeable number of students. One soldier optimistically remarked that these instructions would help him and other of his fellows win the hearts of the laundresses for potential marriage.[46]

Most dances at frontier military posts were arranged, hosted, and attended exclusively by officers and their wives. These were fairly predictable affairs that melded together dancing, conversation, games, and food. Typical was the 1867 welcoming party for newly married Frank and Alice Baldwin at Ft. Harker, Kansas. Although only one large stone building was completed at that time, fellow officers commandeered the space, fixed it up, and organized an ensemble of stringed musicians from among the soldiers and civilian employees. The shindig extended far into the night, and Mrs. Baldwin wrote that "the ladies wore their best 'bib and tucker' and borrowed of each other and exchanged what one possessed and the other did not—a kindly spirit and mutual interest with us all."[47]

On other occasions, fancier facilities were employed to create a more festive ambience than was available in the redecorated administrative buildings of the fort. Assistant surgeon Dr. James Reagles Jr. marveled at the amenities available to revelers who took an afternoon and evening steamboat excursion near Ft. Smith, Arkansas, in 1868. They were entertained with music and dancing all the way home, and the merriment continued at the post until midnight. A similar outing planned for a few days later ended in tragedy when a Lt. Clarke fell overboard and was drowned in the hours preceding the repeat excursion.[48] A decade later, Grant Marsh, captain of the *Far West*, made his steamboat available to officers at Ft. Keogh, Montana, so that they could entertain Gen. William Tecumseh Sherman in grand style during his inspection and game hunt. The celebrated boat provided a colorful setting for the banquet and dances that included reels, polkas, mazurkas, quadrilles, and schottisches, all accompanied with music played by the Fifth Infantry Band.[49]

Officers competed to provide special themes for their parties and to attract unusual entertainment from beyond the fort confines. In February 1886, Whipple Barracks, Arizona, was abuzz with excitement over the Calico Masquerade Ball, whereby officers and their ladies were strongly encouraged to wear disguises. The event was somewhat unique in the sense that two senior officers attended the party—George Crook and Benjamin H. Grierson—and therefore nothing was left to chance in the preparations. Some of the costumes were very ornate, resembling similar festivities in faraway Venice and Florence, Italy.[50] Another outdoor dance held at Ft. Lewis, Colorado, shortly before its deactivation in 1891 attracted high-class entertainers and featured a Scottish Highlanders Piper band playing martial tunes, with its members attired in brightly colored kilts.[51]

Efforts to create an even grander party sometimes led to problems for commanders who exceeded their authority. Lt. Col. William R. Shafter was determined to bring the leading citizens of Eagle Pass, Texas, to Ft. Duncan during March 1868 so that they could share in the revelry of a three-day post fandango. Military charges were subsequently brought against him for using the military hospital for some of the events and for dispatching the army ambulance on several trips to pick up and take home the invited civilian guests. Some months later, Shafter traveled to San Antonio to face a court-martial that could have ended his career over a seemingly trivial issue. The board of affairs dismissed the charges on the grounds that there had been no criminal intent and no damage had been done.[52]

Dances were held throughout the year, but the most spectacular events that bonded officers, their wives, and reputable civilians were the annual Grand Military Balls. Only the forts that housed sufficient numbers of officers and that were located near substantial towns could afford these extravaganzas. The 1874 Grand Ball hosted by elements of the 6th Cavalry at Ft. Hays attracted the elite of society from seven Kansas communities—Wallace, Ellis, Dodge, Victoria, Russell, Ellsworth, and Hayes City—totaling approximately 200 couples.[53] Ft. D. A. Russell, located three miles outside Cheyenne, Wyoming, presented a Grand Military Ball that drew over 300 civilians and military personnel of all ranks during January 1871. The *Cheyenne Daily Leader* reported the event to be a "perfect success," which transpired "without a single difficulty or misunderstanding."[54] At Ft. Leavenworth, a series of hops during the winter of 1868 led up to a Grand Military Ball that included people from near and far. Considerable money was expended on food and decorations, but at an exorbitant price of 18 dollars per ticket, the invited guests had every reason to expect the best.[55]

Army Bands

Army bands were regularly featured at dances, picnics, weddings, parties, and other off-duty functions, but their mandated responsibilities were based upon long-standing military necessity. Bandsmen were recruited, trained, and outfitted to play for guard mount, drill, dress parades, funerals, and special military functions. These responsibilities came before all other musical endeavors, and not until 1885 did the War Department finally approve the practice of bands playing at purely social occasions. In the wake of the Civil War, musicians also had a new list of martial tunes that would be instantly recognized by soldiers and civilians alike. Popular pieces included "Rally 'Round the Flag," "The Battle Hymn of the Republic," "Tenting Tonight on the Old Campground," and even "Dixie," the unofficial battle song of the former Confederacy.[56]

By military order, bandsmen had to perform the same duties that were expected of all enlisted men. In reality, however, musicians were difficult to recruit and retain, so they often received special privileges that allowed them early dismissal from onerous drill or laborious tasks so that they could rehearse or perform. Sgt. Harry H. McConnell defended the band as an essential army component, but he admitted that many rank-and-file soldiers looked down on musicians, clerks, and other "extra duty men" drawn from the ranks.[57] These critics might well have been thinking of the double standard that was applied to a soldier at Ft. Randall, Dakota Territory. Labeled as a chronic drunkard and having deserted several times, the unidentified man faced the severest of military punishments. Yet Col. Francis Lee interceded in the case because he believed the soldier in question to be "the very best Clarionet [*sic*] player in the Army and our band needs that instrument badly."[58]

Col. Benjamin Grierson, a former music instructor in his own right, demanded perfection from the 10th Cavalry regimental band, but he also recognized the difficulty of outfitting the members with proper uniforms, quality instruments, and ample sheet music. He strongly urged that each enlisted man in the regiment contribute 50 cents to the funding effort and that a group of company officers donate a total of 50 dollars. Not until 1873 did army regulations allow for endowing of bands through the sale of surplus rations.[59]

Col. George Crook utilized similar methods to fund his regimental band, but he was more worried about recruiting and retaining loyal bandsmen. In 1872, Crook sent officers to the Castle Garden immigration station in New York City to enlist experienced German musicians from the recently arrived immigrants.[60] The lesson was not lost on the 7th Cavalry, which at the time of its march to Little Big Horn left behind at Ft. Abraham Lincoln a regimental band whose members consisted of more than half German immigrants.[61] Looking in a slightly different direction for European musical talent, the Eighth Infantry allegedly recruited most of its bandsmen "direct from Italy."[62]

Although chief musicians were paid incredibly high salaries of 60 dollars per month, enlisted men serving in the band received only slightly elevated compensation. They were sometimes able to supplement their salaries by playing at unofficial parties and other social gatherings, but once the fee was split among all performing members, no one emerged with a significant amount. Members of the 21st Infantry Band petitioned the government for increased pay based on their specialized skills and their overall value to military life. Petitioners cited the alleged high turnover rate of army musicians, declaring that most left service after one tour of duty to seek more lucrative employment in civilian circles. Their plea fell upon deaf ears in the War Department.[63]

THEATRICAL PERFORMANCES

While army bands continued to perform official military functions for the rest of the nineteenth century, another type of entertainment occupied only an unofficial status at military posts. Theatricals were universally popular among officers, enlisted men, their families, and civilians, all of whom joined hands in common Thespian presentations as either actors or spectators. Unfortunately, martial duties sometimes interrupted rehearsals and performances, especially during the warm months of the year, when major campaigns drew large numbers of men into the field. The Miles City, Montana, *Yellowstone Journal* remarked in November 1879 that the main part of the theatrical season had just begun at nearby Ft. Keogh when troops were reassigned to field duties. No exceptions were made, even for the key cast members who had spent considerable time practicing for their roles. Col. Nelson A. Miles, an ardent supporter of army theatrical groups, added his lament from the same post that even routine patrols created havoc for scheduling these events and that therefore they should mainly be reserved for the winter months.[64]

Large military installations were ideally suited for the formation of theatrical companies because enough eager participants stood ready to form troupes and because sufficient buildings existed to host the events. Various multiple-use facilities were available, including warehouses, dining rooms, barracks, chapels, and gymnasiums as well as open-air spaces for performances during the warmer months. Where necessary, improvisation could solve the space problem, such as at Ft. Sedgwick, Colorado, where two hospital tents were erected in the late 1860s to serve as a temporary theater and entertainment hall. Later in the century, Ft. Niobrara, Nebraska, housed its theater in the chapel, with the stage placed at one end and the altar situated at the other. Audiences simply turned their chairs around to face the direction of the appropriate social function.[65]

Most theaters were relatively small, handling only a few dozen spectators at any one time, but as the century wore on, some of the facilities became quite grand. Ft. Riley, Kansas, supported the largest post theater on the Great Plains, with the building measuring 135 by 68 feet, equipped with a 65-foot stage, and accommodations for 800 people. On the northern plains, Ft. Shaw, Montana, seated approximately 550; Ft. Maginnis, Montana, 400; Ft. Ellis, Montana, 300; and Ft. Abraham Lincoln, Dakota Territory, 380 people. Some of these experimented with sophisticated lighting systems by the 1890s, but the technology of the day limited most stage lighting to candles and kerosene lamps.[66] Preceding all of these was the tiny post at Camp Warner, Oregon, which as early as 1868 supported a theatrical troupe that already owned several hundred dollars' worth of costumes and scenery and possessed its own scene painter. This must have been an energetic group of thespians who were dedicated to their craft because at that time, they had no building in which to perform.[67] In the same vein, soldiers at Ft. Sherman, Idaho,. staged a benefit performance of *The Pirates of Penzance* that raised more than 100 dollars for the struggling Episcopal Church of Couer d'Alene. And Ft. Keogh actors presented *The Widow-Hunt,* a comedy in three acts as a benefit for the St. Paul's Episcopal Church of Miles City. The event was such a success that a second production was arranged for the following night.[68]

Most of the soldier-produced plays remained within the confines of good taste because their creators did not wish to offend their mixed-gender audiences or give the fort commander good reason to suspend the activities. Yet infrequently, deviations in decorum did occur. Officer's wife Julia Gillis noted that during one cold winter's night of 1867 at Ft. Stevens, Oregon, a small group of enlisted men held an improvised show exclusively for themselves and a few trusted civilian employees. From indirect sources, she learned that the performances had been quite bawdy and that no women were allowed to attend.[69] At another time, enlisted men conducted improvised plays in the relative security of their own Ft. Shaw, Montana, barracks. Here, away from the watchful eyes of their superiors, they mocked their own officers with exaggerated speech and gestures.[70]

Although women participated in numerous plays—especially in those that were reserved for audiences of officers and their families—female roles were handled in other ways when women were unavailable. Comedies especially made use of men who dressed as women and assumed melodramatic characterizations of their own.[71] This type of staging sometimes led to unintended consequences, such as when the Ft. Custer Dramatic Troupe presented a version of John Brogham's *Pocahontas*. Professional actor John Maguire starred as Captain John Smith and, for the sake of authenticity, he invited a small group of Crow Indian scouts to participate in the historical rendition. The early acts of its play seemed to move smoothly, until a visibly agitated Crow elder charged into the hall and began shouting at his friends. The Indians bolted out of the building and ran toward their encampment to arm themselves. As it turned out, a Piegan raiding party had driven off almost 100 horses from the Crow's remuda, and the latter set out in hot pursuit. The historical record remains silent on whether the production of *Pocahontas* continued or was ended for the evening.[72]

Despite the presence of theatrical ensembles at most significant military installations, officers and enlisted men also welcomed professional acting groups that traveled throughout the West. These civilian troupes especially flourished in the decades after 1870, when improved transportation networks made it possible to create entertainment circuits among the ever-increasing number of posts and towns. In addition to theatrical companies, more specialized acts also performed for pay before army audiences. Charles Vivian and his wife, Imogene, became a well-known husband-wife team who combined acting, dramatic readings, and singing before appreciative audiences spread across the northern plains. So renowned were the acting skills of Theodore and Maria Bolls that Col. John Gibbon and his wife invited them to settle at Ft. Shaw, Montana, in 1874 so that they could direct and participate in the theatricals. Soldiers used an army ambulance to move them to the post, then constructed for them a small house attached to the existing theater building and helped them earn a living from ticket sales. The entertainers remained there for a year and a half before returning to Chicago. Their numerous productions not only thrilled the military community, but also attracted civilian spectators from far and wide.[73]

Not all the theatrical events presented by traveling civilian groups were so well received. At Ft. Supply, the audience barely tolerated one particular 1878 performance by an unidentified troupe. In addition to labeling the actors as "humbugs," one clever pundit lamented, "The Indians have not taken us yet, but this strolling show has."[74] Soldiers at Ft. Union, New Mexico, became even more agitated with the incompetence and boredom produced by the traveling theatrical group known as Visscher and Crawford. In addition to harassing the actors, the soldiers applauded one of their own who jumped on stage and began giving an impromptu performance better than the one that they paid for.[75]

As in the case of military bands that routinely traveled to civilian communities, army theatrical troupes also made local visits as part of their unofficial public relations campaign. For instance, during the winter of 1885–1886, the Ft. Custer Comic Opera and Burlesque Company put on 10 shows at the fort, then undertook a tour to Billings, Livingston, Bozeman, Ft. Ellis, and Ft. Keogh. Pvt. James O. Purvis reported the entertainment series in the *Billings Daily Gazette* and promised that the success would all but guarantee a similar excursion during the following fall. On another occasion, an unidentified correspondent for *Harper's Magazine* witnessed the off-post performances by the Ft. Ellis Minstrel and Dramatic Association, pronouncing the group to be "one of the best variety companies we have ever seen and would draw crowded houses anywhere."[76]

One of the most spectacular combinations of dramatic action and realism occurred in 1886, when a group of Denverites presented a play entitled *The Siege of Lucknow*. In celebrating the famous 1857 British victory over rebels in India, the civilian actors utilized real muskets and two cannons supplied by visiting military officers. In the midst of the staged attack that marked the high point of the drama, expended gunpowder filled the air to such a degree that the stage was entirely obscured. The dress of the leading lady also caught fire, and one of the cannons blew an eight-foot-square hole through a wall of the theater.[77]

LITERARY SOCIETIES AND LYCEUMS

The popularity of the theater troupes and variety acts at military posts rested upon the physical nature of the acts, the exoticism of the tales, and the unpredictability of the performances. These factors contrasted sharply with the intentions of literary societies that flourished on some of the larger military installations. The groups attempted to reach a higher intellectual plane by educating their audiences rather than merely entertaining them. These were fairly elitist groups that restricted most of their membership to officers, their wives, and a select few noncommissioned officers. Most consisted of small groups of people who read literary classics to discuss among themselves. Typical of the informal groups was Kramer's Literary Association at Ft. Union, which mixed discussion of classic books with some of the newest literature. Members pooled their money to purchase a continuous supply of books and literary magazines from the East, as did the Emerson Encyclic Literary Society at Ft. Pembina, Dakota Territory.[78]

Wherever literary societies organized themselves, lyceum series often followed. These events normally consisted of public lectures given by local officers, but some attracted traveling civilian speakers who were well-known experts within their specialized fields. During January 1888, post commander August V. Kautz at Ft. Niobrara, Nebraska, approved a lyceum consisting of presentations staged over three evenings. The topics would have appealed only to the most intellectually curious residents of the fort or to people who badly needed a reason for social interaction in the dead of winter. Kautz led off the series with a talk entitled "A Field for the Army in Times of Peace." These were followed on successive evenings with officer presentations on "Rear Guard of Armies" and "Hydrogen Light and Sciopticon." In contrast to these narrowly conceived topics, an 1890 lyceum presented by famed Arctic explorer Lt. Frederick Schwatka drew an overflow crowd from all walks of life at the post.[79]

Most lyceums grew out of informal roots and maintained their simplicity throughout their existence, but some matured into structured organizations that addressed more pragmatic goals. At Ft. Robinson, Nebraska, during the 1890s, the post commander served as president of the lyceum, and the majors and captains acted as instructors. This more formal context emerged after an 1891 directive from Commanding General of the Army John M. Schofield that lyceums be instituted wherever possible to enhance the edification and promotion chances for officers and noncoms.[80] During the first years after the directive went into effect, positive reports emanated from departmental commanders

Enlisted men playing chess in quarters at Ft. Stanton, New Mexico, during the late 1880s. (*Collection in Museum of New Mexico*)

such as Gen. Oliver Otis Howard and Gen. Alexander M. McCook. Virtually all of these lyceums, unlike their predecessors of the 1870s and 1880s, dealt with military topics that would have attracted little attention outside military circles. Yet many of the revised presentations found their way into print in interservice publications, such as *Cavalry Journal, United Service,* and *Journal of the Military Service Institution of the United States.* In printed form, the essays reached broad audiences of servicemen since virtually all of the larger posts subscribed to these periodicals. Likewise, they helped articulate officers' concerns on a broad range of issues and helped generate spirited discussions through letters of response that were also published in the journals. Most of these lyceum presentations and subsequent articles addressed real problems dealing with morale, desertion, supply systems, and medical needs as well as provided possible solutions for these problems.[81] Such pragmatic essays were indeed a far cry from most of the earlier lyceum topics that ranged from exotic travelogues to highly esoteric discussions of theoretical issues.

Throughout the full extent of the nineteenth century, the War Department never designed or endorsed a program of off-duty recreation and entertainment for its soldiers. Frontier regulars therefore initiated their own forms of amusement, and most of the unofficial activities were not only tolerated, but encouraged by senior officers, who recognized the benefits of improved health and morale. Rather than inventing a unique set of recreational activities peculiar to military life, they merely applied the popular pursuits that were widely heralded in mainstream society.

Indeed, very few men who joined the frontier army in the decades after the Civil War could be characterized as loners who had turned their backs on the world. Even the most troubled of recruits who were escaping debts, failed marriages, dictatorial fathers, past crimes, and other personal disappointments saw the army not as the ultimate dead end to a fruitless life, but rather as an opportunity to begin a new life. Likewise, instead of turning their backs on "civilization," most soldiers relished the institutions of broader society and participated in the perpetuation and renewal of those institutions at even the most isolated of posts.

NOTES

1. Challenging the traditional view that army officers were socially isolated from their civilian peers are two important studies: John M. Gates, "The Alleged Isolation of U.S. Army Officers in the Late 19th Century," *Parameters: The Journal of the U.S. Army War College* 10 (September 1980): 32–45; and, for the postfrontier era, Richard C. Brown, *Social Attitudes of American Generals, 1898–1940* (New York: Arno Press, 1979), 38.

2. Dale F. Giese, "Soldiers at Play: A History of Social Life at Fort Union, New Mexico, 1851–1891" (PhD diss., University of New Mexico, 1969), 95–96.

3. Margaret Irvin Carrington, *Absaraka, Home of the Crows: Being the Experience of an Officer's Wife on the Plains* (Philadelphia: J. B. Lippincott, 1868), 141–42, 200–10.

4. Stephen Ralph Buss, "The Military Theatre: Soldier-Actor Theatricals on the Frontier Plains" (PhD diss., Washington State University, 1982), 51.

5. Tom Lindmier, *Drybone: A History of Fort Fetterman, Wyoming* (Glendo, WY: High Plains Press, 2002), 103. Thomas Twichel, "Fort Logan and the Urban Frontier," *Montana, Magazine of Western History* 17 (Autumn 1967): 49. Giese, "Soldiers at Play," 96.

6. *Army and Navy Register* (November 10, 1886). A similar article from an army wife appears in *Army and Navy Register* (January 12, 1887). The issue of buying Christmas gifts from afar and crafting them at home is dealt with by Julia Gillis, *So Far from Home: An Army Bride on the Western Frontier, 1865–1869,* ed. Priscilla Knuth (Portland: Oregon Historical Society, 1993), 161–62.

7. Thomas R. Buecker, ed., "Letters of Caroline Frey Winne from Sidney Barracks and Fort McPherson, Nebraska, 1874–1878," *Nebraska History* 62 (Spring 1981): 27.

8. Jere W. Roberson, ed., "A View from Oklahoma, 1866–1868: The Diary and Letters of Dr. James Reagles, Jr., Assistant Surgeon, U.S. Army," *Red River Valley Historical Review* 3 (Fall 1978): 41. Harry H. Anderson, "A History of the Cheyenne River Agency and Its Military Post, Fort Bennett, 1868–1891," *South Dakota Report and History Collections* 28 (1956): 514.

9. Ray H. Mattison, ed., "The Complete Diary of Surgeon Washington Matthews, Fort Rice, D.T.," *North Dakota History* 21 (January 1954): 28–29. Don Rickey Jr., *Forty Miles a Day on Beans and Hay: The Enlisted Soldier Fighting the Indian Wars* (Norman: University of Oklahoma Press, 1963), 206–7. Giese, "Soldiers at Play," 96.

10. Thomas T. Smith, ed., *A Dose of Frontier Soldiering: The Memoirs of Corporal E. A. Bode, Frontier Regular Infantry, 1877–1882* (Lincoln: University of Nebraska Press, 1994), 172–73.

11. Sherry L. Smith, ed., *Sagebrush Soldier: Private William Earl Smith's View of the Sioux War of 1876* (Norman: University of Oklahoma Press, 1989), 123.

12. John G. Bourke, *Mackenzie's Last Fight with the Cheyennes: A Winter Campaign in Wyoming and Montana* (New York: Argonaut Press, 1966), 53. Extensive eyewitness accounts of Christmas celebrations at the forts and privations suffered "in the field" are contained in Lori A. Cox-Paul and James W. Wengert, comps., *A Frontier Army Christmas* (Lincoln: Nebraska State Historical Society, 1996).

13. Examples of the abundant foods and liquors available for Independence Day celebrations are described in Ray H. Mattison, "The Army Post on the Northern Plains, 1865–1885," *Nebraska History* 35 (March 1954): 29. Ray H. Mattison, "Fort Rice, North Dakota's First Missouri River Military Post," *North Dakota History* 20 (April 1953): 95. Donald K. Adams, ed., "The Journals of Ada A. Vogdes, 1868–71," *Montana, Magazine of Western History* 13 (Summer 1963): 8.

14. Mattison, "Army Post," 40. Virtually the same list of 1878 Independence Day activities was given for Ft. Supply in Indian Territory, and these activities are discussed in Robert C. Carriker, *Fort Supply, Indian Territory: Frontier Outpost on the Plains* (Norman: University of Oklahoma Press, 1970), 153. A similar eyewitness account for 1868 is provided in Robert M. Utley, ed., *Life in Custer's Cavalry: Diaries and Letters of Albert and Jennie Barnitz, 1867–1868* (New Haven, CT: Yale University Press, 1977), 167.

15. Giese, "Soldiers at Play," 94–95.

16. Betty Loudon, ed., "Pioneer Pharmacist J. Walter Moyer's Note on Crawford and Fort Robinson in the 1890s," *Nebraska History* 58 (Spring 1977): 103–4.

17. Margaret Bierschwale, *Fort McKavett, Texas: Post on the San Saba* (Salado, TX: Anson Jones Press, 1966), 78–80.

18. Mattison, "Fort Rice," 93–95.

19. Thomas C. Railsback, "Military Bands and Music at Old Fort Hays, 1867–1889," *Journal of the West* 22 (July 1983): 31.

20. Gilliss, *So Far from Home,* 164, 180.

21. Giese, "Soldiers at Play," 105.

22. Ibid., 102.

23. Thomas R. Buecker, "Fort Niobrara, 1880–1906: Guardian of the Rosebud Sioux," *Nebraska History* 65 (Fall 1984): 312.

24. Giese, "Soldiers at Play," 105–6.

25. Ibid., 106.

26. Glendolin Damon Wagner, *Old Neutriment* (Boston: R. Hill, 1934), 92–96.

27. Adams, "Journals of Ada Vogdes," 6.

28. Gillis, *So Far from Home,* 38.

29. Robert A. Murray, "Fort Fred Steele: Desert Outpost on the Union Pacific," *Annals of Wyoming* 44 (Fall 1972): 199. A more negative appraisal of winter skating and sleigh rides on the northern plains appears in Philippe Régis de Trobriand, *Military Life in Dakota: The Journal of Philippe Régis de Trobriand,* ed. Lucile M. Kane (Saint Paul, MN: Alvord Memorial Commission, 1951), 191.

30. Bill Green, *The Dancing Was Lively: Fort Concho, Texas, a Social History, 1867 to 1882* (San Angelo, TX: Fort Concho Sketches, 1974), 99–103. Shirley A. Leckie, "Fort Concho: Paradise for Children," *Fort Concho Report* 19 (Spring 1987): 9.

31. Anderson, "History of the Cheyenne River Agency," 530–31.

32. Giese, "Soldiers at Play," 106–8.

33. Loudon, "Pioneer Pharmacist," 102.

34. Robert F. Bluthardt, "Baseball on the Military Frontier," *Fort Concho Report* 19 (Spring 1987): 17–20. This article (pp. 20–21) also discusses the nature of baseball equipment at that

time and demonstrates how the rules were different from those that are honored today. Merrill J. Mattes, *Indians, Infants and Infantry: Andrew and Elizabeth Burt on the Frontier* (Denver: Old West, 1960), 259–60, 266.

35. Bluthardt, "Baseball," 18. Giese, "Soldiers at Play," 118.

36. Harry H. Anderson, "The Benteen Base Ball Club: Sports Enthusiasts of the Seventh Cavalry," *Montana, Magazine of Western History* 20 (July 1970): 84–87.

37. Don Russell, *Campaigning with King: Charles King, Chronicler of the Old Army,* ed. Paul L. Hedren (Lincoln: University of Nebraska Press, 1991), 31.

38. Buecker, "Fort Niobrara," 313.

39. Lindmier, *Drybone,* 104.

40. Robert Lee, *Fort Meade and the Black Hills* (Lincoln: University of Nebraska Press, 1991), 25.

41. Giese, "Soldiers at Play," 117–20.

42. "New York *Herald* Says," *Army and Navy Journal* (October 1, 1881): 189.

43. S. S. Peters, "Letters of a Sixth Cavalryman Stationed at 'Cantonment' in the Texas Panhandle, 1875," *Texas Military History* 7 (Summer 1968): 80–81.

44. Rickey, *Forty Miles a Day,* 198–99.

45. Ami Frank Mulford, *Fighting Indians in the 7th United States Cavalry* (Corning, NY: Paul Lindsley Mulford, 1879), 47. Rickey, *Forty Miles a Day,* 199.

46. Giese, "Soldiers at Play," 92.

47. Alice Blackwood Baldwin, *Memoirs of the Late Frank D. Baldwin, Major General, U.S.A.* (Los Angeles: Wetzel, 1929), 128.

48. Roberson, "View from Oklahoma," 45.

49. Baldwin, *Memoirs of Frank D. Baldwin,* 189–90.

50. Shirley A. Leckie, ed., *The Colonel's Lady on the Western Frontier: The Correspondence of Alice Kirk Grierson* (Lincoln: University of Nebraska Press, 1989), 169–70.

51. W. Heath Eldridge, "An Army Boy in Colorado," *Colorado Magazine* 32 (October 1955): 308–9.

52. Paul H. Carlson, *"Pecos Bill": A Military Biography of William R. Shafter* (College Station: Texas A&M University Press, 1976), 41–42.

53. Thomas C. Railsback and John P. Langellier, *The Drums Would Roll: A Pictorial History of United States Army Bands on the American Frontier, 1866–1900* (New York: Arms and Armour Press, 1987), 18.

54. Gerald M. Adams, *The Post Near Cheyenne: A History of Fort D. A. Russell, 1867–1930* (Boulder: Pruett, 1989), 45.

55. Utley, *Life in Custer's Cavalry,* 134.

56. William G. Huey, "Making Music: Brass Bands on the Northern Plains, 1860–1930," *North Dakota History* 54 (Winter 1987): 3–4.

57. H. H. McConnell, *Five Years a Cavalryman, or Sketches of Regular Army Life on the Texas Frontier, 1866–1871* (Jacksboro, TX: J. N. Rogers, 1889), 266.

58. Huey, "Making Music," 4.

59. Railsback and Langellier, *Drums Would Roll,* 15–16. Jack D. Foner, "The Socializing Role of the Military," in *The American Military on the Frontier: Proceedings of the Seventh Military History Symposium,* ed. James P. Tate (Washington, DC: Office of Air Force History, 1978), 89.

60. Railsback and Langellier, *Drums Would Roll,* 17. Huey, "Making Music," 4.

61. Huey, "Making Music," 4.

62. Martha Summerhayes, *Vanished Arizona: Recollections of the Army Life of a New England Woman,* 2nd ed. (Salem, MA: Salem Press, 1911), 12.

63. Railsbach and Langellier, *Drums Would Roll,* 18–19.

64. Buss, "Military Theatre," 45–46. Nelson A. Miles, *Personal Recollections and Observations of General Nelson A. Miles* (Chicago: Werner, 1896), 333.

65. Buss, "Military Theatre," 97–102.

66. Ibid., 105–7, 114.

67. Gillis, *So Far from Home,* 180.

68. William H. Bisbee, *Through Four American Wars* (Boston: Meador, 1931), 228. Buss, "Military Theatre," 48.

69. Gillis, *So Far from Home,* 111.

70. Buss, "Military Theatre," 54–55.

71. Ibid., 54, 72–73.

72. Ibid., 13–14.

73. Ibid., 55–58, 145, 154.

74. Carriker, *Fort Supply,* 153.

75. Giese, "Soldiers at Play," 35.

76. Buss, "Military Theatre," 68, 75.

77. Ibid., 135–36.

78. Giese, "Soldiers at Play," 42. William D. Thomson, "History of Fort Pembina: 1870–1895," *North Dakota History* 36 (Winter 1969): 35.

79. Buecker, "Fort Niobrara," 313.

80. Frank N. Schubert, *Buffalo Soldiers, Braves and Brass: The Story of Fort Robinson, Nebraska* (Shippensburg, PA: White Mane, 1993), 120–21.

81. Edward M. Coffman, *The Old Army: A Portrait of the American Army in Peacetime, 1784–1898* (New York: Oxford University Press, 1986), 276–78.

7   MANY MISSIONS: A MULTIPURPOSE ARMY ON THE FRONTIER

American military history was once viewed as the exciting record of battles, tactics, and victorious commanders. Entire books often hinged on a narrow focus where individual units moved about on the battlefield until they ultimately succeeded or failed with their dangerous maneuvers under fire. Such interpretive methodologies produced wonderfully intricate studies of command decisions, personal valor, and the inevitable blunders that accompany the "fog of war." Unfortunately, these examinations provide an incomplete perspective on the army's diverse roles. Nowhere is this better illustrated than in the late nineteenth century, when military leaders were constantly searching for new missions to redefine themselves in the eyes of the public and to warrant continued congressional appropriations. By casting the net widely in search of duties that would justify their existence, officers had to deal with the realities of limited budgets, inadequate manpower, and a public that perpetually feared creation of a large military establishment.

Yet in the face of these limitations, the army undertook a multitude of tasks, some by choice and some by coerced assignment. These nonmartial duties had little to do with the context of Indian fighting but nonetheless were major contributions to the settlement of the West. In his monumental 1953 book *Broadax and Bayonet,* Francis Paul Prucha accurately concluded that the frontier army served as the nation's "orderly purveyor of civilization" and that it "cannot be assigned a single position in the parade to the West; its presence was felt in all stages of the pioneering process."[1] With these words, Prucha presaged the concept that other historians have dubbed the "multipurpose army," and they have documented these nonmartial roles with great precision. For all its virtues and faults, the multipurpose army served as the right arm of the federal government in its nineteenth-century expansionist endeavors, and it is within this larger context that the institution must be considered.

EXPLORATION, MAPPING, AND SCIENCE

Most recognizable of the army's peacetime roles was the exploration, mapping, and publication of information about the vast western landscape. From the time of Lewis and Clark's 1804–1806 ascent of the Missouri River until the 1863 demise of the elite Topographical Engineers, the army was America's primary explorer of terra incognita. The "topogs," as they were affectionately known, were mostly led by West Point–trained officers who combined scientific curiosity with pragmatic notions of expanding the influence of their nation. Prominent names, such as Zebulon Pike, Stephen Long, John C. Frémont, James W. Abert, Randolph B. Marcy, William Emory, James H. Simpson, Amiel Weeks Whipple, Howard Stansbury, and Gouverneur K. Warren, echoed across the public consciousness and energized a people who were relentlessly pushing toward the Pacific basin during the antebellum period.[2]

Although most of the transcontinental exploration was completed before the Civil War, soldiers continued reconnaissances within more confined regions to the end of the century. Some became famous in their own right, such as Lt. Col. George Custer's 1874 massive exploration of the Black Hills that set off a mining rush, provoking the Great Sioux War and the signature battle at Little Big Horn.[3] Other ventures, including the arduous one undertaken in 1875 by Lt. Col. William R. Shafter across the southern areas of the Texas panhandle to the Pecos River, were little more than reinforced reconnaissances.[4] Yet in all of these cases, whether recorded in extensive reports or cryptic journal entries, soldiers were filling in the collective knowledge about the most remote areas of the United States.

A column of cavalry, artillery, and wagons commanded by Lt. Col. George Custer crosses the plains of the Dakota Territory during the 1874 Black Hills expedition. (*Courtesy of the National Archives*)

The last "great survey" undertaken purely as a military effort was the protracted operations coordinated by Lt. George M. Wheeler, who oversaw a series of 14 separate explorations in the vast area between the central plains and California. The grand sweep yielded a seven-volume set entitled *Report upon United States Geographical Surveys West of the One Hundredth Meridian* (1875–1889), complete with topographical and geological atlases collectively containing 164 precise maps. One later text summarized the importance of Wheeler's work by claiming, "The director and his associates had located and examined some 219 mining districts, made observations and delineations of 143 mountain ranges and of the profiles of 202 mountain passes, and charted the course of 90 streams. They determined the elevation of 395 high peaks, explored 25 lakes, discovered 50 terminal springs, and collected a few new species of birds, reptiles, fishes, and insects. The total collection of specimens later placed in the Smithsonian Institution numbered 61,659."[5]

Although best remembered for locating new routes and compiling improved maps, the soldier-explorers worked closely with civilian-scientists to expand the realm of knowledge about the zoology, botany, paleontology, and geology of the West. Sometimes the military aid was of a secondary nature, often in providing escorts through dangerous country or in assisting the scientists with their less technical tasks. For instance, the commander of Ft. Fetterman, Wyoming, arranged for a detail of soldiers to accompany Professor J. A. Allen of the Museum of Comparative Zoology in his ornithological work during 1880.[6] A decade later, soldiers stationed at Ft. D. A. Russell, Wyoming, escorted celebrated Yale professor Othniel C. Marsh and 30 of his paleontology students on a successful dig within the Agate Fossil Beds of Nebraska's panhandle.[7]

On other occasions, officers took the initiative to make their own discoveries and to share their knowledge with the nation's scientific community. West Point–trained officers certainly received a strong grounding in scientific methods, and some of them evidenced a lifelong interest in these endeavors. Army physician Capt. Theophilus H. Turner, while stationed at Ft. Wallace, Kansas, discovered a rare fossil skeleton of a dinosaur, which he carefully excavated and transported to Edward D. Cope, curator of the Academy of Natural Sciences of Philadelphia. For this contribution of a major specimen and for his later amateur paleontological work, Turner was rewarded with membership in the academy. Although not a graduate of West Point, Dr. Turner represented the college-educated elite that made a life in the army.[8]

Even greater fame came to Elliott Coues, who served 19 years as an army assistant surgeon at a number of far-flung posts. Within that time, his off-duty pursuits led to his recognition as one of the country's premier ornithologists. In 1872, he published the classic reference work *Key to North American Birds,* followed by additional books on birds of the Northwest and Colorado Valley. Though primarily recognized as an avian expert today, he also devoted considerable attention to mammals. Together with Joel Allen, he published *Monographs of North American Rodentia* (1877) and *Fur Bearing Animals: A Monograph of North American Mustelidae* (1877). Between the crafting of his books, Coues maintained a lively publication record within the celebrated academic journals of the Academy of Natural Sciences, the Boston Society of Natural History, and the Essex Institute.[9]

Occasionally, ambitious enlisted men also evidenced scholarly interests. German-born Charles E. Bendire rose through the ranks to eventually become a captain of cavalry. His major claim to scholarship rested upon his publication of the two-volume *Life Histories of American Birds* (1892–1896) and upon his years as honorary curator of the Department of Oology at the Smithsonian Institution.[10] Former enlisted man Ivan F. Tidestrom, a Swedish immigrant, served two terms in the cavalry before resigning to pursue academic studies in botany. In 1925, he published *Flora of Utah and Nevada,* followed 16 years later by *Flora of Arizona and New Mexico.*[11]

Officers and enlisted men also contributed to other expanding fields of knowledge: ethnology and linguistics. Virtually all of these studies dealt with Native American cultures and languages. Some were purely utilitarian, such as the extensive Lakota Sioux vocabulary compiled by Col. Philippe Régis de Trobriand to aid his personal communications and army surgeon William Corbusier's Apache vocabulary to help him teach English to Indians at Arizona's Rio Verde Agency. More extensive was Capt. William Philo Clark's *The Indian Sign Language* (1885), which remained the standard source for many years and contributed to numerous future studies.[12]

Perhaps the most celebrated of all the military ethnologists was post surgeon Dr. Washington Matthews, who published extensively in the most revered academic journals as well as the series of books presided over by the Bureau of American Ethnology. His pathbreaking studies on the Hidatsa tribe were followed by even more seminal investigations of the Navajos. Joined in his later efforts by Corp. Christian Barthelmess, Matthews published extensively on Navajo language, ritual, and material culture. With these studies, he became recognized as one of the pioneers in the field of physical anthropology.[13]

Closely approaching Dr. Matthews in terms of his renown in the scholarly community was Capt. John G. Bourke, who was not only an observant recorder of Indian life, but also a participant in some of the most important military campaigns against Sioux, Northern Cheyenne, Ute, Nez Percé, and Apache peoples. Bourke's two best-known books were *On the Border with Crook* (1891) and *An Apache Campaign in the Sierra Madre* (1886), which offered action-packed but honest accounts of military campaigns on the Great Plains and in the Southwest as well as unrelenting defense of Bourke's mentor Gen. George Crook. More scientific in approach was his *The Snake Dance of the Moquis of Arizona* (1884), which offered the best ethnological information on the Hopis and was collected directly from Indian elders of the kivas of Walpi. His 1892 detailed study *The Medicine Men of the Apache* was published as the Ninth Annual Report of the Bureau of American Ethnology. The impressive work attracted the attention of national figures such as Theodore Roosevelt and John Wesley Powell, director of the Bureau of American Ethnology, who worked to have Bourke transferred from routine field duty so that he could devote full time to ethnological publications. Although the reassignment strategy failed, Bourke continued to provide articles for major scientific journals, and he was elected to membership by the leading scientific groups.[14]

ARMY IMPROVEMENTS ON WESTERN RIVERS AND HARBORS

Most Americans have long recognized the U.S. Army's significant contribution to frontier exploration, but its massive efforts at creating and maintaining a western transportation and communication system have been largely overlooked. In addition to the extensive road and bridge building projects of the late nineteenth century that have been discussed in a previous chapter, soldiers engaged in other forms of work projects that not only enhanced the army's ability to move men and supplies, but also simultaneously benefited civilian populations.

One of the national concerns that ultimately affected military policy was the need to improve western river access wherever the natural waterways were deep enough and wide enough to serve commercial needs. One focal point for this expensive work was the Missouri River, which meandered across the northern plains to the continental divide of the Rocky Mountains in present-day Montana. Following the Civil War, the government funded a Missouri River project that had been initiated as early as the 1840s. On the basis of a comprehensive report filed by Maj. Charles W. Howell in December 1867, it provided a meticulous plan for removal of snags, islands, boat wrecks, and boulders from the river. It also directed a rechanneling of some stretches by means of dredging and blasting and the construction of landings at commercially viable locations. Though the improved river conditions could aid military movement of men and supplies, its more important function was to facilitate civilian transportation and commerce over the long term.[15]

Other rivers—including the Rio Grande, Brazos, Colorado, Willamette, and Columbia—drew the attention of the Corps of Engineers throughout the late nineteenth century. Some of these waterways received substantial work from the army, and others were quickly proven to lack commercial potential. Perhaps the most promising endeavor was along the formidable Columbia River. In close association with the powerful Oregon Steam and Navigation Company, Maj. R. S. Williamson proposed taming the three imposing rapids at Umatilla, Homely, and John Day, all of which endangered riverboat traffic. Their blasting on John Day Rock marked the first permanent improvement along the Columbia, and by 1873, the corps had eliminated all major obstacles from the immediate vicinity. Even more complex was the construction of a four million dollar canal around the Cascades, an imposing project that was not fully completed until 18 years later.[16]

Rivers were not the only bodies of water that interested the Army Corps of Engineers in the West. Along the coastline of California and the Pacific Northwest, the army spent considerable time and money in harbor and reclamation work. Congress blessed the massive projects in 1866 by establishing a permanent San Francisco office for the corps and entrusting it with the responsibility of rechanneling rivers that flowed into the port cities. This was done as part of a broader effort to prevent silting of the harbors in key trade centers such as San Francisco, Monterey, Los Angeles, and San Diego. Throughout the 1880s and 1890s, the corps also dredged channels and built jetties at Humboldt Bay, approximately 200 miles north of San Francisco. This newly created deep water port handled much of the interior commerce for northern California and Oregon, especially the burgeoning timber industry.[17]

RAILROADS, MAIL DELIVERY, TELEGRAPH, AND WEATHER SERVICE

Among the most important army contributions to improving western transportation was its connection to the transcontinental railroads. Because the rail lines could build through the most difficult terrain, could economically serve areas with relatively small populations, could convey heavy loads at reasonable rates, and could link frontier communities with eastern industry, they were viewed as the solution for overcoming frontier isolation. Even before private companies began the actual construction projects of laying track, the U.S. Army Corps of Topographical Engineers directed the four Pacific Railroad surveys of the 1850s.[18]

Sectional disputes and economic concerns delayed the building plans until the Civil War, when Republican domination of the White House and Congress opened the door to fulfillment of a party promise to link the continent with a ribbon of iron. Soldiers not only guarded the construction crews of the Union Pacific Railroad and other transcontinentals, but also, the War Department allowed civilian workers to secure timber and stone from military reservations without cost and to erect depots on post lands. In return, the army received discounted rates to move men and supplies by trains that ultimately crisscrossed the West.[19] Thus as surveyor, protector, and frequent user of the railroads, the military had helped introduce the single most important piece of transportation technology for closing the frontier era in the vast region from the Missouri River to the Pacific Ocean.

While railroads certainly represented the most visible improvement in national transportation systems, a more subtle form of improved communication also assumed an army connection: the federal mail service. Although primarily a civilian function administered by the Post Office Department, mail delivery was entrusted to the military in some of the most remote areas. At Ft. Laramie, Sgt. Leodegar Schnyder received the coveted position as postmaster in 1859 and held the position for 17 years during his active service years and into his subsequent retirement. At Wyoming's Ft. D. A. Russell, Lucinda Lester, wife of Sgt. Major Lester of the 17th Infantry, received appointment as postmistress in early 1887. More often than not, the post sutler sought and won the designation, which allowed him to supplement his income without assuming a significant increase in workload.[20]

If mail call provided a welcome relief for soldiers, it furnished an equally important boost to the lives of civilians who drew their mail at nearby forts. Typical beneficiaries of this service were residents of the eastern Texas panhandle—mostly ranchers, sheepherders, railroad construction crews, and townspeople of Mobeetie—who relied upon Ft. Elliott as their mail drop. By the summer of 1879, service had improved considerably at the post, with delivery six times weekly from Ft. Dodge, Ft. Supply, and Ft. Reno. This operation was mainly in the hands of civilian contractor Lee and Reynolds Freighting Company, but at other isolated spots, soldiers carried the mail for both military and civilian clientele.[21]

Closely associated with the fusion of civilian and soldier postal efforts was the combined role for telegraphic services. Soldiers not only guarded construction and repair crews, they also occasionally contributed physical labor to the building of what was otherwise a privately owned business. They dug holes, hauled poles, and repaired wire whenever civilian work crews were unavailable or were frightened off by periodic Indian scares. As new companies established their own lines across the plains in the 1870s and 1880s, they purposely linked themselves to military establishments. Many were under federal contract to transmit military messages, and for this they received generous government subsidies. Although most of these associations proved to be mutually beneficial, some companies took advantage of the army.[22] In 1883, Omaha newspaper correspondent William Annin reported the discontent at Ft. Robinson, Nebraska, where civilian operators let the infrastructure of their line deteriorate, fully aware that soldiers would be sent out to speedily make repairs so that they could maintain official communications between military installations.[23]

Ft. Concho, Texas, stood at the center of the most extensive military telegraph-building project of the mid-1870s. The volume of monthly messages at the post averaged between 600 and 700, ranging from important information on troop deployments to very personal information, such as Col. William Shafter ordering three bottles of the best claret, three quarts of the best champagne, and a dozen lemons. Within three years, 1,218 miles of military telegraph lines linked the frontier defense system across the wilds of western Texas at a total start-up cost of almost 100,000 dollars.[24]

As they did with the army postal services, civilians made frequent use of the military telegraph. Ranchers, farmers, businessmen, and frontier families routinely placed orders for goods with firms as far away as New York and San Francisco. Unfortunately, like their military associates, civilians had to tolerate frequent breaks within telegraphic services. Prairie fires destroyed wooden poles; bison rubbed their backsides against posts and knocked them down; lightning severed lines; teamsters occasionally cut down poles to use for cooking fires; and in some people's estimation, Indians sometimes severed the wire to use it for the fashioning of arrow points. Beginning with the extensive west Texas project of the mid-1870s, soldiers replaced wooden poles with iron poles, some of which still supported telephone lines a century later.[25]

A worthy by-product of military experimentation with agriculture and telegraphic services was evidenced in the army's commitment to the collection of weather and environmental data. As early as 1814, Surgeon General James Tilton instructed all army physicians to maintain regular weather records at their posts and to submit summaries of these observations to the War Department. These cumulative studies supposedly would help officers better understand what food crops could be raised at forts that were situated in variable climates and environments. Four years later, the new surgeon general, Joseph Lovell, greatly expanded the program to require that other weather- and climate-related data be collected by all military doctors so that the medical services could discern the connection between unique environmental conditions and individual diseases. The directive was only lightly adhered to during its first three decades, but by 1853, 97 military reporting stations were active in this record keeping all across the nation.[26] In subsequent decades, many civilian scientists, medical doctors, and agricultural innovators returned to these older records for their own studies of climate, weather, and health.[27]

The most important advance in promoting a practical use for this knowledge occurred during the 1850s, when Professor James Pollard Espy, civilian assistant to Surgeon General Joseph Lovell, applied the systematic record of observations toward the uncertain field of weather prediction. Using the readings of wind speeds, wind directions, barometric pressures, topographical characteristics, and comparative temperatures, he worked out a theory of storms that gained respect in the international scientific community.[28] When Col. Albert James Myer became chief signal officer of the Army Signal Corps in 1867, a natural melding of meteorology and military telegraphy came into being. As separate entities, the two services could not have survived post–Civil War budget cuts, but when combined into a single unit, they were destined to expand operations. As America's fledgling weather service, the Army Signal Corps could now retrieve data quickly from its far-flung observers—military and civilian alike—and it could quickly disseminate national weather information via telegraph to shippers, farmers, commercial businesses, and the public at large.[29]

During the early 1880s, the army's close ties with the national weather service began to fade. The death of longtime champion Myer at the beginning of the decade, a financial scandal unleashed by one of the assistants, and budgetary cuts in military spending prompted new legislation during October 1890. Congress ordered the Signal Corps to transfer all meteorological activities to a new civilian weather bureau that would be housed within the Department of Agriculture. With the exception of remote Alaska Territory, the army was officially out of the weather reporting and predicting business until the exigencies of the two world wars prompted revivals of the service.[30]

PUBLIC RELIEF WORK BY THE ARMY

Despite repeated efforts to restrict the size of the army and its budget, emergency needs periodically brought the military wing of the government to very visible and popular tasks. This gradual evolution of peacetime roles came not from a sustained legislative drive, but rather from small precedent-setting cases that found favor from an appreciative public. Two activities—relief work during natural disasters and protection of federal resources—were truly humanitarian endeavors, and they brought a sense of self-satisfaction to officers and enlisted men alike.

Widely scattered examples of direct federal intervention into the lives of citizens who suffered from natural disasters can be found throughout the antebellum period. Yet not until after the Civil War did public perceptions begin to promote a more activist relief role for the government and the U.S. Army. Most evident was the work of the Freedmen's Bureau in the South during the Reconstruction era. It provided schools, health care, and flood and famine relief to tens of thousands of poor people, without regard for their race. As widespread as this aid was, the army's primary role was limited to protecting the lives and property of Freedmen's Bureau employees and contractors from unrepentant Southerners.[31]

More representative of this new activist role were the following examples of direct army intervention into relief work: the Chicago fire in 1871; the yellow fever epidemics in Memphis and Shreveport in 1873; the Mississippi River floods in 1874; a yellow fever epidemic in the South in 1878; the Missouri River floods in 1881; the Mississippi River floods in 1882; the Mississippi and Ohio River floods in 1884; the Johnstown flood in 1889; the Seattle fire in 1889; the Indian Territory drought in 1890; Minnesota forest fires in 1894; Saint Louis tornadoes in 1896; Mississippi River and Rio Grande floods in 1897; and the Galveston hurricane of 1900.[32] Throughout these tumultuous events, military officers assessed the immediate relief needs, secured supplies, transported them to the affected areas, and maintained order if civil officials could not do so. In most cases, military personnel turned the supplies over to local authorities and allowed them to make the actual distributions.[33]

Because army officers possessed authority to act upon their best judgments in time of crisis, more than a few of them demonstrated initiative and common sense in their actions. During the winter of 1872, local commanders transported food and clothing to Union Pacific crews and passengers who became stranded on the Great Plains by blizzards. At the same time, the senior officer at Ft. Stambaugh made a daring delivery to starving miners at South Pass City, Wyoming, and evacuated some of the worst medical cases to his post for proper care. When coal could not be delivered to the desperate civilians at Cheyenne, the troops at nearby Ft. D. A. Russell hauled their own surplus coal into the town and made it available at no cost. Many such acts of military rescue went virtually unrecorded by the national press because they affected small numbers of people in relatively isolated places.[34]

Where relief work was more comprehensive and sustained, the army response attracted greater public attention, but the officers who implemented the plans also encountered significant legal complications. One of the worst natural disasters occurred when millions of Rocky Mountain locusts descended upon the plains counties of Kansas, Nebraska, Colorado, and the Dakotas. By September 1874, conditions had deteriorated to such an extent that relief efforts could no longer be delayed. Governors of the afflicted states and territories belatedly undertook relief operations, but their shortsighted dependency on voluntary contributions from citizens fell far short of the necessary levels of help. Although the Nebraska legislature finally approved in January the issuance of 50,000 dollars in state bonds for the purchase of supplies, total needs far exceeded the sum.[35]

The clarion call for more comprehensive federal action came when Maj. James S. Brisbin inspected the southwestern sections of Nebraska. Throughout the region, he found desperate families who had little or no food as well as children dressed in ragged and filthy clothing. Even to his untrained eye, Brisbin recognized the effects of malnutrition. A majority of these poor farm families even lacked ammunition to hunt rabbits, and the officer requested that two companies of cavalry be dispatched to kill fresh game for these destitute people.[36]

On October 24, 1874, Gen. Edward O. C. Ord, commander of the Department of the Platte, requested that the adjutant general authorize military personnel to enter the four worst stricken counties of Nebraska to distribute flour and pork from army stocks. Secretary of War William W. Belknap succumbed to heightened public pressure and submitted part of Ord's plan to President Ulysses S. Grant. Belknap further remarked that even though no exact precedent existed for dispensing such a large quantity of food and clothing to civilians, this was a national emergency that warranted immediate action. All told, during the winter of 1874–1875, the army distributed 10,004 infantry coats, 6,285 other coats, 20,664 pairs of shoes and boots, 8,454 woolen blankets, and similar numbers of socks, hats, and trousers.[37]

Despite complaints about some people being bypassed in the delivery process while others allegedly received free food by lying about their status, the improvised system worked well. Ironically, the program worked too well from the vantage point of Gen. Philip Sheridan, commander of the Military Division of the Missouri. Even though he approved the original outlay of supplies, Sheridan worried that a sustained distribution of goods would put a strain on the military budget and would take soldiers away from their regular duties. Before operations finally ended in western Nebraska on September 1, 1875, Gen. Ord had directed the issuance of tons of surplus clothing, plus 1,081,122 ration units to over 29,000 hungry settlers.[38]

PROTECTING THE NATIONAL PARKS

Aiding settlers during natural disasters provided a sense of pride and mission to the soldiers who participated in the relief efforts, and so did another role not foreseen by the Founding Fathers when they first created a national army. The numbers of men who participated in this unique activity were relatively few, but the stakes were immense as the army assumed guardianship over the fledgling National Park System between 1886 and 1918. As with other relief efforts and law enforcement roles, the army was officially assigned this important mandate, but only slowly did Congress grant it sufficient authority to meet the obligations effectively. The officers and enlisted men who were deeply committed to these duties achieved remarkable success, earned the respect of distinguished environmentalists, and established a proper model for the civilian park rangers who would follow in their footsteps.[39]

On August 20, 1886, Capt. Moses Harris led a company of First Cavalry into Yellowstone National Park and assumed control of a landscape that had been routinely abused by tourists and exploiters since creation of the park 14 years earlier. His men immediately extinguished several small forest fires that had been started by careless campers and illegal poachers who drove wild animals out of the park boundaries with the use of raging flames. Although specific legislation for enforcement of park rules was not established until the 1894 Lacey Act, the procession of military commanders followed Harris's commonsense strategy in posting and enforcing their own regulations. Most often, curt warnings proved sufficient for halting minor offenses by tourists, but repeat offenders could be locked in the guardhouse at Ft. Yellowstone, which was constructed in the northwest corner of the park at Mammoth Hot Springs.[40]

As pressures mounted on Yellowstone resources, the army assigned more soldiers to the task, and they were able to establish small camps at all major points within the park boundaries. During tourist season, patrols watched over the major sites and hiked the back trails. But most of their effort remained fixed year-round on the ubiquitous poachers who represented the greatest menace to the park's environmental integrity. Because these trespassers were heavily armed and prone to the larcenous side of life, they also posed an undeniable threat to the soldiers' lives. Other violators included prospectors, illegal timber cutters, fishermen who netted large numbers of trout, and neighboring ranchers who drove their cattle into the lush river valleys for free grazing. Four privates under the command of a noncommissioned officer wintered at each of the log cabin substations, and despite temperatures that sometimes dipped to 40 degrees below zero, they maintained patrols throughout their assigned districts. Several died from exposure during the performance of their duties, and others came away with frostbitten and amputated fingers and toes. With the 1891 addition of 2,000 square miles of forest reserve land to the east of the park, the army now assumed guardianship of over 5,350 square miles of rugged territory with a maximum strength of only three companies of cavalry.[41]

The popularity of Yellowstone led to the creation of three additional national parks in California during 1890: Yosemite, Sequoia, and General Grant. Because of their proximity to San Francisco, which brought a flourishing tourist trade, and their attractiveness to illegal timber cutters, cattle interests, and sheepherders, these parks faced an environmental assault from the moment of their inception. Between 1891 and 1912, two cavalry squadrons followed a routine protective pattern whereby they remained in the three parks throughout the active months but always returned to the Presidio of San Francisco during the winter.[42]

Celebrated preservationist and cofounder of the Sierra Club, John Muir was lavish in his praise for the army's protective role in his beloved Yosemite. In an 1895 speech, the bearded sage of nature proclaimed, "Blessings on Uncle Sam's bluecoats! In what we may call homeopathic doses, the quiet, orderly soldiers have done this fine job, without any apparent friction or weak noise, in the still, calm way that the United States troops do their duty."[43] Muir was especially impressed with the persistence and dedication that Capt. A. E. Wood, first acting superintendent of Yosemite National Park, evidenced during the formative years. Wood shared Muir's almost pathological hatred of the sheepmen, and he made their removal his top priority. By the time of the captain's death in 1894, the sheep menace virtually had been eliminated, and Muir categorized this as the lasting legacy of his military compatriot.[44]

Despite its nearly impossible mandate, the army had made amazing progress toward protection of the national parks. In addition to driving out many of the worst exploiters of the environment, soldiers had created extensive projects for restocking lakes and rivers with fish from hatcheries. They also had mapped the parks; had constructed roads, bridges, and trails; and had aided the many scientific expeditions that undertook studies of flora, fauna, and geology. The National Park Service Act, signed by President Woodrow Wilson on August 26, 1916, signaled the final chapter of military duty within the parks and ushered in a system of Interior Department management that continues to the present.[45]

SOLDIERS IN CIVIL LAW ENFORCEMENT

Of all the wide-ranging roles undertaken by the multipurpose army during the nineteenth century, the most controversial and legally complicated was in the field of law enforcement. This was especially true during the initial stages of settlement in the remote regions of the West, where inadequate numbers of marshals, sheriffs, constables, and policemen made implementation of laws virtually impossible. It also occurred in areas where law officers did exist but were so corrupted by local politics that they could not be counted on to administer justice equitably. Often, the army was the only agency strong enough to maintain legal codes, and thus civilians and elected officials saw a practical need for their intervention into "lawless" situations. Unfortunately, the American people simultaneously drew upon the experiences of their forefathers who, during the American Revolution, had strongly resisted the idea of a large standing army with direct policing powers over civilians. The legalistic impasse was therefore predicated on a need for occasional use of martial power and a concurrent desire to keep the military out of civil affairs. Stuck between the two mandates was an American military establishment that had to walk a tightrope of public opinion and legalistic nuances.

Despite the obvious weakness of enforcement that left military men liable to counterlitigation by civilian prisoners, most officers exercised their own discretion in aiding civil authorities. They decided each issue on its merits, declining some supplications for help while accepting others. Experiences at Ft. Stockton, Texas, were fairly typical of those at many posts during the era. Because the civilian town grew very slowly alongside the fort, and Pecos County was not officially organized until 1875, no jail or courts existed to dispense justice. Hence the post guardhouse held many civilian prisoners between 1869 and 1875, even though they were not supposed to be under military supervision. As soon as possible, the post commander transferred the prisoners under military guard to nearby Ft. Davis, where a civil judge representing Jeff Davis County could try them. At the time of their handover to civil authorities, the prisoners ceased being a military problem.[46]

On a grander scale, Arizona and New Mexico became the scenes of several unofficial uprisings by outlaw groups and feuding parties during the mid-1870s. Most notable was the "state of riot and anarchy" in Colfax County, New Mexico, which was attributed to a group of cowboys under the notorious gunslinger Clay Allison. When the county sheriff admitted that he could not preserve order, Territorial Governor Samuel B. Axtell sent his special agent Ben Stevens to Cimarron in the heart of outlaw country. Accompanying Stevens were regular troops who helped end the "Colfax County War" and persuaded Allison to surrender without a fight.[47]

The extent of lawlessness in the West also drew the attention of Secretary of War William W. Belknap, who, in his 1871 annual report, praised the policing actions by military units. Belknap filled his summary with numerous examples of how soldiers had worked closely with magistrates and law officers to make arrests, deliver prisoners, evict illegal squatters, break up gangs of thieves, and prevent mob activities. Commanding Gen. William Tecumseh Sherman echoed the sentiment and pronounced that civil authorities would not have been able to fulfill their obligations without army help.[48] Only two years earlier, Sherman had vented his own frustration at the lawlessness on the northern plains. In special instructions to the commander of the Department of Dakota, he had stressed the need to abide by the letter of the law when working with civilian authorities. Yet he also concluded the directive with more unrestrained language: "When there are no courts or civil authorities to hold and punish such malefactors, we must of necessity use the musket pretty freely."[49]

The issue of how far military policing powers could be extended was debated throughout the post–Civil War decades, and often with contradictory results. Beginning in the spring of 1878, Representative William Kimmel of Maryland offered an amendment to the year's army appropriation bill. In its final approved version, the act ended all use of federal land and naval forces for policing duty, except in specific cases expressly authorized by the president or Congress. Even more disturbing was an amendment to the bill that assessed a fine of up to 10,000 dollars and two years' imprisonment for any officer or enlisted man who violated the new provision. The amendment passed, and with the stinging promise of retribution, it seemed to have closed the door forever on military aid to civilian law enforcement. The only routine exceptions allowed were for protection of Indians, public lands, and international neutrality laws, all of which were covered by preexisting laws.[50]

In compliance with the new directive, War Department officials issued General Order No. 49 on July 7, 1878, to severely restrict military aid to civilian authorities. But on October 1, a second regulation, General Order No. 71, again restored some discretionary power to local commanders. It stated in less than precise language, "In cases of sudden and unexpected invasion, insurrection or riot, endangering the public property of the United States, or in cases of attempted or threatened robbery or interruption of the United States mails, or any other equal emergency, the officers of the army may, if they think a necessity exists, take such action before the receipt of instructions from the seat of government, as the circumstances of the case and the law under which they are acting may justify."[51] With the second directive, flexibility was restored to the system, but so was the ambiguity.

Predictably, military officers did invoke General Order No. 71 to justify their intervention in isolated events that could best be described as riots. For instance, when many of the white citizens of Rock Springs, Wyoming, attacked the local Chinese community in September 1885, no independent civil force existed to restore order. Alleging that the Chinese would not participate in a strike against the Union Pacific coal mines and that they were taking jobs from white laborers, the rioters killed 28 Chinese, severely wounded 15, and drove the rest into the surrounding countryside. Territorial Governor Francis E. Warren telegraphed Department of the Platte commander Gen. Oliver Otis Howard to deploy troops as quickly as possible. Even before presidential approval had been granted, Secretary of War William C. Endicott and Gen. John M. Schofield, commander of the Division of the Missouri, found an additional justification for using troops against the civilian mob. They reasoned that since the Union Pacific Railroad had been established by an act of Congress, and since it transported federal troops and federal mails, company property warranted special army protection. Slowly, under military escort in some cases, most Chinese residents returned to Rock Springs and resumed their lives, even in the face of continued racism. The army maintained two new camps at Rock Springs and Evanston for several years to assure that no further violence would occur.[52]

Seven years later, in the northeastern counties of Wyoming, a different kind of conflict tested the mettle of officers and enlisted men. The Johnson County War came about when large cattle barons took the law into their own hands against alleged rustlers from among the increasing numbers of small ranchers and homesteaders. The cattle barons, desirous of protecting their open range grazing rights against fencing, hired 22 experienced Texas gunmen and added them to an existing force of 24 men. After killing several suspected rustlers and intimidating other innocent residents, the vigilantes found themselves trapped at a ranch near the town of Buffalo. Acting governor Amos Barber requested immediate deployment of troops from Ft. McKinney to rescue these so-called Regulators before greater bloodshed occurred. Elements of the 6th Cavalry reached the besieged ranch on April 14, accepted the surrender of

Troops of the 7th and 9th Infantries at Rock Springs, Wyoming, protecting Chinese residents from further racial violence in 1885. (*Courtesy of the Wyoming State Archives, Department of State Parks and Cultural Resources*)

the Regulators, and escorted them to Ft. D. A. Russell near Cheyenne. The transfer to civil jurisdiction was delayed until July 5, when the prisoners were placed in the custody of more sympathetic officials in nearby Cheyenne. Although questionable legal practices eventually gained acquittal for the Regulators, bad feelings lingered into the following decade. The army continued to be a target of some of the verbal abuse because it seemingly had demonstrated favoritism toward the wealthy cattle barons.[53]

The problems presented to the army in the Johnson County War case illustrated the endemic weakness of military law enforcement in civil actions. The painful truth was that whenever soldiers intervened in these types of ambiguous conflicts for the sake of preserving peace, their very presence favored one faction over the other. Nowhere was this more evident than in the labor-versus-management controversies that turned violent during the late nineteenth century. The 1877 Railroad Strike provided a wake-up call to military men everywhere because of its expansiveness, depth of public sympathy, and its fast-spreading pattern of violence. During an eight-day interval in July, nine governors called upon President Rutherford B. Hayes to take drastic action, even if it meant calling soldiers to action.[54]

The War Department found itself unprepared for this enormous task. No contingency plans existed, transportation for troops was inadequate, and no one had worked out coordination of the regular army with state militias. Within 11 days of mobilization, however, the regular army had 2,700 troops stationed in the trouble spots. The troops found themselves jeered, spat upon, and threatened with violence wherever they went. Their officers also experienced a jurisdictional nightmare because President Hayes had placed them at the disposal of the various governors. This allowed the state executives to decide tactical issues and to determine how long soldiers would remain at particular sites. Despite these complications, the worst confrontations were over by early August, and the troops were returned to their regular stations. Gen. Winfield S. Hancock, commander of overall operations, praised his men's performance, especially the fact that they had restored order without bloodshed.[55]

Not so fortunate was the handling of another great national labor confrontation, the 1894 Pullman Strike, which erupted after the Pullman Palace Car Company of Chicago reduced workers' wages. By midsummer, 2,000 federal troops, 4,000 militia, and 5,000 deputy marshals patrolled the Chicago streets. Arrayed against them were over 5,000 demonstrators, who pelted the force with rocks, overturned two dozen boxcars, and blocked the tracks to prevent passage of trains. On July 7, soldiers fired into a crowd that had wrecked a train and then dispersed them with a bayonet charge. Four demonstrators died, and 17 were seriously wounded. On the following day, another group of soldiers fired into a crowd at nearby Hammond, Indiana, and President Grover Cleveland warned that anyone obstructing the trains and their federal mail services would be forcibly dealt with.[56]

Soon the strikes spread across the West, and military units found themselves defending railroad property in places such as Green River, Wyoming, Pueblo, Colorado, Pocatello, Idaho, and Lima, Montana. Simultaneously, Lt. Col. William Shafter led almost 300 soldiers into downtown Los Angeles not only to guard rail yards, but also to ride as armed escorts on outbound trains.[57] Friction also developed between Gen. Nelson Miles, who coordinated troops in Chicago, and his superior, Gen. John M. Schofield, commanding general of the army. Miles clearly favored the corporate interests against the strikers, and when he tried to retain troops in the city after the crisis had passed, Schofield and Secretary of War Daniel Lamont criticized his biased approach.[58]

During the last two decades of the nineteenth century, the army increasingly found itself involved with labor strikes and civil disturbances that it was not well trained or legally mandated to handle. Instead of being venerated by the popular image of gallant cavalrymen riding to the rescue of beleaguered settlers under Indian attack, the army encountered growing public dissatisfaction with its domestic constabulary role. As early as 1867, Gen. Christopher C. Augur already recognized the limitations of military policing duties when he wrote, "It is a very delicate and unpleasant duty, and one from which we could gladly be relieved by the establishment and enforcement of civil laws."[59] His words proved prophetic for the rest of the century, and by the beginning of the twentieth century, the army would face an even more difficult role as an international constabulary trying to maintain order in its overseas empire.

Despite its failure to please the American public in handling complex law enforcement issues, the U.S. Army performed admirably in its multipurpose duties as the right arm of the federal government. Throughout the western territories and states, its members served as explorers, scientists, road builders, river and harbor engineers, railroad promoters, mail carriers, telegraphic agents, weather recorders and predictors, purveyors of relief programs, protectors of national parks, and guardians of law and order. No other institution—governmental or privately owned—made as much of an impact on the West in the decades after the Civil War.

NOTES

1. Francis Paul Prucha, *Broadax and Bayonet: The Role of the United States Army in the Development of the Northwest, 1815–1860* (Madison: State Historical Society of Wisconsin, 1953), viii.

2. The definitive work on the topogs is William H. Goetzmann, *Army Exploration in the American West, 1803–1863* (New Haven, CT: Yale University Press, 1959). Two excellent syntheses for general audiences are James P. Ronda, *Beyond Lewis and Clark: The Army Explores the West* (Tacoma: Washington State Historical Society, 2003); and Frank N. Schubert, *Vanguard of Expansion: Army Engineers in the Trans-Mississippi West, 1819–1879* (Washington, DC: Office of the Chief of Engineers, n.d.).

3. Donald Jackson, *Custer's Gold: The United States Cavalry Expedition of 1874* (New Haven, CT: Yale University Press, 1966).

4. Paul H. Carlson, *"Pecos Bill": A Military Biography of William R. Shafter* (College Station: Texas A&M University Press, 1989), 72–87.

5. Le Roy R. Hafen, W. Eugene Hollon, and Carl Coke Rister, *Western America: The Exploration, Settlement, and Development of the Region Beyond the Mississippi River* (Englewood Cliffs, NJ: Prentice Hall, 1970), 391. Richard A. Bartlett, *Great Surveys of the American West* (Norman: University of Oklahoma Press, 1962), 367–70.

6. David P. Robrock, "A History of Fort Fetterman, Wyoming, 1867–1882," *Annals of Wyoming* 48 (Spring 1976): 70–71.

7. Richard Guentzel, "The Department of the Platte and Western Settlement, 1866–1877," *Nebraska History* 56 (Fall 1975): 403–4. Gerald M. Adams, *The Post Near Cheyenne: A History of Fort D. A. Russell, 1867–1930* (Boulder: Pruett, 1989), 44.

8. Kenneth J. Almy, ed., "Thof's Dragon and the Letters of Capt. Theophilus H. Turner, M.D., U.S. Army," *Kansas History* 10 (Fall 1987): 184–89.

9. Michael J. Brodhead, "Of Mice and Mastodons: Contributions to the Literature of Mammalogy by Officers and Men of the United States Army in the Nineteenth Century," *Archives of Natural History* 18, no. 3 (1991): 366–67.

10. Edgar Erskine Hume, *Ornithologists of the United States Army Medical Corps* (Baltimore: Johns Hopkins University Press, 1942), 22–31.

11. Michael J. Brodhead, "The Military Naturalist: A Lewis and Clark Heritage," *We Proceeded On* 9 (November 1983): 9–10. Hume, *Ornithologists,* 413–17.

12. Philippe Régis de Trobriand, *Military Life in Dakota: The Journal of Philippe Régis de Trobriand,* ed. Lucile M. Kane (Saint Paul, MN: Alvord Memorial Commission, 1951), 183–84. James A. Wier, "19th Century Army Doctors on the Frontier and in Nebraska," *Nebraska History* 61 (Summer 1980): 207. William P. Clark, *The Indian Sign Language* (Philadelphia: L. R. Hamersly, 1885).

13. Ray H. Mattison, ed., "The Diary of Surgeon Washington Matthews, Fort Rice, D.T.," *North Dakota History* 21 (January 1954): 5–6. The most complete study of Matthews's Navajo ethnographic work is found in Katheryn Spencer Halpern and Susan Brown McGreevy, eds., *Washington Matthews: Studies of Navajo Culture, 1880–1894* (Albuquerque: University of New Mexico Press, 1996).

14. John A. Turcheneske Jr., "Historical Manuscripts As Sources for Anthropological Study: The Ethnological Correspondence of John Gregory Bourke," *New Mexico Historical Review* 59 (July 1984): 266–72. Joseph C. Porter, *Paper Medicine Man: John Gregory Bourke and His American West* (Norman: University of Oklahoma Press, 1986), 203–5, 302–4. John A. Turcheneske Jr., "John G. Bourke—Troubled Scientist," *Journal of Arizona History* 20 (Fall 1979): 328–42.

15. Charles W. Howell, "An Army Engineer on the Missouri in 1867," *Nebraska History* 53 (Summer 1971): 253–85.

16. Henry R. Richmond III, *The History of the Portland District, Corps of Engineers, 1871–1969* (Portland, OR: U.S. Army Corps of Engineers, 1970), 13–18. William F. Willingham, *Army Engineers and the Development of Oregon: A History of the Portland District, U.S. Army Corps of Engineers, 1929–1973* (Washington, DC: U.S. Government Printing Office, 1983), 28–36.

17. Susan Pritchard O'Hara and Gregory Graves, *Saving California's Coast: Army Engineers at Oceanside and Humboldt Bay* (Spokane, WA: Arthur H. Clark, 1991), 9–10.

18. George L. Albright, *Official Explorations for Pacific Railroads* (Berkeley: University of California Press, 1921), 37–43.

19. Guentzel, "Department of the Platte," 395. Raymond L. Welty, "The Policing of the Frontier by the Army, 1860–1870," *Kansas Historical Quarterly* 7 (August 1938): 253–54. Robert G. Athearn, *Union Pacific Country* (Chicago: Rand McNally, 1971), 210.

20. Merrill J. Mattes, "The Sutler's Store at Fort Laramie," *Annals of Wyoming* 18 (July 1946): 103. Adams, *Post Near Cheyenne,* 97. Paul L. Hedren, "On Duty at Fort Ridgely, Minnesota: 1853–1867," *South Dakota History* 7 (Spring 1977): 187.

21. James M. Oswald, "History of Fort Elliott," *Panhandle-Plains Historical Review* 32 (1959): 25. Robert C. Carriker, *Fort Supply, Indian Territory: Frontier Outpost on the Plains* (Norman: University of Oklahoma Press, 1970), 147–48.

22. Guentzel, "Department of the Platte," 398.

23. William E. Annin, "Fort Robinson during the 1880s: An Omaha Newspaperman Visits the Post," *Nebraska History* 55 (Summer 1974): 193.

24. Mary Sutton, "Glimpses of Fort Concho through the Military Telegraph," *West Texas Historical Association Year Book* 32 (1956): 122–32. Clayton Williams, *Texas' Last Frontier: Fort Stockton and the Trans-Pecos, 1861–1895,* ed. Ernest Wallace (College Station: Texas A&M University Press, 1982), 200. L. Tuffly Ellis, ed., "Lieutenant A. W. Greely's Report on the Installation of Military Telegraph Lines in Texas, 1875–1876," *Southwestern History Quarterly* 69 (July 1965): 67–85. Adolphus W. Greely, *Reminiscences of Adventure and Service: A Record of Sixty-five Years* (New York: Charles Scribner's Sons, 1927), 153–55.

25. Bill Green, *The Dancing Was Lively: Fort Concho, Texas, a Social History, 1867 to 1882* (San Angelo, TX: Fort Concho Sketches, 1974), 74. James H. Ware, "San Angelo and San Antonio: A Comparative Study of the Military City in Texas, 1867–1898" (MA thesis, Southwest Texas State University, 1973), 45. Williams, *Texas' Last Frontier,* 200. Almy, "Thof's Dragon," 183. Edmund B. Tuttle, *Three Years on the Plains: Observations of Indians, 1867–1870* (Norman: University of Oklahoma Press, 2002), 88.

26. Philip A. Kalisch and Beatrice J. Kalisch, "Indian Territory Forts: Charnel Houses of the Frontier, 1839–1865," *Chronicles of Oklahoma* 50 (Spring 1972): 65. Donald R. Whitnah, *A History of the United States Weather Bureau* (Urbana: University of Illinois Press, 1961), 10–11. Charles C. Bates and John F. Fuller, *America's Weather Warriors, 1814–1985* (College Station: Texas A&M University Press, 1986), 4–5.

27. Gary S. Freedom, "Military Forts and Logistical Self-Sufficiency on the Northern Great Plains, 1866–1891," *North Dakota History* 50 (Spring 1983): 7.

28. Edgar Erskine Hume, "The Foundation of American Meteorology by the United States Army Medical Department," *Bulletin of the History of Medicine* 8 (January–May 1940): 208–19.

29. Rebecca Robbins Raines, *Getting the Message Through: A Branch History of the U.S. Army Signal Corps* (Washington, DC: Center for Military History, 1996), 5–31, 49. Paul J. Scheips, "'Old Probabilities': A. J. Myer and the Signal Corps Weather Service," *Arlington Historical Magazine* 5 (October 1974): 36–38. Frederick J. Hughes Jr., "Albert James Myer: Army Physician and Climatologist," *Transactions of the American Clinical and Climatological Association* 81 (1969): 124–26.

30. Raines, *Getting the Message Through,* 54–61. Scheips, "Old Probabilities," 39. Bates and Fuller, *America's Weather Warriors,* 13–14. Joseph M. Hawes, "The Signal Corps and Its Weather Service, 1870–1890," *Military Affairs* 30 (Summer 1966): 74–76.

31. David H. Donald, *Liberty and Union* (Lexington, MA: D. C. Heath, 1978), 178–82.

32. Gaines M. Foster, *The Demands of Humanity: Army Medical Disaster Relief* (Washington, DC: Center for Military History, United States Army, 1983), 16. B. Franklin Cooling, "The Army and Flood and Disaster Relief," in *The United States Army in Peacetime,* ed. Robin Higham and Carol Brandt (Manhattan, KS: Military Affairs/Aerospace Historian, 1975), 62–67.

33. Foster, *Demands of Humanity,* 16–17. Cooling, "Army and Flood," 62.

34. Guentzel, "Department of the Platte," 406.

35. Gilbert C. Fite, "The United States Army and Relief to Pioneer Settlers, 1874–1875," *Journal of the West* 6 (January 1967): 99. Gary D. Olson, ed., "Relief for Nebraska Grasshopper Victims: The Official Journal of Lieutenant Theodore E. True," *Nebraska History* 48 (Summer 1967): 119–20.

36. Fite, "United States Army and Relief," 99–100.

37. U.S. Congress, House, *Relief of Grasshopper Sufferers,* 44th Cong., 1st sess., 1875, H. Exec. Doc. 28, 2.

38. Olson, "Relief for Nebraska," 124–40. Annette Atkins, *Harvest of Grief: Grasshopper Plagues and Public Assistance in Minnesota, 1873–78* (Saint Paul: Minnesota Historical Society Press, 1984), 115–20.

39. Richard A. Bartlett, *Yellowstone: A Wilderness Besieged* (Tucson: University of Arizona Press, 1985), 257.

40. H. Duane Hampton, "The Army and the National Parks," *Montana, Magazine of Western History* 22 (July 1972): 67–72.

41. George S. Anderson, "Work of the Cavalry in Protecting the Yellowstone National Park," *Journal of the United States Cavalry Association* 10 (March 1897): 5–10. Hampton, "Army and the National Parks," 71–72.

42. H. Duane Hampton, *How the U.S. Cavalry Saved Our National Parks* (Bloomington: Indiana University Press, 1971), 130–57.

43. Quoted in N. F. McClure, "The Fourth Cavalry in the Yosemite National Park," *Journal of the United States Cavalry Association* 10 (June 1897): 118.

44. Ibid., 118–19.

45. Hampton, "Army and the National Parks," 76–79. Richard A. Bartlett, "The Army, Conservation, and Ecology: The National Park Assignment," in *The United States Army in Peacetime,*" ed. Robin Higham and Carol Brandt (Manhattan, KS: Military Affairs/Aerospace Historian, 1975), 56.

46. Williams, *Texas' Last Frontier,* 110, 195–96.

47. Larry D. Ball, *The United States Marshals of New Mexico and Arizona Territories, 1846–1912* (Albuquerque: University of New Mexico Press, 1978), 59–60, 80–81. Howard R. Lamar, *The Far Southwest 1846–1912: A Territorial History* (New York: W. W. Norton, 1970), 151–55.

48. *Annual Report of the Secretary of War, 1871,* 16–33.

49. Quoted in Welty, "Policing," 254.

50. Clayton D. Laurie, "Filling the Breach: Military Aid to the Civil Powers in the Trans-Mississippi West," *Western Historical Quarterly* 25 (Summer 1994): 158.

51. Ibid., 160.

52. Murray L. Carroll, "Governor Francis E. Warren, the United States Army, and the Chinese Massacre at Rock Springs," *Annals of Wyoming* 59 (Fall 1987): 18–23. Clayton D. Laurie, "Civil Disorder and the Military in Rock Springs, Wyoming: The Army's Role in the 1885 Chinese Massacre," *Montana, Magazine of Western History* 40 (Summer 1990): 52–59.

53. Helena Huntington Smith, *The War on Powder River: The History of an Insurrection* (New York: McGraw-Hill, 1966), 190–219. Robert A. Murray, "The United States Army in the Aftermath of the Johnson County Invasion, April through November, 1892," in Robert A. Murray, *The Army on the Powder River* (Bellevue, NB: Old Army Press, 1969), 40–46.

54. Elwell S. Otis, "The Army in Connection with the Labor Riots of 1877," *Journal of the Military Service Institution of the United States* 5 (1884): 292–96.

55. Jerry M. Cooper, *The Army and Civil Disorder: Federal Military Intervention in Labor Disputes, 1877–1900* (Westport, CT: Greenwood Press, 180), 45–65. Jerry M. Cooper, "Federal Military Intervention in Domestic Disorders," in *The United States Military under the Constitution of the United States, 1789–1989,* ed. Richard H. Kohn (New York: New York University Press, 1991), 134.

56. Louise Carroll Wade, " 'Hell Hath No Fury Like a General Scorned': Nelson A. Miles, the Pullman Strike, and the Beef Scandal of 1898," *Illinois Historical Quarterly* 79, no. 3 (1986): 168–71. Robert Wooster, *Nelson A. Miles and the Twilight of the Frontier Army* (Lincoln: University of Nebraska Press, 1993), 198–201.

57. Adams, *Post Near Cheyenne,* 119. William H. Bisbee, *Through Four American Wars* (Boston: Meador, 1931), 232–33. Thomas R. Buecker, "Fort Niobrara, 1880–1906: Guardian of the Rosebud Sioux," *Nebraska History* 65 (Fall 1984): 318. Carlson, *Pecos Bill,* 156–57. Clayton D. Laurie, "Extinguishing Frontier Brushfires: The U.S. Army's Role in Quelling the Pullman Strike in the West, 1894," *Journal of the West* 32 (April 1993): 54–63.

58. Wooster, *Nelson A. Miles,* 200–1. Wade, "Hell Hath No Fury," 171–72. John M. Schofield, *Forty-six Years in the Army* (New York: Century, 1897), 491–512.

59. *Annual Report of the Secretary of War, 1867,* 60.

8 "TIGERS OF THE HUMAN SPECIES": MILITARY VIEWS OF THE AMERICAN INDIAN

During the twentieth century, the image of the U.S. Army underwent a radical revision in American popular culture. Throughout the first five decades, the military establishment was, for the most part, viewed through a prism of adulation. Officers and enlisted men alike were identified with the great patriotic efforts of World Wars I and II as well as resisting communist expansion during the early phases of the Cold War. In keeping with this trend, turn-of-the-century paintings and sculptures by Frederic Remington and Charles Shreyvogel idolized the frontier soldier, and they remained popular with each new generation of Americans. Furthermore, they provided a receptive climate for novelists such as Gen. Charles King and Hamlin Garland, who further venerated the heroism of the so-called Old Army in new editions of their books. Nowhere was this image better conveyed than in the movies of director John Ford, whose trilogy of fictionalized films *Fort Apache, She Wore a Yellow Ribbon,* and *Rio Grande* defined what most Americans perceived to be true about the blue-coated veterans of the last century.

But public perceptions changed during the Vietnam War, when many people began to openly question their nation's foreign policy as well as the moral conduct of its overseas army. Movies such as Arthur Penn's *Little Big Man* (1970) and Ralph Nelson's *Soldier Blue* (1970) broke with tradition and cast the frontier army as a racist and bloodthirsty institution that happily murdered and mutilated Indian people at the behest of corrupt politicians and greedy capitalists. In the former movie, history was turned upside down so that the heroic Sioux and Northern Cheyennes could administer righteous vengeance against an insane George Armstrong Custer and his minions. *Soldier Blue* offered an even more impassioned appeal by utilizing the 1864 Sand Creek Massacre as a metaphor for the 1968 My Lai Massacre in Vietnam.

Despite their opposing interpretations of frontier military life, the two popular vantage points shared one thing in common: They both stressed the Indian-fighting role of the army without closely examining the historical record of soldiers' attitudes toward Indians and Indian attitudes toward soldiers. The pattern that emerges from actual accounts demonstrates an ambiguity on both sides, rather than a rigid stereotype of perpetual hatred and conflict between two peoples. Historian Robert Utley captured the essence of this relationship when he declared, "Ambivalence, therefore, marked military attitudes toward the Indians—fear, distrust, loathing, contempt, and condescension on the one hand; curiosity, admiration, sympathy, and even friendship, on the other."[1] What he declared about soldiers' perceptions of Indians might well have been applied to Indians' perceptions of soldiers.

AMBIGUOUS VIEWS OF NATIVE AMERICANS

Military officers left an extensive record of their personal thoughts about Indians as individuals, as specific tribes, and as a generic racial group. These documents—including informal field reports; official summaries filed with the secretary of war; articles in newspapers, magazines, and service journals; and full-length autobiographies—clearly demonstrate the ambivalence identified by Utley and reiterated by other historians, such as Thomas Leonard and Sherry L. Smith. On the one hand, officers portrayed Indian deeds in the most horrific of ways, such as dwelling on the wanton killing of innocent settlers and the desecration of bodies. They also made ethnocentric judgments about Indian material culture and spirituality, for which they had little real understanding. Likewise, they made inaccurate assertions that Native Americans frequently broke their word by promising cooperative behavior, while other members of the band or tribe simultaneously undertook raids. In the worst cases of blatant hypocrisy, some of these officers tolerated the same evils when whites inflicted them upon Native Americans. The cutting off of Indian heads to ship to the Army Medical Museum for scientific study, the forced removal of Indian children from their parents, and the army's enforcement of unjust government policies did not resonate with a sense of justice, but rather with an application of double standards.

Yet amid all the curious value judgments, officers and enlisted men did seem to have a strong admiration for Indian fighting skills, survival techniques, and even their courageous dedication to maintaining traditional lifestyles in the face of overwhelming odds. Virtually none of these observers believed it wise to preserve ancient cultural traditions against the advance of "civilization," but many of them voiced nostalgia about the passing of such a "noble race." Even a man such as Lt. Col. George Custer, who wrote disparagingly of Indians and made his mark in questionable combats at the 1868 Battle of the Washita and the 1876 Battle of Little Big Horn, could write, "If I were an Indian, I often think I would greatly prefer to cast my lot among those of my people [who] adhered to the free open plains, rather than submit to the confined limits of a reservation, there to be the recipient of the blessed benefits of civilization, with its vices thrown in without stint or measure."[2]

Though not a true champion of Indian people, Custer also touched upon a sentiment widely held in military circles, that the costly Indian wars had been initiated more by white selfishness and broken promises than by Indian duplicity or innate savagery. Gen. Philip Sheridan, certainly an outspoken critic of Native Americans on many occasions, could alternatively write,

We took away their country and their means of support, broke up their mode of living, their habits of life, introduced disease and decay among them and it was for this and against this they made war. Could anyone expect less?[3]

More specific in his charges was Gen. James Parker, who alleged that most problems on the southern plains were caused by Texas cowboys, buffalo hunters, and thieves who committed atrocities against Comanches and Kiowas. He even vowed, "I would go on a scouting expedition after renegade Texans and hang up every scoundrel I caught."[4] Equally unforgiving was the 1885 assertion made by Gen. George Crook that "greed and avarice on the part of the whites—in other words, the almighty dollar—is at the bottom of nine-tenths of all our Indian trouble."[5]

From time to time, officers spoke in patronizing and even threatening tones about Indians, but these military men were not the sources of incessant race hatred that some of their contemporaries made them out to be. Nor were they banded together by a grand plan for the physical extermination of America's indigenous peoples. When Thomas Bland published an 1879 article in his *Council Fire* newspaper, he chose to entitle it "Abolish the Army" so as to elicit a visceral reaction. Bland represented one wing of the Indian reform movement of the late nineteenth century that wanted all aspects of federal Indian policy removed from military control and turned over to the civilian-run Interior Department. He alleged that the officer corps was "supported in luxurious style and aristocratic leisure at the public expense." Furthermore, the size and social influence of the army had made its power so great that few citizens dared challenge it, even when it operated in an "ambitious, mercenary and bloodthirsty" way. An angry Bland ended the essay by reminding his audience that even Thomas Jefferson had warned against the maintenance of a large standing army that would become a menace to a free republic.[6]

Bland's argument touched a raw nerve with officers who not only resented the inaccuracy of the allegation, but also the dishonor that it brought to the military establishment. The army was caught between two divergent philosophies of Indian policy. It could never entirely please either advocacy group, and the enforcement tools for carrying out its stated mission were never fully provided by Washington officials. Gen. William Tecumseh Sherman articulated the dilemma best when he wrote, "There are two classes of people, one demanding the utter extinction of the Indians, and the other full of love for their conversion to civilization and Christianity. Unfortunately, the army stands between and gets the cuffs from both sides."[7] Thus military officers placed blame for the so-called Indian problem on misguided reformers, hate-filled racists, and incompetent bureaucrats, but they rarely found any culpability within their own ranks.

Officers' wives also wrote prolifically about Native Americans, capturing the same ambiguity articulated by their husbands. Raised on ubiquitous literary stereotypes about Indian savagery, they feared being captured by raiding parties, suffering the pain of torture and having their captive children raised by their tormentors.[8] Caroline Frey Winne, wife of the post surgeon at Ft. Washakie, Wyoming, wrote in an 1879 private letter how disgusted she was with the filthy habits of the Shoshone men, including their laziness and propensity toward theft. On the one hand, she pitied them for having been robbed of their land and resources by whites, but she had no desire to help them in their time of need. Despite her contempt for Indians in general, Winne spoke favorably of Shoshone chief Washakie because of his polite manners, civilized clothing, and total honesty.[9] Army wife Elizabeth Burt experienced a parallel situation at Ft. Bridger, Wyoming, a full decade earlier when she and her husband invited Washakie to their quarters for an elegant dinner. She marveled at his refined demeanor, proper table etiquette, and social conversation, even though it had to be explained by an interpreter. Burt praised her guest's leadership ability, especially his success at keeping most of the Shoshone men from taking up weapons against whites.[10]

Caroline Frey Winne and Elizabeth Burt exemplified the prevailing ambiguity in late-nineteenth-century national views of Native Americans. When they appraised Indian life from a distance, they tended to lump indigenous behavior in negative categories judged through rigid ethnocentric preconceptions. Yet when they got to know individual Indians within a social setting, and especially when those Indians came from the ranks of tribal leadership and evidenced aspects of the white man's lifestyle, officers and their wives often demonstrated a great curiosity and fondness for their newfound acquaintances. Very few of the relationships were deep, enduring, or even culturally incisive, but they allowed members of both races to gain some empathy and understanding for each other.[11] Furthermore, wives frequently shared the opinion that malevolent and inept civilian institutions were the real causes of Indian wars. The army therefore was like a fire department rushing around to solve the problems that incessantly broke out all across the frontier.[12]

Nor were enlisted men silent in their judgments about Native Americans. Even though lower-ranking servicemen left fewer records on the subject, those that did showed the same contradictions as their so-called social betters. Division of opinion was well illustrated in a conversation between two members of the Second Cavalry who had learned about the recent murder and mutilation of a teamster. One advocated immediate reprisals against all Indians, guilty or not. But trooper Bill Baker sarcastically remarked that Native Americans had an original right to the land and, by inference, a right to protect it from interlopers. A short time later, Cheyennes killed Baker in an ambush.[13]

As in the cases of officers and their spouses who got to know Indians on a more intimate level, enlisted men gained an appreciation for individual Native Americans when they spent time together. Curiosity governed these relationships more than did genuine affection, but the contacts at least tempered some of the worst misunderstandings between the races. For instance, Sgt. John E. Cox, a First Infantryman stationed at Ft. Randall during the mid-1870s, spent considerable time among the nearby Poncas, learned their language, and pronounced that the "Poncas and soldiers were the best of friends." He subsequently taught English to Hunkpapa Sioux children at Standing Rock Reservation and later ended his reminiscences by paying homage to the outstanding virtues of different tribes and stating, "I myself never had any difficulty with Indians of any kind."[14]

Just as Sgt. Cox's positive feelings translated into honorable deeds, other soldiers applied the golden rule to their relationships with individual Native Americans. Sgt. George Neihaus campaigned extensively against the feared Apaches, but he also wrote, "The soldiers did not hold hard feelings about the Indians. I could always make friends with them, when they were treated right." Likewise, Sgt. John H. Barron recalled how members of the First Cavalry forcibly returned panicked Crows to their Montana reservation in 1887, and then proceeded to calm their fears and help erect their tipis at the customary campsites.[15]

PROTECTING INDIAN PEOPLE AND THEIR RESOURCES

Very few white men or women made the full cultural transition that allowed them to see the world through Indian eyes. Yet some officers who served as agents held unique positions that assured them sustained personal contact with Indian people. For this reason, their judgments about Native Americans deserve attention, especially since most of their reactions were positive, albeit somewhat paternalistic.

Capt. Frank Bennett served as agent for the Navajos during the harsh transition years of 1869–1871. The Navajos had only recently returned to their beloved canyon country south of the Four Corners area after several years of confinement on the Bosque Redondo of eastern New Mexico. While living there during the Civil War, many had died because of government neglect. They trusted few white men, but many soon came to view Bennett as a friend and protector. He worked endlessly to rebuild their communities, to reestablish their crops and fruit orchards, and to restore their herds of sheep. He fought with government bureaucrats and local contractors to assure timely delivery of food and other supplies. Most important, Bennett used federal troops and Navajo police to help keep white trespassers from stealing reservation livestock and natural resources. When notified in 1871 that he would be replaced by a civilian appointee, Bennett offered to end his military career so that he could continue his protective role as the Navajos' new civilian agent. The strategy failed, however, when the position went to a far less qualified man.[16]

In the desert Southwest, where notable Indian outbreaks persisted as late as 1886, other officers served as unofficial agents to the Apaches. Capt. Emmett Crawford and his assistant, Lt. Britton Davis, supervised the luckless San Carlos Reservation, while Lt. Charles Gatewood and his assistant, Lt. Hamilton Roach, oversaw events at Ft. Apache. The situation at both locations was somewhat unique since the civilian agent at San Carlos still retained administrative control over the agencies. Yet even with the assistance of loyal Apache police, the agent was unable to control the remote areas of the reservation or to prevent residents from leaving the agencies and joining small groups of raiders. The four military officers gained good reputations because they spent considerable time among the Indian families. As commanders of the Apache scout units, they often participated in tribal ceremonies, and they frequently dined, hunted, and socialized with their Apache friends. On a number of occasions, Apache leaders acknowledged that they trusted these military agents more than their civilian counterparts because the former could more often be counted on. Furthermore, the intensely personal diplomacy that these young officers engaged in was precisely the type of social bonding that was revered in traditional Apache society.[17]

Conflicting Roles for the Military in Indian Matters

Crawford, Davis, Gatewood, and Roach witnessed firsthand in Arizona one of the most befuddling dilemmas faced by the military throughout the entire West. As the primary government institution in frontier areas, the army was entrusted with the protection of Indian lands and resources. At the same time, it had to follow federal directives on the closings of reservations and the public sale of rich timber, mining, and grazing areas formerly guaranteed to Native Americans by treaties. No tribe escaped the avaricious onslaught of economic development and the continuous public outcry for removal of tribes to smaller and less valuable enclaves.

When soldiers tried to arrest illicit gold miners descending upon the Black Hills in 1875, their orders seemed quite simple: move unlicensed white men off of the Great Sioux Reservation. Officers initially followed General Military Order No. 2 without much fanfare. They located the trespassers and detained them for further action in federal courts. Legal rulings by U.S. District Judge Elmer S. Dundy in Omaha declared that the army did have a right to repel trespassers on the Great Sioux Reservation and its westernmost edges of the Black Hills. Unfortunately, his ruling left no real teeth in the law because military forces were allowed to hold these detainees no more than five days, certainly not enough time to transfer them to federal courts in Yankton, Sioux City, or Omaha.[18]

One prospector who correctly judged the army's weakened position proudly claimed that he had been arrested four times within three months. Soldiers had merely escorted him away from his claim, and within a matter of days, he was back working it again. He anticipated a day not too far into the future when no soldiers would be deployed for protecting Sioux lands in the Black Hills.[19] Sgt. Charles Windolph later recalled the futility of enforcement when he wrote, "All the soldiers in the United States couldn't hold back the tide then. You could sign all the Indian treaties you could pack on a mule, but they wouldn't do any good. Men would get through. They'd go after gold in spite of hell and high water."[20] It did not help that during this crisis, federal authorities created an ambiguous set of policies that alternately encouraged and discouraged this mining rush. Ultimately, Indians, soldiers, miners, and settlers paid the price of the bloody Great Sioux War of 1876–1877, and another dark legacy had been affixed to the saga of the westward movement.

Despite the army's frequent attempts to protect Indian lands during the nineteenth century, soldiers experienced the same duality of feelings on this subject that civilians did. Some officers and enlisted men took orders seriously and felt a moral commitment to protecting Indian treaty rights. Others, more likely the majority, were relieved when they no longer had to defend Indian interests against white interests. They did not relish the wars that sometimes erupted from these policies or the harsh campaigns that had to be waged against recalcitrant tribes, but all favored the inevitable white domination of the continental empire.

Ironically, it was in Indian Territory that the army did some of its best work at protecting land and preserving order. These events came very late in the century, too late to help the original Indian claimants in the Cherokee Outlet and the Unassigned Lands, but the circumstances drew national, even international, attention. The initial threat came from "boomers," who illegally crossed from Kansas and tried to establish homesteads in the Outlet. President Rutherford B. Hayes issued a directive as early as 1879 for soldiers to remove the more than 300 white families who had settled on Cherokee land. The unresolved issue dragged on for almost 20 years as the government incrementally opened the region to white occupation. 5th Cavalry Pvt. John H. Brandt later recalled the futility of the army's protective effort and how it earned considerable enmity from civilians: "It was a job none like to do, yet it had to be done and I think we were the best hated men in the United States, at least those people who had to leave thought so."[21]

The unique problems faced by the army were best demonstrated in the 1889 opening of the Unassigned Lands by a chaotic land rush scheme. Perhaps 40,000–50,000 people lined up for the rush to begin at high noon on April 22. Federal authorities in Washington, D.C., had anticipated a fairly orderly movement of people onto the prairies, but they had never anticipated such great numbers of expectant settlers. In the wake of the massive population push, soldiers took up stations at Guthrie, Kingfisher, Purcell, and Oklahoma City. They were instructed to assume the initiative only if so requested by the federal marshals who were assigned to the newly opened area. The 30 marshals soon found their small numbers inadequate for law enforcement, and they called upon soldiers for help. Despite their unclear authority to detain civilians, military officers set about enforcing liquor and gambling prohibitions, carrying out specific orders from the territorial governor, tracking down thieves, and preventing violence that arose over conflicting land claims.[22]

Disputes over specific homesteads and town lots led to the most significant law enforcement problems. On May 26, federal marshals tried to eject an elderly man from a choice town lot in Guthrie after a de facto city "arbitration board" gave the lot to another claimant. By some accounts, a mob of 1,200 citizens drove the marshals out of town and even threatened to destroy the tent that served as a city hall. Capt. H. G. Cavanaugh, commander of troops at Camp Guthrie, wasted no time in dispersing the crowd with a single company of infantry. On another occasion, Cavanaugh faced down a small group of men who were trying to rescue a companion from Guthrie's first jail.[23]

In fledgling Oklahoma City, Capt. D. F. Stiles separated competing factions who were promoting rival town sites. Two or three civilians were slightly wounded by bayonet thrusts and being pushed back by rifle butts, but no serious injuries occurred. These military actions certainly angered some people on the losing side of these debates, but most people seemed to welcome the army's presence. When Oklahoma City residents learned that the soldiers might be withdrawn from the town, prominent citizens petitioned War Department authorities in November 1889 to retain the troops at their present stations until Congress could provide adequate civil authorities. Camp Guthrie remained garrisoned just over two years and received wide praise from citizens and government officials.[24]

Events in the Black Hills and Indian Territory demonstrated both the strengths and weaknesses of the army in protecting Indian rights and federal lands. When soldiers received legal backing from Washington, D.C., and from local populations, they performed well. But when legislative authority and popular support were absent, or where the protective role had to be administered over a large region, they had little chance of fulfilling their goals.

Some Military Assistance for Northern Cheyennes

Yet in some cases that were less visible to the public, army efforts in behalf of Indians could achieve monumental results. The Northern Cheyennes, badly mauled by two decades of disease and intermittent conflict, longed for a reservation in their original Montana homeland. Like other tribes, they found their shrinking enclave under persistent attack from cattlemen, farmers, and land speculators. But unlike most other tribes, their efforts to preserve their ancestral domain paid off. Their 22-year struggle drew upon the support of politicians and eastern reformers to actually produce an enlargement of their reservation. Key to their legal victories were the generous efforts of military officers such as Gen. Nelson A. Miles, Maj. Henry Carroll, and Capt. George W. H. Stouch. Not only did these career military men protect the reservation from trespassers, they also wrote the letters, reports, and petitions that ultimately gave the Northern Cheyennes an unparalleled victory. One lowly private, George Yoakam, shared in this ultimate happy ending for his Indian friends. As agency farmer since the early years of the reservation experience, Yoakam documented their rights to the Tongue River lands, and he taught white agriculture and ranching skills to help tribesmen bridge the gap between old and new economies.[25]

The close contact that Pvt. Yoakam maintained with the Northern Cheyennes yielded positive results for both sides precisely because Yoakam came to understand Cheyenne culture and sensitivities. This was often true of another type of army officer who became more closely involved with Indians: the captain of scouts. Men assigned to these unique positions were a different breed of soldier. Even though well steeped in formal command structure and combat techniques, they were expected to utilize the guerrilla fighting techniques that were endemic to Indian methods of raiding and warfare. The most successful of the junior officers were the ones who lived with their scouts, gained their trust, learned their cultural ways, and made use of their knowledge of the landscape and tribal dynamics.

INDIANS AS ARMY SCOUTS

The U.S. Army had periodically employed Indian scouts and guides ever since 1792, when Congress authorized the president to raise an unspecified number from friendly tribes at a maximum funding of $20,000.[26] Limited numbers were recruited only for short periods of time, mostly during the War of 1812, the Creek and Seminole wars, and on the frontier during the Civil War. In the earliest cases, their limited service was apparently successful because in 1855, native scouts received land bounties equaling those for white soldiers.[27]

Not until after the Civil War did the idea of a large and permanent scout force finally become a reality. An act of July 18, 1866, authorized up to 1,000 Indian scouts for the entire army. They would serve as an official component of the military for fixed terms and would receive pay equal to privates. Signed for either three- or six-month stints, far below the service period for regular soldiers, they answered only to their department commanders, an arrangement that provided them the flexibility necessary for guerrilla operations. Furthermore, instead of spending most of their time with drill and labor projects at the forts, they would remain in the field conducting reconnaissances, gathering intelligence from other Indians, and tracking recalcitrant bands.[28]

Commanders throughout the West requested a share of the scout contingents for their respective military departments, but most found that the War Department kept numbers significantly below the maximum allowed. Gen. Irvin McDowell, commander of the Department of California and the District of Arizona, was more successful than most when he received authorization for 90 Indian scouts in Arizona.[29] The pattern set in 1866 remained constant for the next 25 years as the southwestern territories supported the overwhelming majority of Indian scouts, and most of these were from the various Apache bands.

Why Indians Enlisted As Army Scouts

The motivations that led Indians to enlist as army scouts are as complex as the individuals themselves, but certain factors contributed to the desire for this type of service and to the high reenlistment rates. Jason Betzinez, an Apache who rode with Geronimo as a boy, believed that most men joined the scout units because of the boredom and unemployment of reservation life. As scouts, they could receive regular pay from the army and annuities from the Indian Bureau.[30] James Kaywaykla, a youthful follower of the Warm Springs Apache leader Victorio, remarked that scouts not only received salaries, but they also were able to retain their self-respect as warriors. Supplied with rifles and other military equipment, they retained a respected position among kinsmen and proved their courage through field duty.[31]

The army also took advantage of preexistent tribal conflicts in its recruitment process. Pawnees made excellent scouts on the central plains because of their uncompromising pattern of intertribal warfare with the Lakota, or western Sioux. Throughout the late 1860s and early 1870s, these Pawnee scouts, under the command of brothers Luther and Frank North, happily and efficiently aided military units against their longtime

Sioux adversaries, and especially during the construction of the Union Pacific Railroad. Likewise, Crow scouts from Montana and Arikara scouts from Dakota Territory served with Gen. Alfred Terry and Lt. Col. George Custer in the 1876 Yellowstone Expedition, including the events associated with the Battle of Little Big Horn.[32] From among the Apaches, enterprising officers sought out willing recruits in one band who felt little loyalty to members of another band. The fact that some of Victorio's Warm Springs band had killed a White Mountain Apache chief shortly before the 1879 breakout from San Carlos Agency was reason enough for various White Mountain men to join Company C Apache scouts and to serve alongside white soldiers in the pursuit of Victorio's band.[33]

As with their perceptions of other Native Americans, officers differed in their views about the dependability of Indian scouts. Gen. Nelson Miles, a man who betrayed the loyal Apache scouts by sending them to imprisonment in Florida alongside Geronimo's "renegades," was the ultimate hypocrite in this matter. He wrote a decade later, "I had no confidence in their integrity, and did not believe they could be trusted."[34] Yet he relied on the same scouts to locate Geronimo's camp in northern Mexico, and two of these scouts, Martine and Kayitah, along with Lt. Charles Gatewood, actually negotiated the final surrender of Geronimo's tiny band of 35 men and 8 boys.[35]

Like Miles, who never had much direct contact with scouts, Gen. William Tecumseh Sherman and Gen. Philip Sheridan played down the importance of scouts and, in some cases, even blocked other officers' requests for strengthening their allotted numbers. They preferred to rely on a handful of white scouts to accomplish the same tasks, but even the best of white scouts could not match the insider's knowledge about landscapes and indigenous cultures that Indian scouts possessed.[36] Some officers gradually came to appreciate the importance of Native American auxiliaries, but only after accompanying them in field operations. For instance, Col. Eugene A. Carr of the 5th Cavalry initially

Sgt. Mickey Free (far left) and other Apache Scouts at Ft. Apache, ca. 1890. Indian scouts became the eyes and ears of the U.S. Army, and were a mainstay of operations conducted in the Southwest and Great Plains. (*Courtesy Arizona Historical Society/Tucson/23744*)

opposed the use of Pawnee scouts, except as couriers and interpreters. Yet after his stunning victory over Cheyennes in the 1869 battle of Summit Springs, Carr praised the Pawnees for their valuable service in the overall campaign and in the battle itself.[37]

By far the strongest advocate for Indian scouts was Gen. George Crook, who used both Plains and southwestern tribes as allies. His greatest praise, however, was for the Apache scouts whom he enlisted at maximum numbers during the 1870s and early 1880s. Crook strongly believed that it took an Apache to find an Apache and that no major military operations could succeed without their help. More importantly, he observed that scouts could perform a valuable service on the reservations by acting as role models for a new way of life. Crook explained to *Los Angeles Times* correspondent Charles Lummis in 1886 about Apache renegades:

> They don't fear the white soldiers, whom they easily surpass in the peculiar style of warfare which they force upon us, but put upon their trail an enemy of their own blood, an enemy as tireless, as foxy, and as stealthy and familiar with the country as they themselves, and it breaks them all up. It is not merely a question of catching them better with Indians, but of a broader and more enduring aim—their disintegration.[38]

The superiority of Apache scouts over regular soldiers in guerrilla warfare was demonstrated at almost every stage of the campaign of 1883 against small bands under Juh, Chihuahua, and Geronimo. The scouts covered up to 60 miles a day, while cavalrymen matched only one-third that distance. Their familiarity with the country allowed Crook to use various mountain shortcuts and to map vital water holes that were previously unknown to military personnel. The scouts' mobility and alertness also prevented ambushes against the main cavalry columns and kept their enemies dispersed.[39]

The trip back to San Carlos from the Mexican border with approximately 325 men, women, and children revealed an interesting feature of the relationship between scouts and their Apache prisoners. Rather than abuse the defenseless captives and steal their possessions, the scouts intermingled with them and renewed acquaintances. The White Mountain Apache scouts shared their food and supplies with members of the Chiricahua band and protected them against reprisals from civilian posses. The prisoners could vilify the scouts for aiding the army, and the scouts could criticize the Chiricahuas for disrupting reservation life, but neither side sought harm for the other after surrender.[40]

Whatever the motives of the scouts for participating in the grueling campaign, their officers agreed that their performance had made success possible. Reports accurately recorded that the scouts did all of the tracking and fighting, while the cavalry were held in reserve. At no time did they display any hesitancy about carrying out orders or putting themselves in harm's way. Special praise went to Tsoe, or "Peaches," as the soldiers called him, whose assistance in locating the Chiricahua camps proved crucial. Newspapers that only two years before had strongly condemned the arming and outfitting of Apache scout units now congratulated them and called for additional enlistments.[41]

As the decade of the 1890s dawned, the War Department was in the midst of major deactivation and consolidation of its western forts. The fabled Indian wars were over, and significant budget cuts were undertaken. The national force of Indian scouts was reduced to fewer than 200, and most of those retained for active duty were Apache companies in the Southwest. But the concept of Indians as fighting men was not yet dead.

Gen. George Crook relied on Indian scouts more than any other senior commander and he wrote favorably of their service by pronouncing, "It takes an Apache to catch an Apache." (*Courtesy of the Library of Congress*)

INDIANS AS SOLDIERS IN THE REGULAR ARMY

The possibility of recruiting Native Americans as soldiers in the regular army was first suggested in a November 1889 issue of *United Service* magazine and was followed four months later by a more persuasive essay in the same military journal. Maj. William H. Powell contended in both articles that after almost 20 years of service among Indians, he was convinced that just such a novel experiment should be launched. Why not "educate them to our ways by employing them in that which is most acceptable to their instincts and tastes?—that is, make soldiers of them," he declared. M. P. Wyman, administrative head of the Crow Agency in Montana, added his endorsement of the plan, as did Agent James McLaughlin of the Standing Rock Reservation in Dakota Territory.[42] Most welcomed was a follow-up article in *Harper's Weekly Magazine* by noted artist Frederic Remington, who championed Powell's plan on the grounds that reservation Indians could best bridge the gap between their traditional cultures and the white man's world through military service. They had lived in a warrior culture for generations and would certainly choose a martial career over the agricultural existence that was advocated by most white reformers.[43]

Opposition to the Indian soldier experiment was immediate, but some of the reticence came from an unlikely source. On February 24, 1890, Gen. George Crook wrote to Adjutant General John C. Kelton, criticizing the Indian integration plan. As scouts, Indians had attained the highest level of military performance, and as agency policemen, they had served as reliable agents of acculturation, Crook asserted, but the important quality of individuality that had assured their successes in these roles would undermine their performance as regular soldiers. The military virtues of drill, discipline, and rigid organization would impair their value as fighting men for their native cultures placed little emphasis on these values. Recalling that scouts had functioned best when stationed among their own people, Crook also belittled the idea of removing the Indians from their native environment for three-year terms of service.[44] Several months later, Gen. Benjamin Grierson made similar observations in his annual report to the secretary of war.[45]

Maj. Powell responded that there was already a large population of young Indian graduates of government and mission boarding schools who had mastered the English language, were well versed in white values, and were used to regimentation. Many of these young men, he argued, would be happy to enter military service, and they would begin the process on par or above the quality of white recruits. Furthermore, army life would not only improve their economic prospects, it would also offer the best plan of acculturation yet devised. He suggested that they be trained at eastern posts in basic military matters as well as receiving various forms of mechanical training that could readily support them after they left military service.[46]

In pressing for adoption of the experiment, Powell and other proponents secured a worthy ally in Secretary of War Redfield Proctor. On March 9, 1891, Proctor's views found a vehicle for adoption when Gen. John M. Schofield issued General Order No. 28, which authorized adding Indian companies to 26 of the total 35 regiments in the overall army. The directive followed Maj. Powell's original concept that these companies would be filled entirely with Indian recruits at all enlisted ranks, rather than having Indian soldiers integrated directly into white companies. In the initial years of the experiment, white officers would command the all-Indian companies, but the door was left open for the eventual promotion of Indian commissioned officers from the ranks.[47]

Initial reports from the field indicated that the Indians seemed eager for army service and that recruitment was proceeding smoothly. By the end of May, about one-fourth of the 1,500-man quota had been filled. As much of the initial recruiting took place among the horse-oriented cultures of the Great Plains, cavalry units proved to be the most popular. Officers reported, however, that infantry companies would attract adequate numbers once the cavalry troops had been fully mustered.[48]

The initial phases of the Indian soldier experiment generated mixed reactions among ranking officers of the army. Some remained cautious, most notably Gen. Nelson A. Miles, who withdrew his tepid support two years later when Indian enthusiasm for the program began to decline. Others, such as Gen. Oliver Otis Howard, never took a firm stand on the issue. But Capt. Richard Henry Pratt, who had commanded native scouts in Indian Territory and had subsequently organized the well-known school for Indian children at Carlisle, Pennsylvania, strongly defended the experiment. Maj. George W. Baird, veteran of the Indian wars and Medal of Honor winner, also endorsed the plan, but he cautioned that success or failure would depend primarily upon the quality of white officers assigned to these special units.[49]

Gen. Schofield continued to be one of the strongest advocates of the experiment. In his annual report of September 1891, he surveyed the valuable military skills performed by the Indian soldiers, but he also highlighted the important acculturation benefits of the new program. He pronounced the Indian companies a success and intimated that they would provide the medium through which assimilation of the entire aboriginal population could take place. However, in his 1897 autobiography, Schofield recorded one misgiving about the experiment: He felt that their training prepared them well for frontier duty but that they probably would not function as well in quelling civil disturbances in urban areas. Thus their effectiveness would be significantly circumscribed in emergency situations involving labor strikes and riots.[50]

Despite the preponderance of favorable reports that continued to reach the War Department and military journals during the remainder of 1891, not everything was proceeding according to plan. Recruiters indicated deep suspicions among Bannocks, Shoshones, Utes, Paiutes, and Klamaths, who doubted most white men's promises. Among other tribes, where the recruitment process moved slowly, Indian spokesmen voiced specific reasons for not joining the army. They did not want to leave their families or remain in service among whites for a minimum enlistment period of three years. Others objected to the regulation that only 10 married men per company could take their wives and children with them to each new assignment and that the soldier would have to cover family expenses out of his monthly pay. Still others were adamant about enlisting in the cavalry only and retaining the right to take their own horses with them at government expense. A few also voiced concern that they might lose their tribal rights to annuities and reservation property if they joined the army. Despite efforts by recruiters such as Lt. William H. Johnston to assure Bannocks and Shoshones of their rights and to alleviate their worst fears, only five recruits came forward. Frustrated by the entire experience, Lt. Johnston requested that he be relieved from the recruiting mission.[51]

As the novelty of the Indian soldier experience wore away, some of the initial enthusiasm on both sides diminished. Capt. Richard Henry Pratt came to believe that the acculturation aspects of military service were not advancing quickly enough and that the most promising young men should return to schools to resume their education in agricultural and industrial skills. Capt. W. W. Wotherspoon, who commanded the most unique unit in the army—Company I, 12th Infantry, composed of Apache prisoners of war at Mount Vernon Barracks, Alabama—praised the success of his soldiers, but like Pratt, he doubted the long-term benefits that would accrue for them and their families.[52]

All of these cultural factors worked to weaken the experiment, and when Stephen B. Elkins replaced Redfield Proctor as secretary of war in late 1891, it deprived the program of one of its most outspoken advocates at a crucial juncture. Elkins refused to ardently support the venture because he believed that it kept white men from filling the companies in question. Even though he supported the continued role of Indian scouts on a small scale, he did not think that Indians could match the quality of white soldiers within the regular regiments.[53]

By the end of 1895, most of the Indian soldier companies had been mustered out of service. As the program drew to a close, only a reconstituted Troop L, Seventh Cavalry, was left to wait out its enlisted term. The end came on May 31, 1897, when the men conducted their final drill and surrendered all military equipment to Ft. Sill authorities. Of the 49 Apaches discharged at the time, 12 received employment as scouts. The others were less fortunate. Some applied for distant jobs that would take them away from family and friends. But military officials did little to help, and instead, they denied the Apaches permission to leave the post since they were still technically prisoners of war. Ironically, these were members of the Chiricahua band that had surrendered with Geronimo in 1886, or they had been loyal government scouts who treacherously had been shipped off to a Florida prison with Geronimo's followers at that same time. Six years of loyal service in the U.S. Army had not yet erased all of the animosity that some whites still harbored for Apaches.[54]

Twenty years after leaving Ft. Sill, Gen. Hugh L. Scott, former commander of the last Indian troop, stated in a personal letter that his native soldiers had been cheated out of success by prejudiced minds in the War Department.[55] Gen. Oliver Otis Howard, never a strong supporter of the program, had been even more direct in his charge of racial prejudice. Writing in his autobiography a decade after these events, Howard contended that some officers and enlisted men resented the fact that white soldiers might one day have to take orders from Indian noncommissioned officers.[56]

By the time the Indian soldier experiment ended, military relations with Native Americans had changed in some regards and remained much the same in other ways. At the beginning of the nineteenth century, soldiers routinely regarded most American Indians as the enemy. Although some tribes established close affiliations with the army and even served as scouts and auxiliaries, these were viewed as aberrational cases. Not until after the Civil War did significant numbers of Native Americans find sustained employment as scouts in the army. Officers who served alongside the scouts came to respect them and, in some cases, developed a greater empathy for Native Americans in general. Yet for whatever level of social understanding that might have been attained in these personalized relations, most officers and enlisted men continued to view Native Americans through a prism fashioned by white biases. The majority of white observers—military and civilian alike—viewed Indians as their racial inferiors, a people who had to yield to the "march of civilization" before they could undertake their own assimilation into the white man's world. Even advocates for a "noble redman" image could not escape their cultural predisposition to triumph over and change Indian people forever. Throughout the tortuous twists and turns of the nineteenth century, the U.S. Army had been both a protector and an adversary of Indian rights. Though never as cruel and unjust as some twentieth-century critics made them out to be, frontier soldiers nonetheless served as one vital arm of the government in ultimately producing a catastrophic future for Native Americans everywhere.

NOTES

1. Robert M. Utley, *Frontier Regulars: The United States Army and the Indian, 1866–1891* (New York: Macmillan, 1973), 45.

2. George Armstrong Custer, *My Life on the Plains, or Personal Experiences with Indians* (Norman: University of Oklahoma Press, 1976), 22.

3. Quoted in Thomas C. Leonard, "The Reluctant Conquerors: How the Generals Viewed the Indians," *American Heritage* 27 (August 1976): 36.

4. Quoted in Sherry L. Smith, *The View from Officers' Row: Army Perceptions of Western Indians* (Tucson: University of Arizona Press, 1990), 119–20.

5. John G. Bourke, *On the Border with Crook* (New York: Charles Scribner's Sons, 1891), 464.

6. Thomas A. Bland, "Abolish the Army," *Council Fire* (March 1879): 36.

7. Quoted in Raymond L. Welty, "The Indian Policy of the Army 1860–1870," *Cavalry Journal* 36 (July 1927): 378. Gen. Sheridan made similar statements about the origins of costly Indian wars and how the army became a convenient target for all special interest groups. See Paul A. Hutton, ed., *Soldier's West: Biographies from the Military Frontier* (Lincoln: University of Nebraska Press, 1987), 85–86.

8. Ray H. Mattison, ed., "An Army Wife on the Upper Missouri: The Diary of Sarah E. Canfield, 1866–1868," *North Dakota History* 20 (October 1953): 216–17.

9. Thomas R. Buecker, ed., "Letters from a Post Surgeon's Wife: The Fort Washakie Correspondence of Caroline Winne, May 1879–May 1880," *Annals of Wyoming* 53 (Fall 1981): 48–52.

10. Merrill J. Mattes, *Indians, Infants and Infantry: Andrew and Elizabeth Burt on the Frontier* (Denver: Old West, 1960), 84–89.

11. In addition to Smith, *View from Officer's Row,* see Sandra L. Myres, "Romance and Reality on the American Frontier: Views of Army Wives," *Western Historical Quarterly* 13 (October 1982): 412–14; and "Army Women's Narratives as Documents of Social History: Some Examples from the Western Frontier," *New Mexico Historical Review* 65 (April 1990): 180–82.

12. Buecker, "Letters," 59. Julia Gillis, *So Far from Home: An Army Bride on the Western Frontier, 1865–1869,* ed. Priscilla Knuth (Portland: Oregon Historical Society, 1993), 184.

13. Edward M. Coffman, *The Old Army: A Portrait of the American Army in Peacetime, 1784–1898* (New York: Oxford University Press, 1986), 392.

14. John E. Cox, "Soldiering in Dakota Territory in the Seventies: A Communication," *North Dakota Historical Quarterly* 6 (October 1931): 63–81.

15. Don Rickey Jr., *Forty Miles a Day on Beans and Hay: The Enlisted Soldier Fighting the Indian Wars* (Norman: University of Oklahoma Press, 1963), 234.

16. Norman J. Bender, *"New Hope for the Indians": The Grant Peace Policy and the Navajos in the 1870s* (Albuquerque: University of New Mexico Press, 1989), 23–36. Oakah L. Jones Jr., "The Origins of the Navajo Police 1872–1873," *Arizona and the West* 8 (Autumn 1966): 225–238.

17. Britton Davis, *The Truth about Geronimo* (New Haven, CT: Yale University Press, 1929), viii–xi, 29–54. Jason Betzinez and Wilbur S. Nye, *I Fought with Geronimo* (Harrisburg, PA: Stackpole, 1959), 126–33. Eve Ball and James Kaywaykla, *In the Days of Victorio: Recollections of a Warm Springs Apache* (Tucson: University of Arizona Press, 1970), 159–61.

18. Grant K. Anderson, "The Black Hills Exclusion Policy: Judicial Challenges," *Nebraska History* 58 (Spring 1977): 2–8. Erik Erikkson, "Sioux City and the Black Hills Gold Rush 1874–1877," *Iowa Journal of History and Politics* 20 (July 1922): 334. Watson Parker, "The Majors and the Miners: The Role of the U.S. Army in the Black Hills Gold Rush," *Journal of the West* 11 (January 1972): 79–113.

19. Agnes Wright Spring, *The Cheyenne and Black Hills Stage and Express Routes* (Glendale, CA: Arthur H. Clark, 1949), 67.

20. Frazier Hunt and Robert Hunt, *I Fought with Custer: The Story of Sergeant Windolph, Last Survivor of the Battle of Little Big Horn* (New York: Scribner, 1954), 42.

21. Quoted in *Winners of the West,* June 24, 1926, 6. Stan Hoig, *Fort Reno and the Indian Territory Frontier* (Fayetteville: University of Arkansas Press, 2000), 81–86. Alvin O. Turner, "Order and Disorder: The Opening of the Cherokee Outlet," *Chronicles of Oklahoma* 71 (Summer 1993): 154–73.

22. Donald E. Green, "The Oklahoma Land Run of 1889: A Centennial Re-interpretation," *Chronicles of Oklahoma* 67 (Summer 1989): 117–18. Pamela S. Bocock, "Camp Guthrie: Urban Outpost in the Territory, 1889–1891," *Chronicles of Oklahoma* 62 (Summer 1984): 166–67, 180–81.

23. Green, "Oklahoma Land Run," 123.

24. Ibid., 124–25. Bocock, "Camp Guthrie," 185. The experiences of an enlisted man stationed at Oklahoma City are told in his own words in Bunky [Irving Geffs], *The First Eight Months of Oklahoma City* (Oklahoma City: McMaster, 1890).

25. Orlan J. Svingen, *The Northern Cheyenne Indian Reservation, 1877–1900* (Niwot: University Press of Colorado, 1993), 29–44, 130–47.

26. "An Act of Protection of the Frontiers of the United States," public law, *U.S. Statutes at Large* 1 (1792): 243.

27. Edward Howes, "The Employment of Indian Scouts by the U.S. Army in Arizona, 1865–1886" (MA thesis, University of California at Berkeley, 1947), 49. U.S. Congress, Senate, *Memorial of Richard C. Adams, Representing the Delaware Indians for the Issue of Land-Bounty Warrants for Services Rendered to the Government in Times of War,* 57th Cong., 1st sess., 1902, S. Doc. 294, 1–25.

28. "Act to Increase and Fix the Military Peace Establishment of the U.S.," public law, *U.S. Statutes at Large* 14 (1866): 333–34.

29. Howes, "Employment of Indian Scouts," 50.

30. Betzinez, *I Fought with Geronimo,* 54–55. Paul N. Beck, "Military Officers' Views of Indian Scouts 1865–1890," *Military History of the West* 23 (Spring 1993): 5–6.

31. Ball and Kaywaykla, *In the Days of Victorio,* 80.

32. George Bird Grinnell, *Two Great Scouts and Their Pawnee Battalion* (Cleveland, OH: Arthur H. Clark, 1928). Thomas W. Dunlay, *Wolves for the Blue Soldiers: Indian Scouts and Auxiliaries with the United States Army, 1860–90* (Lincoln: University of Nebraska Press, 1982), 111–64. The best photographic record of scouts from many tribes is Fairfax Downey and J. N. Jacobsen, *The Red-Bluecoats: The Indian Scouts, U.S. Army* (Fort Collins, CO: Old Army Press, 1973).

33. John Rope, as told to Grenville Goodwin, "Experiences of an Indian Scout," *Arizona Historical Review* 7 (January 1936): 58.

34. Nelson A. Miles, *Personal Recollections and Observations of General Nelson A. Miles* (Chicago: Werner, 1896), 495.

35. Angie Debo, *Geronimo: The Man, His Time, His Place* (Norman: University of Oklahoma Press, 1976), 281–86, 298.

36. Beck, "Military Officers' Views," 7–8.

37. James T. King, *War Eagle: A Life of General Eugene A. Carr* (Lincoln: University of Nebraska Press, 1963), 101–17. Donald F. Danker, ed., *Man of the Plains: Recollections of Luther North, 1856–1882* (Lincoln: University of Nebraska Press, 1961), 128.

38. Charles F. Lummis, *General Crook and the Apache Wars,* ed. Turbesé Lummis Fiske (Flagstaff, AZ: Northland Press, 1966), 17. One of the most comprehensive articles explaining Gen. Crook's philosophy of offensive warfare and crucial use of Indian scouts is George Crook, "The Apache Problem," *Journal of the Military Service Institution of the United States* 8 (1886): 257–69.

39. John G. Bourke, *An Apache Campaign in the Sierra Madre: An Account of the Expedition in Pursuit of the Hostile Chiricahua Apaches in the Spring of 1883* (New York: Charles Scribner's Sons, 1958), 45–50.

40. Ibid., 106, 114.

41. Dan L. Thrapp, *General Crook and the Sierra Madre Adventure* (Norman: University of Oklahoma Press, 1972), 128–39. Clippings from *Tombstone Epitaph,* 13 June 1883, and Tucson *Star,* 16 June 1883, both in John G. Bourke, "Diary, 1872–1896," vol. 69, 13–15, 61; original diaries at U.S. Military Academy, West Point, New York.

42. William H. Powell, "Soldier or Granger?" *United Service* 2 (November 1889): 445–53. Quoted in William H. Powell, "The Indian As a Soldier," *United Service* 3 (March 1890): 237.

43. Frederic Remington, "Indians as Irregular Cavalry," *Harper's Weekly Magazine,* 27 December 1890, 1004–6.

44. George Crook to Adjutant General, 24 February 1890. George Crook Letterbook, II, 50–52, Rutherford B. Hayes Memorial Library.

45. Report of Benjamin Grierson, *Annual Report of the Secretary of War, 1890,* 172.

46. Powell, "Indian As a Soldier," 229–38.

47. General Order No. 28, 9 March 1891, in *General Orders and Circulars: Adjutant General's Office, 1891* (Washington, DC: U.S. Government Printing Office, 1892).

48. *Army and Navy Journal* (May 9, 1891), 632; *Army and Navy Journal* (May 30, 1891), 682.

49. *Army and Navy Journal* (April 25, 1891), 601. "The Last Indian Troop," *Leslie's Illustrated Weekly Newspaper,* 8 July 1897, 23. Jack D. Foner, *The United States Soldier between Two Wars: Army Life and Reforms, 1865–1898* (New York: Humanities Press, 1970), 129–30.

50. Report of John M. Schofield, *Annual Report of the Secretary of War, 1891,* 57–59. John M. Schofield, *Forty-six Years in the Army* (New York: Century, 1897), 488–89.

51. Eric Feaver, "Indian Soldiers, 1891–95: An Experiment on the Closing Frontier," *Prologue* 7 (Summer 1975): 112–13.

52. Ibid., 114.

53. Clifford P. Coppersmith, "Indians in the Army: Professional Advocacy and the Regularization of Indian Military Service, 1889–1897," *Military History of the West* 26 (Fall 1996): 178–79. An excellent account of Sioux soldiers' performances within the experiment is Robert Lee, "Warriors in Ranks: American Indian Units in the Regular Army, 1891–1897," *South Dakota History* 21 (Fall 1991): 263–316. Also for Northern Cheyenne participation, see Don Rickey Jr., "Warrior-Soldiers: The All-Indian 'L' Troop, 6th U.S. Cavalry in the Early 1890s," in *Troopers West: Military and Indian Affairs on the American Frontier,* ed. Ray Brandes (San Diego, CA: Frontier Heritage Press, 1970). Further discussion on the national debate about the experiment appears in Bruce White, "The American Indian As Soldier, 1890–1919," *Canadian Review of*

American Studies 7 (Spring 1976): 15–25; and Byron Price, "The Utopian Experiment: The Army and the Indian, 1890–1897," *By Valor and Arms* 3 (Spring 1977): 15–35.

54. "Last Indian Troop," 23.

55. Hugh L. Scott to E. E. Ayer, 19 February 1917. Correspondence of 1911–1917 Pertaining to the Proposed Organization of Indian Cavalry Regiments, File 1669226, Records of the Adjutant General's Office, National Archives. Hugh L. Scott, *Some Memories of a Soldier* (New York: Century, 1928), 170.

56. Foner, *United States Soldier,* 130.

9   BLACK REGULARS: RACIAL REALITIES IN A WHITE MAN'S ARMY

Social experimentation was never a priority of the U.S. Army during the nineteenth century, but at certain times, political exigencies produced significant changes in policy making and command structure. Ironically, the people most affected by these new political pressures were African Americans. Blacks had served in every American war since the colonial era, and yet during periods of so-called peacetime, they had been systematically denied entry into one of the nation's most venerated institutions. Prevailing racial attitudes and Southern fears of large bodies of armed black men moving freely around the country inevitably silenced public debate about the issue. Furthermore, as each new generation paid homage to the proudest moments from the Revolutionary War and the War of 1812, celebrants rarely extended more than lip service to the African American veterans who had helped secure and preserve their country's freedom.

Throughout the antebellum period, military law preserved the army's legacy of a white man's exclusive domain. Recruitment officers rigidly enforced the regulation of February 18, 1820, declaring that "no Negro or Mulatto will be received as a recruit of the Army." The following year, a new regulation affirmed what was already obvious, that only "free white male persons" were eligible for service in the regular army. Despite these restrictions, War Department officials did allow African Americans to serve as mechanics, laborers, and servants when their efforts were needed for construction projects and for domestic duties. An 1842 report from the Engineers Department revealed that it had utilized the labor of 545 slaves and 25 black freemen on various public works projects. The Ordnance Department confirmed that it too had employed 28 slaves in similar capacities during the year. In neither case were these men treated as soldiers, nor were they armed or entitled to regular army pay. This pattern was maintained during the Mexican War, when small numbers of blacks traipsed across the deserts and mountains, but only as personal servants for regular army officers. Some African Americans did join state militia units during the war, though their numbers were negligible.[1]

Given the long-standing tradition of rejecting potential black recruits from regular army service, it is little wonder that when African Americans tried to join Union forces in response to the secessionist bombardment of Ft. Sumter in April 1861, they were summarily turned away. President Lincoln and most members of his government feared, with good reason, that any effort to arm black men would drive the slave-owning border states into the hands of the Confederacy. Not until Union calls for 300,000 additional volunteers during July 1862 went largely unanswered did Lincoln approve the use of blacks as laborers and in other nonmartial capacities. The measure drew upon well-established precedents and thus provoked no systematic opposition since these laborers were not armed or empowered by the government. Finally, with the issuance of the Emancipation Proclamation, effective January 1, 1863, the president was prepared to cast the war in a different light and to begin drawing upon the large numbers of eager black recruits who wanted to fight for the freedom of their race. Recruitment went slowly at first, beginning with organization of the 54th Massachusetts Infantry Regiment under their aristocratic Bostonian officer Col. Robert Gould Shaw. Not until June 15, 1864, did Congress pass legislation to grant equal pay to black soldiers, retroactive to those who were recognized as freemen on April 19, 1861. By war's end, all black soldiers had their pay equalized with white soldiers of the same rank, and special funding was made available for retroactive pay.[2]

By the time of Gen. Robert E. Lee's surrender at Appomattox Courthouse in April 1865, black soldiers had established an enviable war record in some of the bloodiest fighting across the South. Approximately 180,000 black men had worn the uniform of the United States, and their sheer numbers and courage had contributed significantly to the Union victory.[3] Yet wartime maneuvering by politicians and military leaders had raised questions about how dedicated the newly restructured nation would be toward the continuation of this so-called Sable Arm.

CREATION OF THE BLACK REGIMENTS

Most Americans welcomed the postwar reduction of troop strength from 1.5 million at the height of the Civil War to a prewar total of 16,000 men. Tightening of the federal budget would surely lead to taxpayer benefits, allow veterans to resume their normal lives, and prevent the maintenance of a large standing army in peacetime. Even when these numbers were soon increased to approximately 25,000 to handle Reconstruction duties in the South, the French menace on the Mexican border, and Indian problems in the West, most northern citizens accepted the modest expansion of numbers.[4] Yet within this arena of public acceptance, very little sentiment existed to enlist black soldiers for these new duties.

Challenges to the traditional white man's army came from two groups in the immediate post–Civil War era. First, many African Americans advocated that the army should be opened to their race as a means of gaining employment opportunities and to assure their patriotic participation in the nation's future. These voices, however, were scattered, and they had little direct impact on subsequent legislation.[5] More important to the story were the Radical Republicans, activist politicians who advocated a thorough restructuring of the former Confederacy and the extension of legal rights to freedmen. Ohio senator Benjamin Wade took the lead in sponsoring a revision of the March 14, 1866, senate bill that authorized 67 regiments within the army—5 of artillery, 12 of cavalry, and 50 of infantry. Wade's amendment directed that two of the cavalry regiments be reserved exclusively for blacks to supplement the eight black infantry regiments that already had been included in the bill.[6] It passed overwhelmingly, and after further revisions, the army appropriation bill of July 28, 1866, guaranteed 2 black cavalry and 4 black infantry regiments within a 60-regiment army. This suited the Radical Republican agenda as well as making it easier for officers to recruit enough men for the army's expanded roles.[7]

The stationing of black soldiers in the South during Reconstruction was part of a necessary plan for protecting the rights of freedmen and their sympathizers, but this occupation incurred the wrath of most white Southerners. Nowhere was this more strongly felt than in Texas, the one former Confederate state that not only experienced Reconstruction policies but also an increased Indian threat to its westernmost counties. By the end of 1865, black soldiers conducted policing duties across the Lone Star State, mostly in the eastern sections, where postwar animosities still boiled over. The *Bellville Countryman* newspaper summarized majority white opinion when it declared that "the idea of a gallant and high-minded people being ordered and pushed around by an inferior, ignorant race is shocking to the senses."[8]

This verbal attack on black soldiers was paralleled by a shocking event that occurred in Jefferson, Texas, during 1866. Two soldiers of the 80th U.S. Colored Infantry were shot without cause by the deputy town marshal who emptied his double-barreled shotgun and pistol into them. Gen. Philip Sheridan, commander of Reconstruction troops in Texas, chose not to bring charges against the culprit since he knew that an all-white jury from the community would exonerate the man and make a farce of federal authority. Popular prejudices and vigilante violence assured that most black garrisons gradually were removed from the densely populated areas of Texas and rotated to the more remote posts in the frontier areas of the state.[9]

Legislation of 1869 finalized the organizational structure of the army by substantially reducing the number of infantry regiments. Throughout the remainder of the century, black soldiers would serve exclusively in four regiments: 9th and 10th Cavalries and 24th and 25th Infantries.[10] Initially, all commissioned officers were white men, but the door was left open for future black officers to lead these units. Some senior white commanders who had gained their rank during the Civil War turned down offers to lead black troops due to their innate racial views and their perception that promotions would not come quickly in African American regiments. George Armstrong Custer was among that number when he refused appointment to the 9th Cavalry with the full rank of lieutenant colonel. Fortunately for him, political and military friends exerted enough pressure that he won equal rank in the all-white 7th Cavalry rather than having to take a reduction of rank to major or even captain.[11]

Other senior white officers, however, voiced a preference for command of black regiments. Notable were Col. Edward Hatch, who assumed leadership of the 9th Cavalry, and Col. Benjamin Grierson, who took charge of the 10th Cavalry, as well as Lt. Col. William Shafter of the 24th Infantry and Col. George Lippitt Andrews of the 25th Infantry.[12] Although these men were not without their own racial prejudices, they fully dedicated their efforts toward making their regiments among the best in the army.

WHITE ATTITUDES TOWARD BLACK SOLDIERS

Throughout the officers' ranks, opinions remained greatly divided about the reliability of African American soldiers. Frederick Benteen and Eugene A. Carr took substantial reductions in rank rather than command companies within these regiments. In reverse fashion, two West Point officers, John Bigelow Jr. and Walter D. Finley, chose service in black regiments, even though openings were available in white units. Whatever their reasons for these choices, it was not because they saw black men as their racial equals. Both officers used racist language and condescending terms when referring to black enlisted men, and their relationships with these soldiers were patronizing at best. Historian Edward M. Coffman noted that throughout the 1870s and most of the 1880s, rank did indeed have its privilege, for during that extended period, black regiments generally received the lowest-ranking West Point graduates.[13]

Attitudes also differed among officers who got to know black enlisted men firsthand. Dr. William M. Notson, a native of Philadelphia and newly assigned post surgeon for the 9th Cavalry, wrote disparagingly of the soldiers soon after his arrival at Ft. Concho, Texas, in 1869. He recorded that "the negro is essentially a mimic, therefore in the manual [labor] they excel, but they are not as reliable....Lying and thieving are the principal vices." Continuing his private discourse several months later, Notson stated his opposition to the continued social experiment by remarking that "the impracticability of making intelligent soldiers out of the mass of negroes is growing more evident to the Post Surgeon every day." Notson continued to invoke racial stereotypes, even though his accusations rarely dealt with specific examples.[14]

Several years later, Chaplain Norman Badger was on duty at the same post when the 10th Cavalry arrived to transform it into their regimental headquarters. Badger was struck by the high quality of black soldiers who took up residence at Ft. Concho, and he observed that they outperformed the white troops who had occupied the post during the previous two years. He especially noted their superior "moral condition" and their propensity for less drinking and profanity, while simultaneously increasing the attendance at chapel services.[15]

Officers' wives joined their husbands in expressing different opinions about black soldiers. Eveline Alexander, wife of a lieutenant colonel of cavalry, described a trip across Indian Territory to New Mexico in the bleakest of terms, and she concocted a dreadful image of the black infantrymen who helped escort the column. "These Negroes...are indeed the most hideous blacks I have ever seen," she contended, and "there is hardly a mulatto among them; almost all are coal black, with frightfully bad [f]aces."[16] Her harsh racial stereotyping was somewhat rebutted by Emily Andrews under similar circumstances. While traveling to Ft. Davis, Texas, under protection of soldiers of the 25th Infantry, she praised "our gallant '*brunette*' escort" for their stamina and close attention to military details.[17]

The most typical observation from the racially conscious army was attributed to Frances M. A. Roe while stationed with her husband at Camp Supply, Indian Territory, during 1873. She was appalled that the commanding officer allowed the mixing of white and black enlisted men in daily guard details. Roe contended that such unacceptable race mixing made white soldiers more likely to desert and undermined morale throughout the ranks. Worst of all in her mind was the outrageous practice of allowing black sergeants to command white corporals and privates. Rank was not the problem in this case; skin color was. Roe happily noted that the black soldiers had recently been transferred to another military department, and exclusive white authority would soon be reestablished over the post.[18]

As was the case in white regiments, black noncommissioned officers were the key to maintaining order and high performance levels among black troops. This was especially true among the sergeants, who not only had to be tough and serve as good role models, but also had to handle administrative duties that required basic educational skills. In the earliest years of the black regiments, finding enough educated men to fill these positions was somewhat difficult. This problem was gradually answered by the promotion of on-post schools at the largest installations. Highly literate black chaplains took on the enormous task of educating as many black soldiers as possible, especially those who aspired to noncommissioned rank.[19]

In the field, black noncoms had the responsibility of leading patrols, conducting escorts, preparing reconnaissance reports, making sketch maps of the terrain, and serving as the liaison between white officers and black enlisted men. On post, the duty sergeants maintained regulations within the barracks, supervised the issuance of equipment, prepared duty rosters, arranged construction and drill assignments, and kept the daily records regarding matters ranging from sick call to company finances.[20]

COMPOSITION OF BLACK UNITS

African American soldiers probably came from every state in the Union during the late nineteenth century, but an examination of 1870 enlistment statistics reveals an interesting nativity pattern. Rather than the great majority of recruits coming from former slave areas of the Deep South, demographics show a more diverse body of men than the usual stereotype implies. A census of the unusually large garrison of 336 men of the 9th Cavalry and 24th and 25th Infantries that were temporarily congregated at Ft. McKavett, Texas, provides a reliable sample for study. Only 6.5 percent of the total were born in Alabama, Georgia, South Carolina, Mississippi, or Florida, but virtually the same percentage were born in the free states of New York and Pennsylvania. Kentucky was well represented at 34.8 percent, far ahead of the next-highest state, Virginia, which represented 13.9 percent. Thus the free states and border states of the upper South were more heavily represented than were the Deep South states that contained a far higher proportion of the nation's total black population. How many of these were freedmen and how many were slaves at the end of the Civil War is unrevealed in the census, as is their degree of literacy.[21]

Further research also raises the question about the origins of the term *buffalo soldier,* which has assumed iconic proportion in the twentieth century. Historian William H. Leckie helped popularize the phrase in his choice of title for the first systematic study of the combat records of the 9th and 10th Cavalries: *The Buffalo Soldiers: A Narrative of the Negro Cavalry in the West* (1967). Like others before him, he repeated the story that Comanche Indians noticed the similarity between the texture of many black soldiers' hair and that of the buffalo. Supposedly, Comanches began using the phrase because of this similarity or, in another version of the story, because of their respect for the courage of the black soldiers, who were spiritually powerful like the buffalo. Although no independent proof of these stories has ever been uncovered, the term *buffalo soldier* was occasionally used by late-nineteenth-century writers, such as Frederic Remington.[22]

More recent investigations into this question have been carried out by historians William A. Dobak and Thomas D. Phillips. They found that veterans of the four African American regiments almost never used the term in print, either at the time of their service or in their retirement years. Furthermore, the term does not show up in soldiers' frequent letters to the *Cleveland Gazette, Huntsville Gazette,* or other black newspapers. Accordingly, Dobak and Phillips opted for the phrase *black regulars* to replace *buffalo soldiers* as a description more authentic to the time.[23] Nevertheless, the 10th Cavalry's regimental insignia clearly carried the image of the buffalo by the end of the frontier period.

Black soldiers of the 25th Infantry, some wearing buffalo robes, Ft. Keogh, Montana, ca. 1890. (*Courtesy of the Library of Congress*)

Combat Records of African American Units

Combat records of the four black regiments reveal an impressive array of military actions across the Great Plains and the Southwest. These narratives have been encapsulated in the individual regimental histories as well as in the syntheses offered by William Leckie and Arlen Fowler.[24] Rather than merely repeat their detailed stories, it is more worthwhile to look at the overall activities of a single troop of cavalry within a single regiment that operated in the field continuously from 1867 to 1898. The experiences of this smaller group of men generally mirrors the accomplishments of other black units of the same time period.

Troop L, 10th Cavalry, began its existence at Ft. Riley, Kansas, on September 21, 1867, but within a month, it was dispatched to Ft. Arbuckle, Indian Territory, for larger operations against the Comanches and Kiowas, while the rest of the regiment continued protecting Union Pacific Railroad construction crews in Nebraska. During its stationing at Ft. Arbuckle, the troop suffered its first casualty, Pvt. Fillmore Roberts, who drowned while carrying mail to and from Ft. Gibson.[25]

Following its redeployment to Ft. Cobb and subsequent sweep of the Washita River area of western Indian Territory, Troop L helped construct the region's pivotal post known as Ft. Sill. From 1869 through the end of 1872, it conducted many patrols across western Indian Territory and occasionally south of the Red River into Texas. Rising problems with Comanche and Kiowa resistance led to transfer to Ft. Richardson, another pivotal center of operations across northwest Texas. Troop L participated in the 1874 rescue of personnel at the Wichita Agency and in the larger operations collectively known as the Red River War, which eliminated all organized opposition by the Comanches, Kiowas, and Southern Cheyennes. From the mid-1870s to 1880, its members were stationed at Ft. Concho and Fort Davis and along the line of subposts that extended between these two primary west Texas installations. Their operations against Mescalero and Lipan Apaches took them throughout the mountainous terrain of Texas's Pecos River country and into southern New Mexico. By the summer of 1885, the entire 10th Cavalry was rotated to stations in Arizona, where it participated in the final operations against Geronimo.[26]

Throughout its 23-year service on the frontier, Troop L of the 10th Cavalry had taken part in 11 significant Indian combats, constructed a number of forts, built and maintained military roads across the southern plains and in the Southwest, and helped establish an economic impact wherever it went. By 1897, only two of the troop's original enlistees still remained in service. One of these, David Haskins, had risen to first sergeant of the unit. The other, Courtney Matthew, still remained a private.[27]

Despite the enviable record that black regulars were establishing in the West, debates in Washington, D.C., raised questions about whether the four regiments would continue in service. The central issues had to do with the gradual fading of federal Reconstruction efforts in the South and new mandates to economize on army budgets. House Military Affairs Committee chairman Henry B. Banning (Democrat from Ohio) promoted a bill in 1875 whose purpose was to terminate the services of all black soldiers. Couched in budget-cutting terms, and hidden among false promises of promoting racial equality, the Banning Bill passed the House of Representatives but failed in the Senate. The bill would have ended the black regiments in the name of promoting racial integration, while simultaneously providing no guarantee that the army would have to accept African Americans into other existing regiments.[28] An 1878 attempt to revive the subterfuge came in the form of the Burnside Bill, which Senator James G. Blaine of Maine attacked with the warning "do not let us deceive ourselves." Again, the bill failed in the Senate, and ironically, an important black institution was saved by segregationist logic.[29]

Problems for Black Soldiers: Housing, Advancement, Training, and Education

Black servicemen certainly exercised some control over their daily lives, but always within the strict parameters of military protocol and under the tutelage of white officers who shared most of the popular prejudices of the day. One of the most persistent complaints printed within black-owned newspapers was the charge that African American soldiers were never stationed in the settled areas of the East. Unlike white regiments that periodically rotated to preferred assignments east of the Mississippi River, the four black regiments spent the entire period of 1869–1898 moving from one frontier post to another. Luxuries and opportunities were comparatively scarce at the more remote forts, and in the smallest subposts, living conditions were abysmal. Even *The New York Times* joined the chorus of complaint when it remarked in 1891 that very few Americans had even seen a black soldier since their initial stationing in the western states and territories. When the Spanish-American War began seven years later and large numbers of black regulars proudly marched off to battle, much of the nation seemed stunned that so many African Americans had been in uniform for such a long time.[30]

Another source of complaint expressed within African American newspapers was the total exclusion of black soldiers from the army's most elite units. Specialized branches, such as artillery, ordnance, engineers, and signal corps, were entirely closed to their membership. Only in the case of artillery service was the issue of black access raised in Congress. As early as 1866, Senator Henry Wilson of Massachusetts sponsored just such a bill, but it faced strong opposition from important men such as Gen. Ulysses S. Grant, who warned that African Americans could not easily master the technology. On the basis of the testimony of Grant and like-minded officers, the Senate Military Committee opposed this provision, and it was ultimately removed from the bill.[31]

Articles addressing this issue sometimes appeared in service publications during the following two decades, but not until 1889 was it again seriously addressed at the highest levels. In his annual report to the secretary of war, Gen. John M. Schofield called for the number of artillery regiments to be raised from five to seven. Secretary of War Redfield Proctor endorsed the plan, with a further observation that at least one of the new units should be reserved for black enlisted men. A member of the 9th Cavalry wrote to the *New York Age* expressing his enthusiasm for the proposal and declaring, "We need a colored artillery regiment badly, and I see no reason why we cannot have one."[32]

Expectations were soon dashed, despite Proctor's valiant efforts. The bill failed to pass Congress, as did a similarly conceived effort during the following year. As if to add insult to injury, the creation of two additional white artillery regiments during the Spanish-American War was tinged with racism. When a newspaper correspondent asked Capt. Henry H. Wright why African Americans were not included in the artillery, this white officer of the 9th Cavalry sarcastically responded, "He lacks the brains.... He is brave enough and willing enough; but if we let him enlist in the artillery our shooting will very much resemble the fine marksmanship of the Spaniards."[33]

An even more critical issue for African Americans was the lack of black commissioned officers. Although no specific legislation existed to officially preserve racial purity within the officer corps, tradition and prejudice safeguarded the existing system. Even the passage of new legislation in 1878 failed to alleviate the problem. The law authorized the promotion of outstanding enlisted men into the commissioned ranks if they were recommended by their company officers, were approved by a military board, and passed qualifying examinations. More liberal legislation in 1892 allowed the individual soldier to initiate his own application rather than wait for action from his superiors. A relatively small percentage of white enlisted men were elevated through the ranks by these reforms, but not a single black infantryman or cavalryman attained his commission between 1866 and 1898.[34]

Another method existed for obtaining a regular commission: graduation from the U.S. Military Academy. Twenty-two black men did obtain admission to West Point between 1870 and 1889, largely through the efforts of Republican congressmen, including some southern black congressmen who held seats during Reconstruction. Unfortunately, only 12 of these passed the difficult entrance exam. In the entirety of the experiment, only three of the select few managed to persevere through the "silent treatment," physical abuse, and other forms of harassment to actually graduate. Henry Ossian Flipper became the first African American graduate of West Point in 1877, and he subsequently served as a lieutenant of the 10th Cavalry in west Texas. Flipper was court-martialed and removed from service five years later amid controversial charges that were steeped in racial prejudice.[35] The second graduate, John Hanks Alexander, died while on active duty with the 9th Cavalry in 1887. The only black graduate to survive the ordeal of the academy and field service was Charles Young, but his position within the army was one of virtual invisibility. He served in all four black regiments before being assigned to the all-white 7th Cavalry in 1896. Young was subsequently ordered to the all-black campus of Wilberforce University in Ohio to teach military science. By this act of trickery, his superiors were able to eliminate the possibility of white soldiers having to take orders from a black officer.[36]

An anonymous 9th Cavalryman stationed at Ft. Robinson, Nebraska, during the height of the Plains Indian wars best summarized the bleak prospects that awaited black

Portrait of American officer, Lt. Henry Ossian Flipper in uniform, the first Black graduate of the U.S. Military Academy at West Point, ca. 1877. (© *Getty Images*)

soldiers who aspired to a second lieutenancy. He wrote, "It is not that they do not possess the necessary qualifications for the office, but that the sentiment of the army is decidedly against it, and any ambitious aspirant for shoulderstraps in the ranks is promptly and effectually given to understand that 'spades are not trumps' here."[37]

RACIAL PREJUDICE IN WESTERN COMMUNITIES

If the military establishment stacked its cards against the advancement of black soldiers, how then did white civilians react to the presence of these same troops in their own frontier communities? As in all other cases, preconceptions and reactions varied considerably, depending on region, time period, and the prejudices of individuals. But in most cases, racism was so entrenched that black regulars could hope to gain little more than a grudging respect from their white neighbors. These same neighbors often lived off army revenues, and they welcomed the protection of black troopers in times of trouble, but they merely tolerated the convergence of the races when it was necessary to daily life. In private matters, however, the racial divide between black soldiers and white civilians was maintained with the same determination as it had been in the antebellum period.

Racial Violence on the Frontier

On far too many occasions, racial animosities boiled over and led to violence on the frontier. These events began soon after the deployment of the first African American forces to the plains of Kansas. One of the earliest episodes occurred in Hays City during 1867, when three black soldiers were refused service in a local bordello. In a series of events that are still unclear, the angry men shot and killed a civilian employee of the fort who was guarding military contract items at the rail yard. The county sheriff proceeded to the post, talked with the commanding officer, and escorted the three alleged assassins back to the town's jail. A mob broke into the building, seized the three, and hanged them from a railroad bridge west of town.[38]

In a reversal of the story line some years later, Hays City citizens found themselves threatened by a large group of black soldiers who sought revenge after one of their unit had been killed by a local law officer while allegedly resisting arrest. Only the forceful intervention of Capt. Lloyd Wheaten prevented the escalation of violence. In summarizing the early history of Ft. Hays and Hays City, historian James N. Leiker noted the sad irony that "the average black soldier had more reason to fear civilians or even comrades than Indians; more injuries and killings resulted from altercations in camp or nearby Hays City than from combat."[39]

Beginning in the mid-1870s, Ft. Concho, Texas, repeatedly proved to be a magnet for racial violence as unreconstructed Southerners provoked trouble with members of the 10th Cavalry at the sprawling headquarters post. The most serious confrontation occurred in January 1881, when local sheep rancher Tom McCarthy got into an altercation with Pvt. William Watkins in McDonald's Saloon. After an exchange of angry words on both sides, McCarthy shot and killed the unarmed trooper. Post guards captured the fugitive as he tried to escape from the adjacent town of San Angelo (called Saint Angela at the time). Commanding officer Colonel Benjamin Grierson turned the prisoner over to the local sheriff, who then freed the man while he awaited a court hearing. Three days later, members of the 10th Cavalry circulated a handbill throughout San Angelo that threatened, "We the soldiers of the U.S. Army, do hereby warn for the first and last time, all citizens, cow-boys, etc. of San Angela and vicinity, to recognize our right-of-way as just and peaceable men. If we do not receive justice and fair play, which we must have, some one will suffer—if not the guilty, the innocent. It has gone far enough! Justice or death! U.S. Soldiers, one and all."[40]

In response to the threat, the local judge requested that Texas Rangers be dispatched from Hackberry Springs, some 70 miles away. Col. Grierson did his most to calm fears, but rumors abounded that McCarthy's friends were headed for town. The following day, the defendant's brother, John C. McCarthy, rode into town and registered at the Nimitz Hotel. This led to a confusion of identities, and a false report was circulated among the soldiers that the judge had already released the murderer. After several white men fired upon members of the fort's picket guard during the evening, approximately 40 irate soldiers crossed the Concho River and attacked the Nimitz Hotel, firing as many as 150 shots, by some estimates. The military arrest of 3 noncommissioned officers and two privates, plus the arrival of 21 Texas Rangers, quieted the situation. Tom

McCarthy's trial was eventually moved to Austin, where a jury found him not guilty. The five soldiers faced severe disciplinary action but no further charges in civil court. Col. Grierson, much to his credit, sent a lengthy report to the Texas governor outlining a litany of soldier complaints against the citizens of San Angelo. Unfortunately, nothing ever came from the report, and the regiment was transferred to Ft. Davis a year later.[41]

Even the most mundane situation revealed the popular prejudices of the day. For instance, black troopers frequently rode escort during the 1870s for civilian stage coaches traveling between Ft. Concho and El Paso, Texas. Even though they protected the lives and property of company employees, the soldiers were often subject to mistreatment by those same employees. The station master at Leon's Hole was especially notorious because of his racial insults and refusal to feed black soldiers who were traveling with the coaches. Col. William R. Shafter wrote a sharply worded note intended for the company executives. He warned that patrols would continue their protective role for the company, but only if the soldiers were guaranteed ample food and sleeping facilities at the stations. On another occasion, a heated exchange erupted between a stage driver and Pvt. Frank Tall of the 25th Infantry, who was riding escort. After the driver struck Pvt. Tall with a hard blow to the face and fired a revolver at him, the soldier shot the abusive man dead in his tracks.[42]

Not all community prejudice manifested itself with violent acts; sometimes it made itself known in more subtle ways. In June 1890, Capt. Edward T. Comegys sharply criticized Texans who refused to help a black trooper as he traversed the state after departing the Army General Hospital at Hot Springs, Arkansas, to join his regiment at Ft. Bayard, New Mexico. He had to endure the 48-hour train trip without food or even a cup of coffee because white vendors on the train and in the towns refused to serve him because of his skin color.[43]

Not all racial prejudice was confined to communities in the South and Southwest. One of the worst cases of violence occurred near Ft. Meade, situated at the northeast corner of South Dakota's Black Hills. The nearby town of Sturgis drew considerable revenue from the army's presence, but in the fall of 1885, citizens submitted a petition demanding that white regiments replace all black military personnel in the district. A number of incidents had helped create an ugly climate of resentment that boiled over with the murder of Dr. H. P. Lynch. Evidence was circumstantial at best, but Corp. Ross Hallon of the 25th Infantry was arrested because he had been involved in a running feud with the doctor over charges that Hallon had continuously mistreated a black woman of the community. Two nights later, a mob broke into the jail, removed the prisoner, and hanged him from a tree just outside the town limits. With no arrests forthcoming during the following month, tensions mounted, and some black soldiers got into a gunfight with local white cowboys, resulting in the death of one of the latter. Sixteen soldiers of Company H were confined to the guardhouse, but of these, only three were convicted of the killing. Two of them managed to escape before being transferred to the penitentiary.[44]

Tensions did not decrease in the wake of the convictions, especially when some Sturgis residents again threatened violence if the 25th Infantry was not immediately reassigned outside the region. Department of Dakota commander Gen. Alfred Terry responded with his own blast against the citizens, warning that legal action would be taken if the real source of trouble was not quickly removed—the illegal saloons, gambling parlors, and brothels that graced the streets of Sturgis. Tensions remained high in the wake of these events and did not fully subside until soldiers of the 7th Cavalry finally replaced those of the 25th Infantry during the following year.[45]

Another unwelcoming locale was Salt Lake City, where many people opposed the redeployment of the 24th Infantry to Ft. Douglas, just to the east of town. The Salt Lake City *Tribune* ran an editorial entitled "An Unfortunate Change," which played upon public fears of "direct contact with drunken colored soldiers." Pvt. Thomas A. Ernest of Company E responded with a letter that the *Tribune* printed in its own pages. Ernest appealed to the readers to not make hasty judgments based upon ugly racial stereotypes, and he reiterated the outstanding service record of the regiment everywhere it had been stationed. With the passage of a year and with more intimate contact established between the races, the *Tribune* retracted its original sentiments. In the best spirit of an apology, the newspaper declared, "The regiment has lived down the apprehensions awakened when the announcement of their coming was made and they are now appreciated at their worth, as citizens and soldiers above reproach."[46]

A similar sequence of events was set in motion during the summer of 1887, when a single company of soldiers was deployed from Ft. Robinson to Ft. D. A. Russell on the outskirts of Cheyenne, Wyoming. Their task was a fairly simple one: to remove illegal barbed wire fences on government land in southeastern Wyoming. Despite the fact that they were to be stationed at Ft. D. A. Russell only for a brief period, they were greeted with considerable animosity. Four months later, when the troops prepared for their return trip to Ft. Robinson, the Cheyenne *Daily Leader* printed its own note of apology. The editor wrote, "Although every resident of this section had solemnly resolved to hate and detest the colored troops before their arrival, they first tolerated them, but contempt soon turned to respect."[47]

BLACK SOLDIERS' POLICING DUTIES IN THE WEST

The most controversial use of black troops occurred when they intervened in large-scale civil insurrections. These types of events also elicited harsh public feelings toward white regiments when they engaged in similar policing duties against angry civilian groups, but in the former cases, racial tensions exacerbated the problems even more. The first of three significant confrontations took place in December 1877, when Col. Edward Hatch led men of the 9th Cavalry into the streets of El Paso, Texas, to restore order amid a feud that pitted Anglos against Hispanics. The financial and political stakes were high for both factions, especially over who would control the valuable salt deposits 70 miles to the east, and over which machine would control county offices and patronage. A number of assassinations within a three-month period, a bloody siege at nearby San Elizario, and the intervention of Texas Rangers to defend Anglo interests worsened the explosive situation. Before the crisis abated, Hispanic residents decried the army's alleged favoritism toward the Anglo faction and their attempt to monopolize the valuable salt deposits. Anglos simultaneously condemned the army for allowing the suspected murderers of their leader to escape unmolested. Both sides directed repeated racial epithets against 9th Cavalrymen throughout the crisis.[48]

A year later, in New Mexico, an equally violent series of events attracted national attention and stirred passions on both sides about whether the army could maintain an impartial role when settling domestic disturbances. Within Lincoln County, two factions vied for government contracts and economic domination of ranching interests and mercantile trade. Entrepreneur Lawrence G. Murphy and his associates James J. Dolan and James H. Riley initially held the upper hand in the contest for power. Arrayed against them were the mercantile partners Alexander McSween and John Tunstall, whose connections were with the local cattle baron John Chisum. The February 1878 murder of

Tunstall by a Dolan-controlled posse set off the infamous Lincoln County War. Col. Nathan A. Dudley, commander at nearby Ft. Stanton, repeatedly resisted calls to enter the fray on the grounds that the president had not issued specific instructions for military intervention. Finally, on July 19, Dudley led 11 black soldiers of the 9th Cavalry and 24 white infantrymen into Lincoln to demand that the justice of the peace issue warrants for the arrest of McSween, William Bonny (Billy the Kid), and other of their Regulator associates. The colonel justified this action on the grounds that Regulators had previously accosted a 9th Cavalry private while he was delivering military communiqués. In addition to the 35 soldiers that accompanied him, Dudley displayed formidable firepower with a Gatling gun and a mountain howitzer.[49]

Even though the McSween faction was in a purely defensive position, Dudley's mere presence encouraged the opposing faction to continue their bloody siege. McSween and four other men were killed, which prompted Mrs. McSween to prefer charges against the colonel. Although the court of inquiry exonerated the commander, his partisanship for the Murphy-Dolan faction had become widely apparent. Enlisted men of the 9th Cavalry had not been responsible for the tragic events of Lincoln County, but their conduct was repeatedly questioned in the hearings and in the territorial press. Additional assassinations occurred, and the level of violence did not completely subside until Billy the Kid was killed in 1881 and John Chisum died of natural causes three years later.[50]

The third major case involving black regulars' intervention into white domestic conflicts happened in Wyoming's 1892 Johnson County War. The story has been told many times by many authors (see chapter 6), always with an emphasis on "cattle barons" versus "small livestock raisers," but the tale had a significant racial dimension, too. In the wake of the Sixth Cavalry's April rescue of the besieged "Invaders" who represented the cattle barons, President Benjamin Harrison authorized additional troop deployments to northeastern Wyoming to keep the peace. During early June, Maj. Charles S. Ilsley led 310 officers and men of the 9th Cavalry from Ft. Robinson to the Burlington and Missouri railroad crossing on the Powder River. There they established Camp Bettens in eastern Sheridan County, five miles from the small town of Suggs.

Local townspeople accepted the influx of soldiers, but the transient population that frequented the saloons and bordellos directed abusive language and gestures at the black soldiers. A saloon altercation sent two troopers fleeing back to camp, barely escaping the gunshots that were directed at them. On the following evening, approximately 20 soldiers returned to Suggs seeking justice, and in the melee that followed, one trooper was killed. The Cheyenne *Daily Leader* printed an inflammatory article that began "PITCHED BATTLE—Soldiers Attacked Private Citizens in the Town of Suggs," but it did not indicate that the soldiers were African Americans. Other newspapers followed suit by placing virtually all the blame on black enlisted men. Rather than confront the racially charged issue, senior officers downplayed it in their reports and confined the soldiers to camp. By the end of September, four companies of the 9th Cavalry were on their way back to Ft. Robinson, having suffered a severe blow to their morale and self-respect. A month and a half later, the remaining two companies returned to their home post.[51]

One of the unique policing duties undertaken by black regulars was protection of federal lands in Indian Territory during the late 1880s. On April 26, 1879, President Rutherford B. Hayes issued a proclamation to prevent trespassers from entering the area known as the Cherokee Strip. Some sought to illegally cut timber or utilize grazing lands, but the majority wanted to settle the area before Indian land titles had been completely transferred to the government. Tribes and their agents petitioned for greater enforcement of the proclamation because the number of "boomers" was increasing.

As early as January 1882, elements of the 9th Cavalry found themselves on continuous patrol duty, looking for trespassers and escorting them north of the territorial line into Kansas. Soldiers operated even in the winter, and on one occasion, during February 1883, calamity befell troopers from Companies F and I when they were caught in storms that dropped the temperature to 11 degrees below zero. Amid high winds and intermittent snow, 10 of the soldiers suffered frostbite, and 50 were not fit for duty for 10 days. Men of the 9th and 10th Cavalries continued to participate in these patrols until part of the territory was opened to settlers in 1889.[52]

ENTERTAINMENT AND PERSONAL IMPROVEMENT FOR AFRICAN AMERICAN SOLDIERS

Because black soldiers felt somewhat isolated in their remote assignments, and because of racial prejudices that separated them from white regiments and the very civilian communities they were sent to protect, they created their own institutions to preserve their identity and promote their interests. Some of these mirrored the institutions found throughout the army—athletic teams, literary societies, musical ensembles, and theatrical groups—activities that provided entertainment and cultural value alike. Other creations represented more important forums for celebrating black identity and maintaining connections with African American communities in the East.

Wherever they went, African American soldiers created their own fraternal lodges, including branches of the Odd Fellows at installations as far-flung as Ft. McKinney, Wyoming, and Ft. Grant, Arizona. Enlisted men of the 9th Cavalry created the Crispus Attucks Lodge, No. 3 of the Knights of Pythias at Ft. Robinson to do charitable work. At other posts, soldiers created clubs that had no national affiliation but that filled an important social niche in off-duty hours. At various times, Ft. Robinson hosted the "Diamond Club" of Troop K, 9th Cavalry, and the "Dog Robbers" and "Syndicate" within the ranks of the 10th Cavalry. In addition to providing social outlets designed by the men themselves, the clubs and fraternal organizations undertook service projects. For instance, Sgt. Joseph Moore rallied fellow soldiers of the 9th Cavalry to collect funds to aid impoverished black settlers who had suffered from recent floods in Custer County, Nebraska. In 1890, he also encouraged fellow troopers to donate money to purchase and commemorate the Harper's Ferry arsenal where John Brown had begun his famous insurrection in 1859.[53]

Black veterans of the 1898 Spanish-American War also began to participate in activities of the Young Men's Christian Association (YMCA), and they carried that association to western military posts when they returned from the war. This organization, with its national recognition and established programs, was attractive to African Americans who preferred that a wholesome environment be available during the off-duty hours. At Ft. Robinson, YMCA activities sometimes involved over half of the garrison. Such unified activities also encouraged black soldiers to pool their money for the purchase of African American newspapers that had a national circulation. Without any supplementary funds from the War Department, black garrisons throughout the West subscribed to outstanding publications such as *The Colored American Magazine, Voice of the Negro, A.M.E. Church Review, Church Review, Howard's American, Richmond Planet, Cleveland Gazette, Indianapolis Freeman,* and *New York Age.*[54] Corporal Joseph Wheelock of the 10th Cavalry stated the situation best in an article published in *The Colored American Magazine.* He encouraged fellow soldiers and the reading audience at large to patronize the race magazines and newspapers: "Do we buy our papers and magazines from other people whose greatest aim is to show us in the worst possible form to the world? Do we patronize the man who at all times is ready to minimize our true manliness?"[55]

Racial prejudice remained one of the nation's most persistent problems at the end of the nineteenth century. Many decades of intimidation, lynchings, and Jim Crow hypocrisy still lay ahead, and progress often seemed to come only at a snail's pace. In retrospect, one could easily argue that race relations had advanced little during the century and that conditions for most black people had not appreciably changed since the demise of the peculiar institution. Likewise, public acknowledgment of the important contributions of black soldiers had never been forthcoming, nor had many white Americans familiarized themselves with the basic history of African American military accomplishments.

Yet by the end of the twentieth century, public perceptions had changed considerably as a new climate of opinion helped rescue these accomplishments from oblivion. In a brief 1996 essay, historian William Leckie could proudly point out that in the preceding eight years, the black regulars had become quite visible for the first time. Countless books, four documentary films, a new U.S. postage stamp, numerous commemorative events, and the dedication of a splendid statue at Ft. Leavenworth, Kansas, which included an address by then chairman of the joint chiefs of staff Gen. Colin Powell, brought about a high level of public awareness that did not exist in earlier times.[56] The new consciousness was long in coming, but when it was finally instilled in a broad cross section of Americans, it affirmed the proud words of the 25th Infantry insignia: "Onward."

NOTES

1. Jack D. Foner, *Blacks and the Military in American History: A New Perspective* (New York: Praeger, 1974), 27–30.

2. Ibid., 34–43. Quintard Taylor, "Comrades of Color: Buffalo Soldiers in the West: 1866–1917," *Colorado Heritage,* Spring 1996, 4.

3. Frank N. Schubert, *Voices of the Buffalo Soldiers: Records, Reports, and Recollections of Military Life and Service in the West* (Albuquerque: University of New Mexico Press, 2003), 5.

4. Taylor, "Comrades of Color," 4.

5. William A. Dobak and Thomas D. Phillips, *The Black Regulars, 1866–1898* (Norman: University of Oklahoma Press, 2001), xi–xii.

6. Jack D. Foner, *The United States Soldier between Two Wars: Army Life and Reforms, 1865–1898* (New York: Humanities Press, 1970), 128.

7. Dobak and Phillips, *Black Regulars,* xv.

8. Quoted in Taylor, "Comrades of Color," 5.

9. Ibid.

10. Foner, *Blacks and the Military,* 52–53.

11. Robert M. Utley, *Cavalier in Buckskin: George Armstrong Custer and the Western Military Frontier* (Norman: University of Oklahoma Press, 1988), 39–40.

12. William H. Leckie, *The Buffalo Soldiers: A Narrative of the Negro Cavalry in the West* (Norman: University of Oklahoma Press, 1967), 7–8. John M. Carroll, ed., *The Black Military Experience in the American West* (New York: Liveright, 1973), 53–59.

13. Edward M. Coffman, *The Old Army: A Portrait of the American Army in Peacetime, 1784–1898* (New York: Oxford University Press, 1986), 366–67.

14. Bill Green, *The Dancing Was Lively: Fort Concho, Texas, a Social History, 1867 to 1882* (San Angelo, TX: Fort Concho Sketches, 1974), 56–57.

15. Ibid., 58.

16. Sandra L. Myres, ed., *Cavalry Wife: The Diary of Eveline M. Alexander, 1866–1867* (College Station: Texas A&M University Press, 1977), 73.

17. Sandra L. Myres, ed., "A Woman's View of the Texas Frontier, 1874: The Diary of Emily K. Andrews," *Southwestern Historical Quarterly* 86 (July 1982): 61–62.

18. Frances M. A. Roe, *Army Letters from an Officer's Wife, 1871–1888* (New York: D. Appleton, 1909), 103–4.

19. Douglas C. McChristian, "'Dress on the Colors, Boys!': Black Noncommissioned Officers in the Regular Army, 1866–1898," *Colorado Heritage,* Spring 1996, 40–41.

20. Ibid. McChristian provides specific examples of black sergeants who did not always serve as good role models for their men (pp. 42–43).

21. Coffman, *Old Army,* 331–32.

22. Leckie, *Buffalo Soldiers,* 26. Frederic Remington, "A Scout with the Buffalo Soldiers," *Century* 15 (April 1889): 899–912. Schubert, *Voices of the Buffalo Soldiers,* 47–49.

23. Dobak and Phillips, *Black Regulars,* xvii, 287n.

24. E.L.N. Glass, comp., *The History of the Tenth Cavalry, 1866–1921* (n.p., 1921). William G. Muller, comp., *The Twenty-fourth Infantry: Past and* Present (n.p., 1923). John H. Nankivell, *History of the Twenty-fifth Regiment, United States Infantry, 1869–1926* (Denver: Smith-Brooks, 1927). Leckie, *Buffalo Soldiers.* Arlen L. Fowler, *The Black Infantry in the West, 1869–1891* (Westport, CT: Greenwood Press, 1971).

25. Richard T. Roome, "A Cavalry Company on the Indian Frontier: A Short History of Troop L, 10th U.S. Cavalry," *Permian Historical Annual* 34 (December 1994): 27–28.

26. Ibid., 28–40.

27. Ibid., 40–41.

28. Coffman, *Old Army,* 369–70.

29. Foner, *United States Soldier,* 138–40. Coffman, *Old Army,* 369–70.

30. Foner, *United States Soldier,* 133–34.

31. Ibid., 135–36.

32. Ibid., 136.

33. Ibid., 136–37.

34. Foner, *Blacks and the Military,* 63–64.

35. Ibid. Bruce J. Dinges, "The Court-Martial of Lieutenant Henry O. Flipper: An Example of Black-White Relationships in the Army, 1881," *American West* 9 (January 1972): 12–17, 59–61. Theodore Harris, ed., *Negro Frontiersman: The Western Memoirs of Henry O. Flipper* (El Paso: Texas Western College Press, 1963).

36. Foner, *Blacks and the Military,* 64. Schubert, *Voices of the Buffalo Soldiers,* 200–3.

37. Quoted in Foner, *Blacks and the Military,* 63.

38. Leo E. Oliva, *Fort Hays, Frontier Army Post, 1865–1889* (Topeka: Kansas State Historical Society, 1980), 36.

39. Ibid., 36–37. James N. Leiker, "Black Soldiers at Fort Hays, Kansas, 1867–1869: A Study in Civilian and Military Violence," *Great Plains Quarterly* 17 (Winter 1997): 4. For the story of a near race riot at nearby Ft. Larned, see Leo E. Oliva, *Fort Larned on the Santa Fe Trail* (Topeka: Kansas State Historical Society, 1982), 51.

40. Patricia E. Lamkin, "Blacks in San Angelo: Relations between Fort Concho and the City, 1875–1889," *West Texas Historical Association Year Book* 66 (1990): 26–37. Susan Miles, "The Soldiers' Riot," *Fort Concho Report* 13 (Spring 1981): 1–12.

41. Miles, "Soldiers' Riot," 12–18. A similar event at Crawford, Nebraska, in 1893 is detailed in Frank N. Schubert, *Buffalo Soldiers, Braves, and the Brass: The Story of Fort Robinson, Nebraska* (Shippensburg, PA: White Mane, 1993), 89–92. Another case of black soldiers joining together to threaten the life of their own white post surgeon, whose neglect had caused the death of an enlisted man, is found in Clayton Williams, *Texas' Last Frontier: Fort Stockton and the Trans-Pecos, 1861–1895,* ed. Ernest Wallace (College Station: Texas A&M University Press, 1982), 169–71.

42. Douglas C. McChristian, "Apaches and Soldiers: Mail Protection in West Texas," *Periodical: Journal of the Council on America's Military Past* 13 (1985): 10–11.

43. Foner, *United States Soldier,* 133.

44. Robert Lee, *Fort Meade and the Black Hills* (Lincoln: University of Nebraska Press, 1991), 80–85.

45. Ibid., 84–85.

46. Foner, *Blacks and the Military,* 70–71.

47. Gerald M. Adams, *The Post Near Cheyenne: A History of Fort D. A. Russell, 1867–1930* (Boulder: Pruett, 1989), 96.

48. C. L. Sonnichsen, *Ten Texas Feuds* (Albuquerque: University of New Mexico Press, 1957), 135–54. Walter Prescott Webb, *The Texas Rangers: A Century of Frontier Defense* (Austin: University of Texas Press, 1965), 345–54.

49. Maurice G. Fulton, *History of the Lincoln County War,* ed. Robert N. Mullin (Tucson: University of Arizona Press, 1968), 70–120. Frederick Nolan, *The Lincoln County War: A Documentary History* (Norman: University of Oklahoma Press, 1992), 314–16, 362–70, 378–90.

50. Nolan, *Lincoln County War,* 395–419. Robert M. Utley, *High Noon in Lincoln: Violence on the Western Frontier* (Albuquerque: University of New Mexico Press, 1987), 66–78, 92–124, 125–36. Monroe Lee Billington, *New Mexico's Buffalo Soldiers, 1866–1900* (Niwot: University Press of Colorado, 1991), 69–86.

51. Frank N. Schubert, "The Suggs Affray: The Black Cavalry in the Johnson County War," *Western Historical Quarterly* 4 (January 1973): 57–68.

52. W. Sherman Savage, "The Role of Negro Soldiers in Protecting the Indian Territory from Intruders," *Journal of Negro History* 36 (January 1951): 25–34. The larger story of the illegal "boomer" efforts of the 1880s is related in Carl Coke Rister, *Land Hunger: David L. Payne and the Oklahoma Boomers* (Norman: University of Oklahoma Press, 1942).

53. Frank N. Schubert, "The Fort Robinson Y.M.C.A., 1902–1907: A Social Organization in a Black Regiment," *Nebraska History* 55 (Summer 1974): 165–68.

54. Ibid., 177–79.

55. Ibid., 171.

56. William H. Leckie, "Foreword," in Arlen L. Fowler, *The Black Infantry in the West, 1869–1891,* new ed. (Norman: University of Oklahoma Press, 1996), xvi.

10 TWILIGHT OF THE OLD ARMY

Few Americans would have realized it at the time, but 1890 marked something of an emblematic conclusion to the history of the so-called old army. In December of that year, soldiers fought their last major engagements against Native Americans in the Pine Ridge country of southwestern South Dakota. These tragic events, which evolved from white overreaction to the Ghost Dance, were not the result of careful military planning, but rather were an anticlimax to a century of Indian-Army conflict. The massacre of more than 200 Lakota people at Wounded Knee Creek never should have happened. Poor military decision making, rough searches of frightened Indian prisoners, and a war hysteria created by an irresponsible corps of journalists contributed to the final debacle in a long history of Indian wars. The Lakota forever regarded these events as the "breaking of the sacred circle" and the beginning of catastrophic times in the new century ahead. For the regular army, the event attracted an unflattering federal investigation and harsh condemnation from reformers. Even the awarding of a record number of 28 Medals of Honor following the Wounded Knee episode seemed more a mockery of the military profession than an honoring of battlefield heroism.[1]

The year 1890 also served as a different kind of milestone for the old army. By that time, the vast majority of far-flung posts and substations that once had dotted the western landscape were now closed. The so-called Indian threat was over, communities were being rapidly settled even in the most remote areas, and reliable transportation networks had reached a level hardly imaginable at the time of the Civil War. Virtually overnight, a venerable old fortress could be turned into a ghost town as soldiers and civilians alike abandoned its environs. When companies of the 9th Cavalry departed Ft. Selden, New Mexico, in 1890, they carried with them everything that was potentially usable—furniture, supply wagons, livestock, field guns, clothing, cooking equipment, books, and miscellaneous equipment. They also stripped off the doors, windows, window frames, and salvageable lumber to transport to their next duty assignment at Ft. Bayard. All surplus items—tents, firewood, hay, coal, pack saddles, and water wagons—were sold at auction or shipped to other southwestern posts.[2]

CLOSING THE FRONTIER FORTS

In two years alone, 1890 and 1891, approximately one-fourth of all military posts were closed. By one estimate, 255 forts, subposts, and temporary stations had existed in the continental United States in 1869, a record high. By the same estimate in 1892, only 96 forts remained active, 33 of which were located east of the Mississippi River.[3] Though there was no significant decrease in the numbers of soldiers allotted by Congress, consolidation of regiments at one or two posts rather than a scattering of companies at six or seven installations became the norm. Noting the inevitable pattern of consolidation as early as 1881, Gen. William Tecumseh Sherman pronounced great value in the closing of many obsolete posts, but only after thorough consideration by senior officers in the field. He especially championed significant savings in the closing of harbor forts, many of which traced their origins to the first three decades of the nation.[4]

In this same report, Sherman echoed the sentiment of other career officers that economics and politics more often decided the fate of posts than did sound military judgment. One of the specific examples he referred to was Ft. Stanton, New Mexico, which had been built just north of the Mescalero Apache reservation to keep a watchful eye on its residents and upon white interlopers who periodically trespassed on reservation land. When Col. John Pope tried to deactivate the post in 1870 on the grounds that it was too isolated, too expensive to supply, and too far away to protect settlements on the Rio Grande, his efforts were rebuffed by civilians throughout the area. It seems that a majority of the petitioners lived directly or indirectly off of the government contracts at Ft. Stanton and on the reservation. A frustrated Pope observed, "The removal of the garrison, however (as indeed, of any other), will occasion loud outcry and endless petitions and representations. Once establish a post and it seems nearly impossible, without infinite clamor and objection, ever to remove it."[5] Indeed, Ft. Stanton remained an active post until 1896, and after its closing, it was subsequently reopened by the Public Health Service as a U.S. Marine hospital.[6]

Some communities launched successful efforts to keep their forts open, and others watched their economies dry up soon after the soldiers marched away. At Ft. Robinson, in the northernmost point of Nebraska's panhandle, discussions began in 1887 about the installation's closing. Residents of nearby Crawford and Chadron marshaled their efforts to fight the budgetary axe, even arguing that the Lakota warriors on nearby Pine Ridge Reservation would begin killing settlers as soon as the army left Dawes County. They found an influential supporter in Nebraska senator Charles Manderson, who was a member of the powerful Committee on Military Affairs. Further endorsements by Gen. George Crook and Quartermaster Maj. George B. Dandy not only helped rescue the post from oblivion, but also helped wrangle additional funds for its expansion.[7]

Not so fortunate were the residents of Mobeetie in the eastern section of the Texas panhandle, who, in 1890, were desperate to stop the closing of Ft. Elliott. Though the last significant Indian fighting in the area had occurred 15 years earlier, civilians petitioned the state governor and their congressional delegation that the removal of troops would result in a massacre by Comanches and Kiowas located on reservations near Ft. Sill, Indian Territory. Despite their plea that "we ask assistance in our behalf for the sole purpose of securing the needed protection of life and property to our citizens," congressmen rightly judged that economic concerns were the real motive behind the petition. Ft. Elliott was closed in October 1890, and Mobeetie gradually declined, even losing its county seat status in 1907.[8]

The case of Bozeman, Montana, turned out quite differently, although its citizens also panicked upon hearing initial reports that Ft. Ellis might soon close. Petitioners warned about potential Indian problems and how the loss of military contracts would devastate the entire region. Yet by the time the closing occurred in 1886, the public clamor had quieted itself. When the citizens of Bozeman discovered that the large military reservation would be opened for private purchase of lands, they saw a unique financial opportunity for themselves. The local newspaper did not even mention the final exodus of the troops, but the *Helena Independent* did. In an ebullient tone, it congratulated the citizens of Bozeman for gaining access to the government land "as it will contribute more to the development of the thrifty little city than its maintenance as a dilapidated two-company post."[9]

If some installations could be closed with so little emotion, then what was the nature of public reaction to the passing of the soldiers who comprised the Indian-fighting army? The answer was partly evident in the handling of soldier burials, both at the time of interment and in the long-term maintenance of the cemeteries that held their remains. By regulation, no more than 10 dollars could be allocated for burial of an enlisted man who died while on active duty. More often than not, members of his own company would have to pass the hat for contributions or initiate a tax among themselves to pay for a better coffin than the plain pine box each deceased trooper was entitled to.[10] When a popular sergeant of Company D, 3rd Cavalry, was killed by Indians near Ft. Washakie, Wyoming, in 1882, his men pooled their money so that his body could be shipped back to Massachusetts for a proper burial among his family members.[11] Likewise, when Sgt. Bowers was killed by Sioux near Ft. Phil Kearny in 1866, the enlisted men of his company swore vengeance in his name, and Capt. Frederick H. Brown placed his own corps badge across the man's body as it was lowered into the grave. Capt. Brown was killed by the same Indians two weeks later in what became known as the Fetterman disaster.[12]

Class also played a significant role in the burials. The remains of officers who died while on active duty often made their way back to their familial homes when relatives paid the full costs of transferring the bodies to cemeteries where they could be buried among friends and loved ones. Most enlisted men were not so fortunate, especially since many of them came from relatively poor families or were first- and second-generation immigrants. Their final resting place was most often in the post cemetery. Yet at that most melancholy of moments, soldiers' debts followed them to the grave. When a company commander wrote to the parents or wife of a deceased trooper, expressing his deep emotions about the loss, he usually included any pay and allowances that the soldier was entitled to at the time of his death. However, the company commander was also empowered to seek economic restitution to cover the expenses incurred by a soldier prior to his death.[13]

Care of cemeteries was a low priority for the War Department, at least prior to the 1880s, when some protective regulations were finally issued. Most lacked fences, few had permanent gravestones, and all were subject to removal to other nearby locations if the post needed to use the cemetery space for construction of new buildings.[14] Ft. Fred Steele, Wyoming, was a typical example of the widespread neglect, for in every year between 1881 and 1884, inspectors drew attention to the deteriorating condition of the post cemetery. The report of 1886 concluded that it "is a very dreary spectacle": an unpainted fence surrounding the rocky hillside, few headboards to mark the graves, no walkways, no shrubs or trees, and the graves not even arranged in a symmetrical pattern. When Ft. Fred Steele was deactivated from service later that year, its cemetery contained the graves of 1 officer, 24 soldiers, 3 children of officers, 5 children of soldiers, 2 soldiers' wives, and 45 civilians.[15]

As more western installations closed during the 1890s, belated efforts were made to protect the remains of military burials by removing the bodies to a small number of national military cemeteries that could be properly maintained. Most of the soldiers who originally had been buried at Nebraska, Wyoming, and Colorado forts had their remains moved to the sprawling Ft. McPherson National Cemetery east of North Platte, Nebraska. Likewise, many of the Texas military burials were moved to the San Antonio National Cemetery. In these and other cases, the deceased received better treatment decades after their deaths than they did at the original burial sites. At these large national cemeteries, they would also rest beside veterans of America's twentieth-century wars, amid tree-lined roads and carefully manicured environs. But even at the time of the reinterment, the issue of long-term neglect was widely evident. For instance, when a private contractor removed the bodies of officers, enlisted men, and their wives and children from Ft. Davis to San Antonio in 1891, many of the identities could not be confirmed. The absence and deterioration of markers as well as the relocation of some burials over the years made proper identification an inexact process. Contractor David Merrill reported that he removed 100 bodies in 1891 for shipment to San Antonio, but in 1968, National Park Service excavations turned up additional bodies on the premises—several soldiers and two children.[16]

PENSIONS FOR VETERANS AND THEIR FAMILIES

If the dead were so easily neglected and forgotten amid military regulations, then what of the families of those men who died while on active service? One merely has to examine the collective fates of the widows of the officers and enlisted men who died in the battle of Little Big Horn to understand one of the army's greatest ambiguities throughout the entire span of the nineteenth century. Women and children simply had no official place on a military reservation. They were permitted to be with their husbands only at the discretion of each fort's commanding officer. With the death of their husbands, they lost even that unofficial claim to residence, and they were expected to leave the post as soon as they could get their affairs in order. Elizabeth Custer found herself in that situation late in June of 1876, as did at least 12 other officers' widows and between two and three dozen soldiers' widows who were living at Ft. Abraham Lincoln, Dakota Territory.[17]

Within three weeks after the first reporting of the destitute status of these women and their children, the interservice magazine *Army and Navy Journal* initiated a national fund-raiser in their behalf. The response was gratifying, for during the first six weeks, donations totaled 5,057 dollars. The Philadelphia sugar refiners McKean, Newhall, and Borie contributed 500 dollars to the fund, followed by 250 dollars from Potter Palmer of Chicago hotel fame. While civilian businesses and individuals contributed generously, most gifts came from military personnel, averaging from 20 dollars down to 50-cent donations from not-so-affluent enlisted men. The full garrison at Ft. Lyon, Colorado, forwarded a 100-dollar money order, a contribution that was tripled by the residents of the Soldiers' Home in Washington, D.C. Aid also came from the Chicago and North Western Railway Company, which offered free transit for the widows and orphans from St. Paul to Chicago. Midway through the campaign, Elizabeth Custer and two other officers' wives requested that a larger percentage of the accrued funds be reserved for the enlisted men's widows because their suffering was the greatest. In the eventual distribution of these funds, officers' wives received 7,500 dollars, while families of deceased enlisted men shared from the total of 6,300 dollars.[18]

Meanwhile, several additional attempts were made to provide financial assistance to the bereaved families. On July 15, Representative Alpheus Williams sponsored two bills advocating a 50-dollar monthly pension for Mrs. Custer and an 80-dollar monthly award to her husband's destitute parents. Following passage by the House of Representatives, the two bills languished in committee in the Senate. Not until six years later would Elizabeth Custer finally receive a 50-dollar monthly pension. Despite her rather meager financial status at that time, she turned down several questionable efforts to raise money for her. She likewise set out to pay family debts so as to preserve her husband's reputation in the face of possible future criticism.[19]

Attempts to gain congressional aid for the other widows proved even more problematic. On July 24, 1876, the House received a bill to provide a special pension fund for all the women and children left destitute by the Little Big Horn disaster. Opponents of the bill, arguing that each case should be handled individually, transferred it to the Committee on Invalid Pensions for further study. Effectively killed by inaction, this piece of legislation never returned to the House floor for further consideration. Subsequent attempts to assure special pensions for six other officers' wives encountered such stiff resistance that none of the pleas produced any results.[20]

The pension issue for surviving spouses and children remained controversial to the end of the nineteenth century, but a new law in 1890 did establish some degree of coverage. At that time, government records showed 104,456 army widows, minor children, and dependent relatives on the pension rolls. Of the total, approximately 96,000 pensioners of deceased enlisted men received 12 dollars per month, the great majority of these being from the Civil War era rather than from frontier service. Larger amounts were allowable for families of deceased officers, but the stipends had to be established on a case-by-case basis, a procedure that required months or years of diligent effort. The average payment in these cases was no more than 20 dollars per month.[21]

If the issue of pensions for dependents proved to be a continuing source of complaint, the situation for surviving veterans was not much better. Those who suffered incapacitating wounds in combat were eligible to seek compensation at the time they were mustered out of service. Throughout the late nineteenth century, they were paid a fixed monthly amount, depending on the perceived severity of the wound. A soldier who suffered the loss of an arm was entitled only to 15 dollars per month, and other significant injuries were compensated in similarly small amounts. Amputees were eligible for artificial limbs and extended treatment at the Soldier's Home in Washington, D.C., but only if spaces were available and if they were willing to accept relocation to the nation's capital.[22]

A perceived breakthrough in veterans' legislation did occur in 1885, with even the interservice journal *Army and Navy Journal* proudly declaring that "faithful soldiers have now something to look forward to, and another inducement for the performance of duty during the allotted period." This new military retirement law guaranteed that each enlisted man who had served 30 years could henceforth receive three-fourths of the pay and allowances that he was collecting at the time of his retirement. Unfortunately, this legislation would have helped very few veterans since only a tiny percentage of the army's enlisted men would have ever completed three decades of active duty.[23]

Amid the frequent complaints against the pension system, the most strident criticism came from veterans of the frontier-era army who were paid, on average, half the amount that Civil War–era servicemen received. The double standard of compensation was clearly unfair, and it reflected the growing power of the Grand Army of the Republic to represent Civil War veterans, while at the same time, former members of the numerically smaller frontier army had no such influential organization to press their claims. Not until December 1923 did an independent group, the National Indian War Veterans, promote the issue and gain national attention. Their mouthpiece was the monthly *Winners of the West,* published in St. Joseph, Missouri, and competently edited by George W. Webb. The newspaper became a forum for Indian war veterans to explain their often dire economic circumstances and to build a lobbying force for congressional action. *Winners of the West* declared itself to be "the only paper in the United States of America devoted exclusively to the pension interests of veterans, widows and orphan children of Indian wars and survivors of the old army of the plains."[24]

Perhaps as many as 200 pension-related letters and articles written by retired officers and enlisted men filled the newspaper during the first several years. Veterans who wrote these letters—many of them in their seventies and eighties—evidenced great pride at having served in the Indian-fighting army, and many wrote descriptions of their most memorable experiences. But the one issue that linked all their efforts was the desire for equality within the capricious pension system. James E. Foreman, formerly of the 19th Infantry, complained that although he had joined the army during the Civil War to fight southern rebels, his unit had been dispatched to Kansas and Indian Territory. By happenstance, he was now entitled to a pension less than half the size of other veterans who had fought in the eastern theater of combat.[25] C. W. Ames, who had served as a frontier infantryman for 10 years, reported the same irregularity in pension awards as well as the fact that he was not entitled to a homestead claim, while many veterans of the Civil War were.[26] C. A. Bills, formerly of the 19th Kansas Volunteer Cavalry, had enlisted in 1868 for service against Comanches and Kiowas, but under the alias of Frank Button. When he later applied for a pension under the Disability Act of 1890, he was denied coverage, even though he could prove that he indeed had been a veteran honorably discharged.[27]

If historians reduced all the sad tales of Indian war veterans to the story of one man, it might well be that of Pvt. John Burkman, who joined the 7th Cavalry in 1870, served in the Yellowstone Expedition of 1873, the Black Hills Expedition of 1874, the Little Big Horn campaign of 1876, and the Nez Percé Pursuit a year later. He was discharged for disability on May 17, 1879, a soldier who had never advanced through the ranks, but one who left his name on the fringes of the George and Elizabeth Custer legacy. He had served as Custer's striker, or what Elizabeth affectionately referred to as a "military servant." Although illiterate, moody, and much the loner, Burkman remained steadfast in his loyalty to the Custer family. Throughout the rest of her life, Elizabeth periodically wrote letters in his behalf hoping to boost his pension because he lived in such impoverished conditions. Except for brief stays in the Montana's Soldiers' Home and the California Soldiers' Home, he remained in Billings, Montana, where he became more frustrated and ill tempered. By the World War I era, he was drawing a disability check of six dollars per month when he asked for and received a two-dollar increase. In the last several years of his life, he was advanced to a payment of 70 dollars per month, largely because of the efforts of powerful people in Montana. Elizabeth Custer wrote him a final letter, which he dearly treasured, a letter congratulating him on finally securing a worthy pension.[28]

Despite improvements in his financial situation, 86-year-old John Burkman continued to live like a hermit, immersed in romanticized memories and with his temper driving away many of his remaining friends. On a Friday afternoon, following a rare meal taken at a Billings restaurant, he returned to his shack, sat down on the front porch, and "fired his own salute" by shooting himself in the head. He was buried among fellow soldiers at Little Big Horn battlefield, honoring a request that he had made many times throughout his life. Clearly John Burkman's 1925 suicide was not primarily caused by his impoverishment at the hands of the capricious military pension system. His personal demons were traceable back to Custer's Last Stand, the death of the man he most venerated, and the fact that he had survived combat that day rather than falling beside the other 7th Cavalrymen. Furthermore, he lamented how quickly the nation had forgotten about those heroic events of June 25, 1876, on the plains of Montana, and on so many other western battlefields of the late nineteenth century. It was as if the events had never happened, and the nation could not care less about understanding those long-ago events.[29]

THE LEGACY OF THE SOLDIERS OF 1865–1898

Four years prior to Burkman's suicide, another group of veterans—exclusively from the officer corps—convened for their 5th annual meeting. These members of the Order of the Indian Wars exchanged greetings, conducted organizational business, and listened to the keynote address by Gen. Charles King, formerly of the 5th Cavalry and author of a series of popular novels about frontier military life. The subject of his address was the Sioux campaign of 1876, including the battle of Little Big Horn. The events he described were already quite familiar to the audience, but in the closing moments of the talk, he offered the following words of praise to all ranks of the old army:

> A more thankless task, a more perilous service, a more exacting test of leadership, soldiership, morale and discipline no army in Christendom has ever been called upon to undertake than that which for eighty years was the lot of the little fighting force of regulars who cleared the way across the continent for the emigrant and settler, whose summer and winter stood guard over the wide frontier, whose lives were spent in almost utter isolation, whose lonely death was marked and mourned only by sorrowing comrade, or mayhap grief-stricken widow and children left destitute and despairing. There never was a warfare which, like this, had absolutely nothing to hold the soldier stern and steadfast to the bitter end, but the solemn sense of Soldier Duty.[30]

Gen. King thus paid homage to veterans of the U.S. Army, and with these nostalgic words, he implied that this bygone era of the blue-coated soldier would never again return. America's continental empire had become internationalized in 1898 with the outcome of the Spanish-American War, and the nation further expanded its influence as a world power in the wake of World War I. Few Americans seemingly cared about the old veterans, their accomplishments, or their problems. No official grand parades recognized their long service, as had celebratory parades at the end of the Civil War, Spanish-American War, and World War I.

Not until the Second World War did Americans enter an era of national unity and patriotic fervor that led to a newfound interest in the old army. Starting in the 1950s, the National Park Service began to acquire and interpret properties associated with the frontier soldier and the fabled Indian wars. Director John Ford's army trilogy of the late 1940s and early 1950s gave a positive voice to old soldiers now consummately portrayed on the silver screen by the likes of John Wayne, Victor McLaglen, and Henry Fonda. The emerging television medium also presented a spate of "westerns" that generally portrayed the frontier army in a favorable light. Unfortunately, the War in Vietnam and other challenges to the American "Establishment" during the late 1960s and 1970s brought into question much of the perceived righteousness of the military system and recast Indians as Vietnamese freedom fighters at Sand Creek, Little Big Horn, and Wounded Knee. In the wake of these negative portrayals, the old army virtually disappeared from American popular culture in the closing decades of the twentieth century.

The story of the American army during the years 1865 and 1898 will always be viewed in myopic terms. For some, it will remain a vital part of an intensely romanticized era of the nation's history. Images of grueling campaigns, courageous last stands, and establishment of "civilization" in the midst of "savagery" mark the centerpiece of this immensely popular but simplistic view. Others will continue to see the frontier army as a bloody tool of political and economic special interests that not only destroyed the land base of Native Americans, but also exploited the labor of the American underclass, while rushing toward the acquisition of wealth and power.

Amid these two polarized views, there stands another stereotype of the age that dominates modern interpretations of the frontier army. Because it is often referred to in retrospect as a "peacetime army," its vital mission in American history is unfairly trivialized. This tendency to gloss over the military's diverse roles during the closing decades of the nineteenth century misses the important point that the army was the right arm of the federal government in developing the western landscape. For all its contributions to the history of the Trans-Mississippi West—both its positive and negative influences—the army was a dynamic and active agency for social change. It can no longer be viewed as a passive entity, biding its time between the glory days of the Civil War and the intoxicating future of global expansion. To perpetuate these three myopic views is to neglect and misinterpret an important institution in American history and to dishonor those who made their lives in the old army.

NOTES

1. Robert M. Utley, *The Last Days of the Sioux Nation* (New Haven, CT: Yale University Press, 1963), 200–85.

2. Monroe Billington, "Black Soldiers at Fort Selden, New Mexico, 1866–1891," *New Mexico Historical Review* 62 (January 1987): 79–80.

3. Edward M. Coffman, *The Old Army: A Portrait of the American Army in Peacetime, 1784–1898* (New York: Oxford University Press, 1986), 282, 345–46. Robert M. Utley, *Frontier Regulars: The United States Army and the Indian, 1866–1891* (New York: Macmillan, 1973), 46–47. Jack D. Foner, *The United States Soldier between Two Wars: Army Life and Reforms, 1865–1898* (New York: Humanities Press, 1970), 2.

4. Coffman, *Old Army,* 345–46.

5. Raymond L. Welty, "Supplying the Frontier Military Posts," *Kansas Historical Quarterly* 7 (May 1938): 160.

6. Robert W. Frazer, *Forts of the West: Military Forts and Presidios and Posts Commonly Called Forts West of the Mississippi River to 1898* (Norman: University of Oklahoma Press, 1965), 103–4.

7. Thomas R. Buecker, "The 1887 Expansion of Fort Robinson," *Nebraska History* 68 (Summer 1987): 86–87.

8. David E. Kyvig, "Policing the Panhandle: Fort Elliott, Texas, 1875–1890," *Red River Valley Historical Review* 1 (Fall 1974): 231–32. James M. Oswald, "History of Fort Elliott," *Panhandle-Plains Historical Review* 32 (1959): 50–53.

9. Thomas C. Rust, "Settlers, Soldiers, and Scoundrels: Economic Tension in a Frontier Military Town," *Military History of the West* 31 (Fall 2002): 137–38.

10. Foner, *United States Soldier,* 73.

11. Don Rickey Jr., *Forty Miles a Day on Beans and Hay: The Enlisted Soldier Fighting the Indian Wars* (Norman: University of Oklahoma Press, 1963), 332–33.

12. Margaret Irvin Carrington, *Absaraka, Home of the Crows: Being the Experiences of an Officer's Wife on the Plains* (Philadelphia: J. B. Lippincott, 1868), 197–98.

13. Dale F. Giese, "Soldiers at Play: A History of Social Life at Fort Union, New Mexico, 1851–1891" (PhD diss., University of New Mexico, 1969), 195. Rickey, *Forty Miles a Day,* 334.

14. Mary L. Williams, "Care of the Dead (and Lack of It) at 19th Century Posts," *Periodical: Journal of the Council on America's Military Past* 13, no. 1 (1984): 14.

15. Robert A. Murray, "Fort Fred Steele: Desert Outpost on the Union Pacific," *Annals of Wyoming* 44 (Fall 1972): 195.

16. Louis A. Holmes, *Fort McPherson, Nebraska, Cottonwood, N.T.: Guardian of the Tracks and Trails* (Lincoln: Johnson, 1963), 62, 93–94. Williams, "Care of the Dead," 23–27.

17. Edgar I. Stewart, "The Custer Battle and Widows' Weeds," *Montana, Magazine of Western History* 22 (January 1972): 53–57.

18. Michael L. Tate, "The Girl He Left Behind: Elizabeth Custer and the Making of a Legend," *Red River Valley Historical Review* 5 (Winter 1980): 8–9.

19. Ibid., 9.

20. Ibid., 9–10.

21. Patricia R. Blackman, "The History of Disability Legislation for Regular Army Widows of the Indian Wars: 1790–1890" (MA thesis, University of Nebraska at Omaha, 1982), 154–55.

22. Rickey, *Forty Miles a Day,* 330–31.

23. Foner, *United States Soldier,* 84.

24. Lora Taylor Gray, " 'Winners of the West': A Personal Reminiscence of Lauren Winfield Aldrich," *Journal of the West* 33 (January 1994): 98. "Introduction," *Winners of the West,* December 1923, 4.

25. "Letter of James E. Foreman," *Winners of the West,* February 1924, 11.

26. "Letter of C. W. Ames," *Winners of the West,* October 1924, 9

27. "Letter of C. A. Bills," *Winners of the West,* April 1926, 3.

28. Glendolin Damon Wagner, *Old Neutriment,* with an introduction by Brian W. Dippie (Lincoln: University of Nebraska Press, 1989), v–viii, 19–24.

29. Ibid., 32–33. Shirley A. Leckie, *Elizabeth Bacon Custer and the Making of a Myth* (Norman: University of Oklahoma Press, 1993), 298.

30. John M. Carroll, ed., *The Papers of the Order of Indian Wars* (Fort Collins, CO: Old Army Press, 1975), 46.

BIBLIOGRAPHY

GENERAL STUDIES

Athearn, Robert G. *Forts of the Upper Missouri.* Englewood Cliffs, NJ: Prentice Hall, 1967.

Chambers, John Whiteclay, II. "The New Military History: Myth and Reality." *Journal of Military History* 55 (July 1991): 395–406.

Clendenen, Clarence C. *Blood on the Border: The United States Army and the Mexican Irregulars.* New York: Macmillan, 1969.

Coffman, Edward M. *The Old Army: A Portrait of the American Army in Peacetime, 1784–1898.* New York: Oxford University Press, 1986.

Cooper, Jerry M. "The Army's Search for a Mission, 1865–1890." In *Against All Enemies: Interpretations of American History from Colonial Times to the Present,* ed. Kenneth J. Hagan and William R. Roberts. Westport, CT: Greenwood Press, 1986.

Dupuy, Raoul. "A Study of the Cavalry of the United States." *Journal of the United States Cavalry Association* 12 (March 1899): 68–92.

Foner, Jack D. *The United States Soldier between Two Wars: Army Life and Reforms, 1865–1898.* New York: Humanities Press, 1970.

Hale, Henry. "The Soldier, the Advance Guard of Civilization." *Mississippi Valley Historical Association Proceedings* 7 (1913–1914): 93–98.

Hutton, Paul A. "The Frontier Army." In *American Frontier and Western Issues: A Historiographical Review,* ed. Roger L. Nichols. New York: Greenwood Press, 1986.

———, ed. *Soldiers West: Biographies from the Military Frontier.* Lincoln: University of Nebraska Press, 1987.

Knight, Oliver. *Life and Manners in the Frontier Army.* Norman: University of Oklahoma Press, 1978.

Linn, Brian McAllister. "The Long Twilight of the Frontier Army." *Western Historical Quarterly* 27 (Summer 1996): 141–67.

Matloff, Maurice, ed. *American Military History.* Office of the Chief of Military History. Washington, DC: U.S. Government Printing Office, 1969.

Mattison, Ray H. "The Army Post on the Northern Plains, 1865–1885." *Nebraska History* 35 (March 1954): 17–43.

Millett, Allan R., and Peter Maslowski. *For the Common Defense: A Military History of the United States of America.* New York: Free Press, 1984.

Morton, Desmond. "Cavalry or Police: Keeping the Peace on Two Adjacent Frontiers, 1870–1900." *Journal of Canadian Studies* 12 (Spring 1977): 27–37.

Nevin, David. *The Soldiers.* New York: Time-Life Books, 1973.

Richardson, Rupert N. *The Frontier of Northwest Texas, 1846 to 1876: Advance and Defense by the Pioneer Settlers of the Cross Timbers and Prairies.* Glendale, CA: Arthur H. Clark, 1963.

Smith, Sherry L. "Lost Soldiers: Re-searching the Army in the American West." *Western Historical Quarterly* 29 (Summer 1998): 149–63.

Smith, Thomas T. *The Old Army in Texas: A Research Guide to the U.S. Army in Nineteenth-Century Texas.* Austin: Texas State Historical Association, 2000.

Tate, James P., ed. *The American Military on the Frontier: Proceedings of the Seventh Military History Symposium.* Washington, DC: Office of Air Force History, 1978.

Tate, Michael L. *The Frontier Army in the Settlement of the West.* Norman: University of Oklahoma Press, 1999.

Urwin, Gregory J. W. *The United States Cavalry: An Illustrated History, 1776–1944.* Norman: University of Oklahoma Press, 2003.

Utley, Robert M. *Frontier Regulars: The United States Army and the Indian, 1866–1891.* New York: Macmillan, 1973.

———. *Frontiersmen in Blue: The United States Army and the Indian, 1848–1865.* New York: Macmillan, 1967.

———. *The Indian Frontier of the American West 1846–1890.* Albuquerque: University of New Mexico Press, 1984.

Weigley, Russell F. *The American Way of War: A History of United States Military Strategy and Policy.* New York: Macmillan, 1973.

Welty, Raymond L. "The Army Fort of the Frontier, 1860–1870." *North Dakota Historical Quarterly* 2 (April 1928): 155–67.

———. "The Daily Life of the Frontier Soldier." *Cavalry Journal* 36 (1927): 584–94.

Wooster, Robert. "The Army and the Politics of Expansion: Texas and the Southwestern Borderlands, 1870–1886." *Southwestern Historical Quarterly* 93 (October 1989): 151–67.

———. *The Military and United States Indian Policy, 1865–1903.* New Haven, CT: Yale University Press, 1988.

———. *Soldiers, Sutlers and Settlers: Garrison Life on the Texas Frontier.* College Station: Texas A&M University Press, 1987.

Wormser, Richard. *The Yellowlegs: The Story of the United States Cavalry.* Garden City, NY: Doubleday, 1966.

Young, William D. "The Military and Kansas History." *Kansas History* 27 (Winter 2004–2005): 264–82.

ADMINISTRATION

Altshuler, Constance Wynn. *Chains of Command: Arizona and the Army.* Tucson: Arizona Historical Society, 1981.

Archambeau, Ernest R., ed. "Monthly Reports of the Fourth Cavalry 1872–1874." *Panhandle-Plains Historical Review* 38 (1965): 95–154.

Barr, Ronald J. *The Progressive Army: U.S. Army Command and Administration, 1870–1914.* New York: St. Martin's Press, 1998.

Brereton, T. R. *Educating the U.S. Army: Arthur L. Wagner and Reform, 1875–1905*. Lincoln: University of Nebraska Press, 2000.

Conway, Walter C., ed. "Colonel Edmund Schriver's Inspector-General Report on Military Posts in Texas, November 1872–January 1873." *Southwestern Historical Quarterly* 67 (April 1964): 559–83.

Clary, David A., and Joseph W. A. Whitmore. *The Inspectors General of the United States Army, 1777–1903*. Washington, DC: Office of the Inspector General and Center for Military History, U.S. Army, 1987.

Derthick, Martha. *The National Guard in Politics*. Cambridge, MA: Harvard University Press, 1965.

Emerson, William K. *Marksmanship in the U.S. Army: A History of Medals, Shooting Programs, and Training*. Norman: University of Oklahoma Press, 2004.

Freedom, Gary S. "Military Forts and Logistical Self-Sufficiency on the Northern Great Plains, 1866–1891." *North Dakota History* 50 (Spring 1983): 4–11.

Guentzel, Richard. "The Department of the Platte and Western Settlement, 1866–1877." *Nebraska History* 56 (Fall 1975): 389–417.

Harte, John Bret. "Conflict at San Carlos: The Military-Civilian Struggle for Control, 1882–1885." *Arizona and the West* 15 (Spring 1973): 27–44.

Hill, Jim Dan. *The Minute Man in Peace and War: A History of the National Guard*. Harrisburg, PA: Stackpole, 1964.

Holt, W. Stull. *The Office of the Chief of Engineers of the Army: Its Non-military History, Activities, and Organization*. Baltimore: Johns Hopkins University Press, 1923.

Jamieson, Perry D. *Crossing the Deadly Ground: United States Army Tactics, 1865–1899*. Tuscaloosa: University of Alabama Press, 1994.

Kime, Wayne R., ed. *The Sherman Tour Journals of Colonel Richard Irving Dodge*. Norman: University of Oklahoma Press, 2002.

Langley, Lester D. "The Democratic Tradition and Military Reform, 1878–1885." *Southwestern Social Science Quarterly* 48 (September 1967): 192–200.

Logan, John A. *The Volunteer Soldier of America*. Chicago: R. S. Peale, 1887.

Merritt, Wesley. "Some Defects in Our Cavalry System." *United Service* 1 (October 1879): 557–61.

Miller, Darlis A. "The Role of the Army Inspector in the Southwest: Nelson H. Davis in New Mexico and Arizona, 1863–1873." *New Mexico Historical Review* 59 (April 1984): 137–64.

Temple, Frank M. "Colonel B. H. Grierson's Administration of the District of the Pecos." *West Texas Historical Association Year Book* 38 (1962): 85–96.

Upton, Emory. *The Armies of Asia and Europe*. New York: D. Appleton, 1878.

———. *The Military Policy of the United States from 1775*. Washington, DC: U.S. Government Printing Office, 1904.

Wade, Arthur P. "The Military Command Structure: The Great Plains, 1853–1891." *Journal of the West* 15 (July 1976): 5–22.

Weigley, Russell F. *Towards an American Army: Military Thought from Washington to Marshall*. New York: Columbia University Press, 1962.

MILITARY LAW

Callan, John F. *The Military Laws of the United States*. Baltimore: John Murphy, 1858.

De Hart, William Chetwood. *Observations on Military Law, and the Constitution and Practice of Courts-Martial, with a Summary of the Law of Evidence, As Applicable to Military*

Trials; Adapted to the Laws, Regulations and Customs of the Army and Navy of the United States. New York: D. Appleton, 1869.

Glasson, William H. *Federal Military Pensions in the United States.* New York: Oxford University Press, 1918.

Graham, Stanley S. "Duty, Life and Law in the Old Army, 1865–1890." *Military History of Texas and the Southwest* 12, no. 4 (1970): 273–81.

"Lawlessness in the Army." *Frank Leslie's Illustrated Weekly* 85 (December 9, 1897): 370.

McDermott, John D. "Crime and Punishment in the United States Army: A Phase of Fort Laramie History." *Journal of the West* 7 (April 1968): 246–55.

Shindler, Henry. *History of the United States Military Prison.* Fort Leavenworth, KS: Army Service Schools Press, 1911.

Sibbald, John R. "Frontier Inebriates with Epaulets." *Montana, Magazine of Western History* 19 (Summer 1969): 50–57.

Woodward, George A. "The Difference Between Military and Martial Law." *United Service* 1 (October 1879): 635–43.

RECONSTRUCTION DUTY

Dawson, Joseph G., III. *Army Generals and Reconstruction: Louisiana, 1862–1877.* Baton Rouge: Louisiana State University Press, 1982.

Donald, David H. *Liberty and Union.* Lexington, MA: D. C. Heath, 1978.

Foner, Eric. *Reconstruction: America's Unfinished Revolution, 1863–1877.* New York: Harper and Row, 1988.

Gillette, William. *Retreat from Reconstruction, 1869–1879.* Baton Rouge: Louisiana State University Press, 1979.

Moneyhon, Carl H. *Texas after the Civil War: The Struggle of Reconstruction.* College Station: Texas A&M University Press, 2004.

Randall, J. G., and David Donald. *The Civil War and Reconstruction.* 2nd ed. Lexington, MA: D. C. Heath, 1969.

Richter, William L. *The Army in Texas during Reconstruction, 1865–1870.* College Station: Texas A&M University Press, 1987.

Sefton, James E. *The United States Army and Reconstruction, 1865–1877.* Baton Rouge: Louisiana State University Press, 1967.

Singletary, Otis. *Negro Militia and Reconstruction.* Austin: University of Texas Press, 1957.

OFFICERS

Altshuler, Constance Wynn. *Cavalry Yellow and Infantry Blue: Army Officers in Arizona between 1851 and 1886.* Tucson: Arizona Historical Society, 1991.

Armes, George A. *Ups and Downs of an Army Officer.* Washington, DC, 1900.

Athearn, Robert G. *William Tecumseh Sherman and the Settlement of the West.* Norman: University of Oklahoma Press, 1956.

Bailey, John W. *The Life and Works of General Charles King, 1844–1933.* Lewiston, NY: Edwin Mellen Press, 1998.

———. *Pacifying the Plains: General Alfred Terry and the Decline of the Sioux.* Westport, CT: Greenwood Press, 1979.

Baldwin, Alice Blackwood. *Memoirs of the Late Frank D. Baldwin, Major General, U.S.A.* Los Angeles: Wetzel, 1929.

Bourke, John G. *On the Border with Crook.* New York: Charles Scribner's Sons, 1891.

Brimlow, George F. *Cavalryman Out of the West: Life of General William Carey Brown.* Caldwell, ID: Caxton, 1944.

Brown, Richard C. *Social Attitudes of American Generals, 1898–1940.* New York: Arno Press, 1979.

Carlson, Paul H. *"Pecos Bill": A Military Biography of William R. Shafter.* College Station: Texas A&M University Press, 1989.

Carpenter, John A. *Sword and Olive Branch: Oliver Otis Howard.* Pittsburgh, PA: University of Pittsburgh Press, 1964.

Carroll, John M. *Camp Talk: The Very Private Letters of Frederick W. Benteen to His Wife, 1871 to 1888.* Mattituck, NY: J. M. Carroll, 1983.

Crane, Charles J. *Experiences of a Colonel of Infantry.* New York: Knickerbocker, 1923.

Croffut, W. A., ed. *Fifty Years in Camp and Field: Diary of Major General Ethan Allen Hitchcock, U.S.A.* New York: G. P. Putnam's Sons, 1909.

Cruse, Thomas. *Apache Days and After.* Caldwell, ID: Caxton, 1941.

Custer, George Armstrong. *My Life on the Plains, or Personal Experiences with Indians.* Norman: University of Oklahoma Press, 1976.

Davis, Britton. *The Truth about Geronimo.* New Haven, CT: Yale University Press, 1929.

De Trobriand, Philippe Régis. *Military Life in Dakota: The Journal of Philippe Régis de Trobriand.* Edited by Lucile M. Kane. Saint Paul, MN: Alvord Memorial Commission, 1951.

Dinges, Bruce J. "The Irrepressible Captain Armes: Politics and Justice in the Indian-Fighting Army." *Journal of the West* 32 (April 1993): 38–52.

———. "Leighton Finley: A Forgotten Soldier of the Apache Wars." *Journal of Arizona History* 29 (Summer 1988): 163–84.

Dixon, David. *Hero of Beecher Island: The Life and Military Career of George A. Forsyth.* Lincoln: University of Nebraska Press, 1994.

Ellis, Richard N. *General Pope and U.S. Indian Policy.* Albuquerque: University of New Mexico Press, 1970.

Forsyth, George A. *The Story of the Soldier.* New York: D. Appleton, 1909.

———. *Thrilling Days in Army Life.* New York: Harper and Brothers, 1902.

Gaff, Alan, and Maureen Gaff, eds. *Adventures on the Western Frontier: Major General John Gibbon.* Bloomington: Indiana University Press, 1994.

Gates, John M. "The Alleged Isolation of U.S. Army Officers in the Late 19th Century." *Parameters: The Journal of the U.S. Army War College* 10 (September 1980): 32–45.

Godfrey, E. S. "Some Reminiscences, Including the Washita Battle, November 27, 1868." *Cavalry Journal* 37 (October 1928): 481–500.

Greene, Duane N. *Ladies and Officers of the United States Army; or American Aristocracy, A Sketch of the Social Life and Character of the Army.* Chicago: Central, 1880.

Greene, Jerome A. *Yellowstone Command: Colonel Nelson A. Miles and the Great Sioux War, 1876–1877.* Lincoln: University of Nebraska Press, 1991.

Hagedorn, Herman. *Leonard Wood: A Biography.* 2 vols. New York: Harper, 1931.

Hancock, Almira R. *Reminiscences of Winfield Scott Hancock.* New York: Charles L. Webster, 1887.

Heitman, Francis B. *Historical Register and Dictionary of the United States Army, from Its Organization, September 29, 1789, to March 7, 1903.* 2 vols. Washington, DC: U.S. Government Printing Office, 1903.

Howard, Oliver Otis. *My Life and Experiences Among Our Hostile Indians.* Hartford, CT: Worthington, 1907.

Hutton, Paul A. *Phil Sheridan and His Army.* Lincoln: University of Nebraska Press, 1985.

Jacob, Richard T., Jr. "Reminiscences of Army Life in Oklahoma, 1867–1871." *Chronicles of Oklahoma* 2 (March 1924): 9–36.

Johnson, Virginia W. *The Unregimented General: A Biography of Nelson A. Miles.* Boston: Houghton Mifflin, 1962.

Jordan, Weymouth T., Jr., ed. "A Soldier's Life on the Indian Frontier, 1876–1878: Letters of 2 Lt. C. D. Cowles." *Kansas Historical Quarterly* 38 (Summer 1972): 144–55.

Kemble, C. Robert. *The Image of the Army Officer in America: Background for Current Views.* Westport, CT: Greenwood Press, 1983.

Kime, Wayne R. *Colonel Richard Irving Dodge: The Life and Times of a Career Army Officer.* Norman: University of Oklahoma Press, 2006.

Kindred, Marilyn Anne. "The Army Officer Corps and the Arts: Artistic Patronage and Practice in America, 1820–85." PhD diss., University of Kansas, 1980.

King, James T. *War Eagle: A Life of General Eugene A. Carr.* Lincoln: University of Nebraska Press, 1963.

Kramer, Adam. "An Army Officer in Texas, 1866–1867." *Southwestern Historical Quarterly* 72 (October 1968): 242–52.

Kroeker, Marvin E. *Great Plains Command: William B. Hazen and the Frontier West.* Norman: University of Oklahoma Press, 1976.

Marcy, Randolph B. *Thirty Years of Army Life on the Border.* New York: Harper and Brothers, 1866.

McChristian, Douglas C., ed. *Garrison Tangles in the Friendless Tenth: The Journal of First Lieutenant John Bigelow, Jr., Fort Davis, Texas.* Bryan, TX: J. M. Carroll, 1984.

McClernand, Edward J. "Service in Montana, 1870 and 1871." *Military Affairs* 15 (Winter 1951): 192–98.

Miles, Nelson A. *Personal Recollections and Observations of General Nelson A. Miles.* Chicago: Werner, 1896.

———. *Serving the Republic: Memoirs of the Civil and Military Life of General Nelson A. Miles.* New York: Harper and Brothers, 1911.

Mills, Anson. *My Story.* 2nd ed. Edited by C. H. Claudy. Washington, DC: Byron S. Adams, 1921.

Mills, Charles K. *Harvest of Barren Regrets: The Army Career of Frederick William Benteen, 1834–1898.* Glendale, CA: Arthur H. Clark, 1985.

Palmer, George Henry. "'We Do Not Know What the Government Intends to Do…,': Lt. Palmer Writes from the Bozeman, 1867–68." *Montana, Magazine of Western History* 28 (1978): 17–35.

Parker, James. *The Old Army: Memories, 1872–1918.* Philadelphia: Dorrance, 1929.

Pierce, Michael D. *The Most Promising Young Officer: A Life of Ranald Slidell Mackenzie.* Norman: University of Oklahoma Press, 1993.

Pohanka, Brian C. *Nelson A. Miles: A Documentary Biography of His Military Career, 1861–1903.* Glendale, CA: Arthur H. Clark, 1985.

Porter, Joseph C. *Paper Medicine Man: John Gregory Bourke and His American West.* Norman: University of Oklahoma Press, 1986.

Post, Marie Caroline. *The Life and Memoirs of Comte Régis de Trobriand.* New York: E. P. Dutton, 1910.

Price, George F. *Across the Continent with the Fifth Cavalry.* New York: Van Nostrand, 1883.

Robinson, Charles M., III. *Bad Hand: A Biography of General Ranald S. Mackenzie.* Austin, TX: State House Press, 1993.

———, ed. *The Diaries of John Gregory Bourke.* Vol. 1, *November 20, 1872–July 28, 1876.* Denton: University of North Texas Press, 2003.

———. *General Crook and the Western Frontier.* Norman: University of Oklahoma Press, 2001.

Russell, Don. *Campaigning with King: Charles King, Chronicler of the Old Army.* Edited by Paul L. Hedren. Lincoln: University of Nebraska Press, 1991.

Schmitt, Martin, ed. *General George Crook: His Autobiography.* Norman: University of Oklahoma Press, 1960.

Schofield, John M. *Forty Six Years in the Army.* New York: Century, 1897.

Scott, Hugh L. *Some Memories of a Soldier.* New York: Century, 1928.

Sheridan, Philip H. *Personal Memoirs of P. H. Sheridan.* 2 vols. New York: Charles L. Webster, 1888.

Sherman, William Tecumseh. *Memoirs of General Gen. William Tecumseh Sherman.* 2 vols. 2nd rev. ed. New York: D. Appleton, 1904.

Skelton, William B. *An American Profession of Arms: The Army Officer Corps, 1784–1861.* Lawrence: University Press of Kansas, 1992.

Smith, Cornelius C., Jr. *Don't Settle for Second: Life and Times of Cornelius Smith.* San Rafael, CA: Presidio Press, 1977.

Smith, Dwight L., ed. "The Kansas Frontier, 1869–1870: Lt. Samuel Tillman's First Tour of Duty." *Kansas History* 12 (Winter 1989–1990): 202–9.

Splitter, Henry Winfred, ed. "Tour in Arizona: Footprints of an Army Officer." *Journal of the West* 1 (July 1962): 74–97.

Steele, James W. *Frontier Army Sketches.* Albuquerque: University of New Mexico Press, 1969.

Thorndike, Rachel Sherman, ed. *The Sherman Letters: Correspondence between General and Senator Sherman from 1837 to 1891.* New York: Charles Scribner's Sons, 1894.

Utley, Robert M. *Cavalier in Buckskin: George Armstrong Custer and the Western Military Frontier.* Norman: University of Oklahoma Press, 1988.

Wheeler, Homer W. *Buffalo Days, Forty Years in the Old West: The Personal Narrative of a Cattleman, Indian Fighter, and Army Officer.* Indianapolis, IN: Bobbs-Merrill, 1925.

Woodruff, Lt. Charles A. "Letters from the Big Hole." *Montana, Magazine of Western History* 2 (October 1952): 53–56.

Wooster, Robert. *Nelson A. Miles and the Twilight of the Frontier Army.* Lincoln: University of Nebraska Press, 1993.

———, ed. *Soldier, Surgeon, Scholar: The Memoirs of William Henry Corbusier, 1844–1930.* Norman: University of Oklahoma Press, 2003.

ENLISTED MEN

Bluthardt, Robert F. "The Men of Company F." *Fort Concho Report* 15 (Summer 1983): 3–9.

Brimlow, George F., ed. "Two Cavalrymen's Diaries of the Bannock War, 1878." *Oregon Historical Quarterly* 68, no. 3/4 (1967): 221–58, 293–316.

Burdick, Usher L. *The Army Life of Charles "Chip" Creighton.* Paris, MD: National Reform Associates, 1937.

Carroll, John M., and Lawrence A. Frost, eds. *Private Theodore Ewert's Diary of the Black Hills Expedition of 1874.* Piscataway, NJ: CRI Books, 1976.

Carter, Robert G., ed. *The Old Sergeant's Story: Winning the West from the Indians and Bad Men in 1870 to 1876.* New York: Frederick H. Hitchcock, 1926.

———. *On the Border with Mackenzie.* Washington, DC: Eynon, 1935.

Comfort, John W. "Of Memory and Massacre: A Soldier's Firsthand Account of the 'Affair on Wounded Knee.'" *Princeton University Library Chronicle* 64 (Winter 2003): 333–62.

Cox, John E. "Soldiering in Dakota Territory in the Seventies: A Communication." *North Dakota Historical Quarterly* 6 (October 1931): 62–81.

Dinges, Bruce J., ed. "A New York Private in Arizona Territory: The Letters of George H. Cranston, 1867–1870." *Journal of Arizona History* 26 (Spring 1985): 53–76.

Ellis, Catherine. "A Common Soldier at Camp Douglas, 1866–68." *Utah Historical Quarterly* 65 (Winter 1997): 49–63.

Gressley, Gene M., ed. "A Soldier with Crook: The Letters of Henry Porter." *Montana, Magazine of Western History* 8, no. 3 (1958): 33–47.

Hedren, Paul L., ed. "'The Worst Campaign I Ever Experienced': Sergeant John Zimmerman's Memoir of the Great Sioux War." *Annals of Wyoming* 76 (Winter 2004): 2–14.

Hershler, N. *The Soldier's Hand-Book: For the Use of the Enlisted Men of the Army.* Washington, DC: U.S. Government Printing Office, 1884.

Hill, Michael D., and Ben Innis, eds. "The Fort Buford Diary of Private Sanford, 1876–1877." *North Dakota History* 52 (Summer 1985): 2–40.

Hunt, Frazier, and Robert Hunt. *I Fought with Custer: The Story of Sergeant Windolph, Last Survivor of the Battle of the Little Big Horn.* New York: Scribner, 1954.

Landrum, Francis S., ed. "From the Sketchbook of 1st Sergeant Michael McCarthy, Troop H, 1st US Cavalry: Excerpts, 1873." *Journal of the Shaw Historical Library* 9 (1995): 1–18.

Larned, Charles W. "The Regeneration of the Enlisted Soldier." *International Quarterly* 12 (January 1906): 189–207.

Larson, James. *Sergeant Larson, 4th Cavalry.* San Antonio, TX: Southern Literary Institute, 1925.

McConnell, H. H. *Five Years a Cavalryman, or Sketches of Regular Army Life on the Texas Frontier, 1866–1871.* Jacksboro, TX: J. N. Rogers, 1889.

Molchert, William. "Sergeant Molchert's Perils: Soldiering in Montana." *Montana, Magazine of Western History* 34 (Spring 1984): 60–65.

Mulford, Ami Frank. *Fighting Indians in the 7th United States Cavalry.* Corning, NY: Paul Lindsley Mulford, 1879.

Pate, J'Nell. "The Red River War of 1874: An Enlisted Man's Contribution." *Chronicles of Oklahoma* 54 (Summer 1976): 263–75.

Peters, S. S. "Letters of a Sixth Cavalryman Stationed at 'Cantonment' in the Texas Panhandle, 1875." *Texas Military History* 7 (Summer 1968): 77–102.

"Poetry of an Army Private." *Frank Leslie's Illustrated Weekly* 78 (1894): 372.

Quaife, Milo M., ed. "*Yellowstone Kelly*": *The Memoirs of Luther S. Kelly.* New Haven, CT: Yale University Press, 1926.

Rea, Bob, ed. "The Red River War Diary of Private John Hechner." *Panhandle-Plains Historical Review* 71 (1998): 24–38.

Reneau, Susan C. *The Adventures of Moccasin Joe: The True Life Story of Sgt. George S. Howard.* Missoula, MT: Blue Mountain, 1994.

Rickey, Don, Jr. *Forty Miles a Day on Beans and Hay: The Enlisted Soldier Fighting the Indian Wars.* Norman: University of Oklahoma Press, 1963.

Sanford, Wilmont P. "The Fort Buford Diary of Private Wilmont P. Sanford." *North Dakota History* 33 (Fall 1966): 335–78.

Smith, Sherry L., ed. *Sagebrush Soldier: Private William Earl Smith's View of the Sioux War of 1876.* Norman: University of Oklahoma Press, 1989.

Smith, Thomas T., ed. *A Dose of Frontier Soldiering: The Memoirs of Corporal E. A. Bode, Frontier Regular Infantry, 1877–1882.* Lincoln: University of Nebraska Press, 1994.

Wagner, Glendolin Damon. *Old Neutriment.* Boston: R. Hill, 1934.

Walker, Henry P. "The Enlisted Soldier on the Frontier." In *The American Military on the Frontier: Proceedings of the Seventh Military History Symposium,* ed. James P. Tate. Washington, DC: Office of Air Force History, 1978.

———, ed. "The Reluctant Corporal: The Autobiography of William Bladen Jett." *Journal of Arizona History* 12 (Spring 1971): 1–50.

Woodhull, Alfred A. "The Enlisted Soldier." *Journal of the Military Service Institution of the United States* 8 (March 1887): 18–70.

Zimmer, William F. *Frontier Soldier: An Enlisted Man's Journal of the Sioux and Nez Perce Campaigns, 1877.* Edited by Jerome A. Greene. Helena: Montana Historical Society Press, 1998.

ETHNICITY

Adams, Kevin. "'Pat Has a Small Chance of Showing His Blood Out in the Wilderness': Class and Ethnicity in the Ideas and Institutions of the Frontier Army, 1865–1890." Paper presented at the Western History Association Meeting, Las Vegas, NV, 2004.

Burton, William L. *Melting Pot Soldiers: The Union's Ethnic Regiments.* Ames: Iowa State University Press, 1988.

Lindberg, Christer, ed. "Foreigners in Action at Wounded Knee." *Nebraska History* 71 (Winter 1990): 171–81.

Mulroy, Kevin. "Wearing of the Army Blue: The Irish in the U.S. Army, 1776–1876." In *Myles Keogh: The Life and Legend of an Irish Dragoon in the Seventh Cavalry,* ed. John P. Langellier, Kurt Hamilton Cox, and Brian C. Pohanka. El Segundo, CA: Upton and Sons, 1991.

White, William Bruce. "The Military and the Melting Pot: The American Army and Minority Groups, 1865–1924." PhD diss., University of Wisconsin, 1968.

BLACK SOLDIERS

Alexander, Charles. *Battles and Victories of Allen Allensworth.* Boston: Sherman French, 1914.

Bigelow, John, Jr. *On the Bloody Trail of Geronimo.* Edited by Arthur Woodward. Los Angeles: Westernlore Press, 1958.

Billington, Monroe. "Black Soldiers at Fort Selden, New Mexico, 1866–1891." *New Mexico Historical Review* 62 (January 1987): 65–80.

———. *New Mexico's Buffalo Soldiers, 1866–1900.* Niwot: University Press of Colorado, 1991.

Buecker, Thomas R. "Confrontation at Sturgis: An Episode in Civil-Military Race Relations, 1885." *South Dakota History* 14 (Fall 1984): 238–61.

———. "One Soldier's Service: Caleb Benson in the Ninth and Tenth Cavalry, 1875–1908." *Nebraska History* 74 (Summer 1993): 54–62.

Carlson, Paul H. *The Buffalo Soldier Tragedy of 1877.* College Station: Texas A&M University Press, 2003.

Carroll, John M., ed. *The Black Military Experience in the American West.* New York: Liveright, 1971.

Clark, Michael J. "Improbable Ambassadors: Black Soldiers at Fort Douglas, 1896–1899." *Utah Historical Quarterly* 46 (Summer 1978): 282–301.

Dinges, Bruce J. "The Court-Martial of Lieutenant Henry O. Flipper: An Example of Black-White Relationships in the Army, 1881." *American West* 9 (January 1972): 12–17, 59–61.

———. "Scandal in the Tenth Cavalry: A Fort Sill Case History." *Arizona and the West* 28 (Summer 1986): 125–40.

Dobak, William A., and Thomas D. Phillips. *The Black Regulars, 1866–1898.* Norman: University of Oklahoma Press, 2001.

Dollar, Charles M. "Putting the Army on Wheels: The Story of the Twenty-Fifth Infantry Bicycle Corps." *Prologue* 17 (Spring 1985): 7–23.

Eppinga, Jane. "Henry O. Flipper in the Court of Private Land Claims: The Arizona Career of West Point's First Black Graduate." *Journal of Arizona History* 36 (Spring 1995): 33–54.

Fletcher, Marvin E. "The Army and Minority Groups." In *The United States Army in Peacetime,* ed. Robin Higham and Carol Brandt. Manhattan, KS: Military Affairs/Aerospace Historian, 1975.

———. "The Black Bicycle Corps." *Arizona and the West* 16 (Autumn 1974): 219–32.

———. *The Black Soldier and Officer in the United States Army, 1891–1917.* Columbia: University of Missouri Press, 1974.

Foner, Jack D. *Blacks and the Military in American History: A New Perspective.* New York: Praeger, 1974.

Fowler, Arlen L. *The Black Infantry in the West, 1869–1891.* Westport, CT: Greenwood Press, 1971.

Glass, E.L.N., comp. *The History of the Tenth Cavalry, 1866–1921.* N.p., 1921.

Harris, Theodore, ed. *Negro Frontiersman: The Western Memoirs of Henry O. Flipper.* El Paso: Texas Western College Press, 1963.

Kenner, Charles L. *Buffalo Soldiers and Officers of the Ninth Cavalry 1867–1898.* Norman: University of Oklahoma Press, 1999.

Lamkin, Patricia E. "Blacks in San Angelo: Relations between Fort Concho and the City, 1875–1889." *West Texas Historical Association Year Book* 66 (1990): 26–37.

Leckie, William H. "Black Regulars on the Texas Frontier, 1866–85." In *The Texas Military Experience: From the Texas Revolution through World War II,* ed. Joseph G. Dawson III. College Station: Texas A&M University Press, 1995.

———. *The Buffalo Soldiers: A Narrative of the Negro Cavalry in the West.* Norman: University of Oklahoma Press, 1967.

Leiker, James N. "Black Soldiers at Fort Hays, Kansas, 1867–1869: A Study in Civilian and Military Violence." *Great Plains Quarterly* 17 (Winter 1997): 3–17.

———. *Racial Borders: Black Soldiers along the Rio Grande.* College Station: Texas A&M University Press, 2002.

McChristian, Douglas C. " 'Dress on the Colors, Boys!': Black Noncommissioned Officers in the Regular Army, 1866–1898." *Colorado Heritage,* Spring 1996, 38–44.

———. *Fort Bowie, Arizona: Combat Post of the Southwest, 1858–1894.* Norman: University of Oklahoma Press, 2005.

Miles, Susan. "The Soldiers' Riot." *Fort Concho Report* 13 (Spring 1981): 1–20.

Muller, William G., comp. *The Twenty-fourth Infantry: Past and Present.* N.p., 1923.

Nankivell, John H., comp. *History of the Twenty-fifth Regiment, United States Infantry, 1869–1926.* Denver: Smith-Brooks, 1927.

Remington, Frederic. "A Scout with the Buffalo Soldiers." *Century* 15 (April 1889): 899–912.

Robinson, Charles M., III. *The Court Martial of Lieutenant Henry Flipper.* University of Texas at El Paso Southwestern Studies, no. 100. El Paso: Texas Western Press, 1994.

Roome, Richard T. "A Cavalry Company on the Indian Frontier: A Short History of Troop L, 10th U.S. Cavalry." *Permian Historical Annual* 34 (December 1994): 25–43.

Savage, W. Sherman. "The Role of Negro Soldiers in Protecting the Indian Territory from Intruders." *Journal of Negro History* 36 (January 1951): 25–34.

Schubert, Frank N. *Black Valor: Buffalo Soldiers and the Medal of Honor, 1870–1898.* Wilmington, DE: Scholarly Resources, 1993.

———. "The Fort Robinson Y.M.C.A., 1902–1907: A Social Organization in a Black Regiment." *Nebraska History* 55 (Summer 1974): 165–79.

———, ed. *On the Trail of the Buffalo Soldier: Biographies of African Americans in the U.S. Army, 1866–1917.* Wilmington, DE: Scholarly Resources, 1995.

———. "The Suggs Affray: The Black Cavalry in the Johnson County War." *Western Historical Quarterly* 4 (January 1973): 57–68.

Schubert, Frank N. *Black Valor:* "Ten Troopers: Buffalo Soldier Medal of Honor Men Who Served at Fort Robinson." *Nebraska History* 78 (Winter 1997): 151–57.

———. "The Violent World of Emanuel Stance, Fort Robinson, 1887." *Nebraska History* 55 (Summer 1974): 203–19.

———. *Voices of the Buffalo Soldier: Records, Reports, and Recollections of Military Life and Service in the West.* Albuquerque: University of New Mexico Press, 2003.

Seraile, William. "Theophilus G. Steward, Intellectual Chaplain, 25th U.S. Colored Infantry." *Nebraska History* 66 (Fall 1985): 272–93.

———. *The Voice of Dissent: Theophilus Gould Steward (1843–1924) and Black America.* Brooklyn, NY: Carlson, 1991.

Steward, Theophilus G., ed. *Active Service, or Religious Work among United States Soldiers.* New York: U.S. Army Aid Association, [1890?].

———, ed. *From 1864 to 1914: Fifty Years in the Gospel Ministry.* Philadelphia: A.M.E. Book Concern, 1921.

———. "Starving Laborers and the 'Hired' Soldier." *United Service* 15 (1895): 363–66.

Stover, Earl F. "Chaplain Henry V. Plummer, His Ministry and His Court-Martial." *Nebraska History* 56 (Spring 1975): 21–50.

Taylor, Quintard. "Comrades of Color: Buffalo Soldiers in the West: 1866–1917." *Colorado Heritage,* Spring 1996, 3–27.

Temple, Frank M. "Discipline and Turmoil in the Tenth U.S. Cavalry." *West Texas Historical Association Year Book* 59 (1982): 103–18.

Thompson, Erwin N. "The Negro Soldiers on the Frontier: A Fort Davis Case Study." *Journal of the West* 7 (April 1968): 217–35.

SOLDIERS' FAMILIES

Adams, Donald K., ed. "The Journal of Ada A. Vogdes, 1868–71." *Montana, Magazine of Western History* 13 (Summer 1963): 2–17.

Baker, Anni P. "Daughters of Mars: Army Officers' Wives and Military Culture on the American Frontier." *Historian* 67 (Spring 2005): 20–42.

Biddle, Ellen McGowan. *Reminiscences of a Soldier's Wife.* Philadelphia: J. B. Lippincott, 1907.

Blackburn, Forrest R. "Army Families in Frontier Forts." *Military Review* 49 (October 1969): 17–28.

Blackman, Patricia R. "The History of Disability Legislation for Regular Army Widows of the Indian Wars, 1790–1890." MA thesis, University of Nebraska at Omaha, 1982.

Boyd, Mrs. Orsemus Bronson. *Cavalry Life in Tent and Field.* New York: J. S. Tait, 1894.

Buecker, Thomas R., ed. "Letters of Caroline Frey Winne from Sidney Barracks and Fort McPherson, Nebraska, 1874–1878." *Nebraska History* 62 (Spring 1981): 1–46.

———, ed. "Letters from a Post Surgeon's Wife: The Fort Washakie Correspondence of Caroline Winne, May 1879–May 1880." *Annals of Wyoming* 53 (Fall 1981): 44–63.

Carr, Mary Patience Magwire. "Fort McPherson in 1870: A Note by an Army Wife." *Nebraska History* 45 (March 1964): 99–107.

Carriker, Robert C., and Eleanor R. Carriker, eds. *An Army Wife on the Frontier: The Memoirs of Alice Blackwood Baldwin, 1867–1877.* Salt Lake City: University of Utah Library, 1975.

Carrington, Frances C. *My Army Life and the Fort Phil Kearney Massacre.* Philadelphia: J. B. Lippincott, 1910.

Carrington, Margaret Irvin. *Absaraka, Home of the Crows: Being the Experience of an Officer's Wife on the Plains.* Philadelphia: J. B. Lippincott, 1868.

Custer, Elizabeth B. *Boots and Saddles or, Life in Dakota with General Custer.* Norman: University of Oklahoma Press, 1961.

———. *Following the Guidon.* New York: Harper and Brothers, 1890.

———. *Tenting on the Plains, or General Custer in Kansas and Texas.* New York: C. L. Webster, 1887.

Eales, Anne Bruner. *Army Wives on the American Frontier: Living within the Sound of Bugles.* Boulder, CO: Johnson Books, 1996.

Eldridge, W. Heath. "An Army Boy in Colorado." *Colorado Magazine* 32 (October 1955): 299–310.

Fisher, Barbara E., ed. "Forrestine Cooper Hooker's Notes and Memoirs on Army Life in the West, 1871–1876." MA thesis, University of Arizona, 1963.

FitzGerald, Emily McCorkle. *An Army Doctor's Wife on the Frontier: Letters from Alaska and the Far West, 1874–1878.* Edited by Abe Laufe. Pittsburgh, PA: University of Pittsburgh Press, 1962.

Foote, Cheryl J. "'My Husband Was a Madman and a Murderer': Josephine Clifford McCrackin, Army Wife, Writer and Conservationist." *New Mexico Historical Review* 65 (April 1990): 199–224.

Fougera, Katherine Gibson. *With Custer's Cavalry.* Caldwell, ID: Caxton, 1940.

Frost, Lawrence A. *General Custer's Libbie.* Seattle, WA: Superior, 1976.

Gilliss, Julia. *So Far From Home: An Army Bride on the Western Frontier, 1865–1869.* Edited by Priscilla Knuth. Portland: Oregon Historical Society, 1993.

Heistand, Mary Ripply. "Scraps from an Army Woman's Diary: An Old Army Christmas." *Army and Navy Life* 9 (December 1907): 626–31.

Lane, Lydia Spencer. *I Married a Soldier.* Albuquerque: University of New Mexico Press, 1987.

Laurence, Mary Leefe. *Daughter of the Regiment: Memoirs of a Childhood in the Frontier Army, 1878–1898.* Edited by Thomas T. Smith. Lincoln: University of Nebraska Press, 1996.

Leckie, Shirley A., ed. *The Colonel's Lady on the Western Frontier: The Correspondence of Alice Kirk Grierson.* Lincoln: University of Nebraska Press, 1989.

———. *Elizabeth Bacon Custer and the Making of a Myth.* Norman: University of Oklahoma Press, 1993.

———. "Fort Concho: Paradise for Children." *Fort Concho Report* 19 (Spring 1987): 1–15.

———. "Reading Between the Lines: Another Look at Officers' Wives in the Post-Civil War Frontier Army." *Military History of the Southwest* 19 (Fall 1989): 137–60.

Leckie, William H., and Shirley A. Leckie. *Unlikely Warriors: General Benjamin H. Grierson and His Family.* Norman: University of Oklahoma Press, 1984.

Mattes, Merrill J. *Indians, Infants and Infantry: Andrew and Elizabeth Burt on the Frontier.* Denver: Old West, 1960.

Mattison, Ray H., ed. "An Army Wife on the Upper Missouri: The Diary of Sarah E. Canfield, 1866–1868." *North Dakota History* 20 (October 1953): 191–220.

Merington, Marguerite, ed. *The Custer Story: The Life and Intimate Letters of General George A. Custer and His Wife Elizabeth.* New York: Devin-Adair, 1950.

Miles, Susan, ed. "Mrs. Buell's Journal, 1877." *Edwards Plateau Historian* 2 (1966): 33–43.

Miller, Darlis, ed. *Above a Common Soldier: Frank and Mary Clarke in the American West and Civil War, 1847–1872.* Rev. ed. Albuquerque: University of New Mexico Press, 1997.

———. "Foragers, Army Women, and Prostitutes." In *New Mexico Women: Intercultural Perspectives,* ed. Joan M. Jensen and Darlis A. Miller. Albuquerque: University of New Mexico Press, 1986.

Myres, Sandra L., ed. "An Arizona Camping Trip: May Banks Stacey's Account of an Outing to Mount Graham in 1879." *Arizona and the West* 23 (Spring 1981): 53–64.

———. "Army Women's Narratives as Documents of Social History: Some Examples from the Western Frontier." *New Mexico Historical Review* 65 (April 1990): 175–98.

———, ed. *Cavalry Wife: The Diary of Eveline M. Alexander, 1866–1867.* College Station: Texas A&M University Press, 1977.

———. "Evy Alexander: The Colonel's Lady at McDowell in Arizona." *Montana, Magazine of Western History* 24 (July 1974): 26–38.

———. "Frontier Historians, Women, and the 'New' Military History." *Military History of the Southwest* 19 (Spring 1989): 27–37.

———. "Romance and Reality on the American Frontier: Views of Army Wives." *Western Historical Quarterly* 13 (October 1982): 409–27.

———, ed. "A Woman's View of the Texas Frontier, 1874: The Diary of Emily K. Andrews." *Southwestern Historical Quarterly* 86 (July 1982): 49–80.

Nacy, Michele J. *Members of the Regiment: Army Officers' Wives on the Western Frontier, 1865–1890.* Westport, CT: Greenwood Press, 2000.

Roe, Frances M. A. *Army Letters from an Officer's Wife, 1871–1888.* New York: D. Appleton, 1909.

Sargent, Alice Applegate. *Following the Flag: Diary of a Soldier's Wife.* 2nd ed. Kansas City, MO: E. B. Barnett, 1928.

Schreier, Jim, ed. "'For This I Had Left Civilization': Julia Davis at Camp McDowell, 1869–1870." *Journal of Arizona History* 29 (Summer 1988): 185–98.

Shields, Alice Mathews. "Army Life on the Wyoming Frontier." *Annals of Wyoming* 13 (October 1941): 331–43.

Smith, Sherry L. "Officers' Wives, Indians and Indian Wars." *Journal of the Order of Indian Wars* 1 (Winter 1980): 35–46.

Stallard, Patricia Y., ed. *Fanny Dunbar Corbusier: Recollections of Her Army Life, 1869–1908.* Norman: University of Oklahoma Press, 2003.

———. *Glittering Misery: Dependents of the Indian Fighting Army.* Fort Collins, CO: Old Army Press, 1978.

Steinbach, Robert H. *A Long March: The Lives of Frank and Alice Baldwin.* Austin: University of Texas Press, 1990.

Stewart, Edgar I. "The Custer Battle and Widow's Weeds." *Montana, Magazine of Western History* 22 (January 1972): 52–59.

Stewart, Miller J. "Army Laundresses: Ladies of the 'Soap Suds Row.'" *Nebraska History* 61 (Winter 1980): 421–36.

Summerhayes, Martha. *Vanished Arizona: Recollections of the Army Life of a New England Woman.* 2nd ed. Salem, MA: Salem Press, 1911.

Tate, Michael L. "The Girl He Left Behind: Elizabeth Custer and the Making of a Legend." *Red River Valley Historical Review* 5 (Winter 1980): 5–22.

Twitchell, Phillip G., ed. "Camp Robinson Letters of Angeline Johnson, 1876–1879." *Nebraska History* 77 (Summer 1996): 89–95.

Utley, Robert M., ed. *Life in Custer's Cavalry: Diaries and Letters of Albert and Jennie Barnitz, 1867–1868.* New Haven, CT: Yale University Press, 1977.

Wales, Martha Gray. "When I Was a Little Girl: Things I Remember from Living at Frontier Military Posts." *North Dakota History* 50 (Spring 1983): 12–22.

Welter, Barbara. "The Cult of True Womanhood, 1820–1860." *American Quarterly* 18 (Summer 1966): 151–74.

Williams, Mary L. "Ladies of the Regiment: Their Influence on the Frontier Army." *Nebraska History* 78 (Winter 1997): 158–64.

SOCIAL LIFE

Anderson, Harry H. "The Benteen Base Ball Club: Sports Enthusiasts of the Seventh Cavalry." *Montana, Magazine of Western History* 20 (July 1970): 82–87.

Bigelow, Donald N. *William Conant Church and the Army and Navy Journal.* New York: Columbia University Press, 1952.

Bluthardt, Robert F. "Baseball on the Military Frontier." *Fort Concho Report* 19 (Spring 1987): 17–26.

Brumbaugh, Thomas B. "Fort Laramie Hijinks: A New Manuscript Account." *Annals of Wyoming* 58 (Fall 1986): 4–9.

Brust, James S. "Photojournalism, 1877: John H. Fouch, Fort Keogh's First Post Photographer." *Montana, Magazine of Western History* 50 (Winter 2000): 32–39.

Brust, James S., and Lee H. Whittlesey. " 'Roughing It up the Yellowstone to Wonderland': The Nelson Miles-Colgate Hoyt Party in Yellowstone National Park, September 1878." *Montana, Magazine of Western History* 46 (Spring 1996): 56–64.

Buchanan, John S. "Functions of the Fort Davis Military Band and Musical Proclivities of the Commanding Officer, Colonel Benjamin H. Grierson, Late Nineteenth Century." MA thesis, Sul Ross State University, 1968.

Buss, Stephen Ralph. "The Military Theatre: Soldier-Actor Theatricals on the Frontier Plains." PhD diss., Washington State University, 1982.

Butler, Anne. "Military Myopia: Prostitution on the Frontier." *Prologue* 13 (Winter 1981): 233–50.

Carlson, Paul H. "Baseball's Abner Doubleday on the Texas Frontier, 1871–1873." *Military History of Texas and the Southwest* 12, no. 4 (1974): 236–43.

Carroll, John M. "The Doubleday Myth and Texas Baseball." *Southwestern Historical Quarterly* 92 (April 1989): 597–612.

Cox-Paul, Lori A., and James W. Wengert, comps. *A Frontier Army Christmas.* Lincoln: Nebraska State Historical Society, 1996.

Culpin, Alan. "A Brief History of Social and Domestic Life among the Military in Wyoming, 1849–1890." *Annals of Wyoming* 45 (Spring 1973): 93–108.

Dobak, William A. "Licit Amusements of Enlisted Men in the Post-Civil War Army." *Montana, Magazine of Western History* 45 (Spring 1995): 35–45.

———. "Yellow-Leg Journalists: Enlisted Men as Newspaper Reporters in the Sioux Campaign, 1876." *Journal of the West* 13 (January 1974): 86–112.

Frink, Maurice, and Casey Barthelmess. *Photographer on an Army Mule.* Norman: University of Oklahoma Press, 1965.

Giese, Dale F. "Soldiers at Play: A History of Social Life at Fort Union, New Mexico, 1851–1891." PhD diss., University of New Mexico, 1969.

Huey, William G. "Making Music: Brass Bands on the Northern Plains, 1860–1930." *North Dakota History* 54 (Winter 1987): 3–13.

Huseas, Marion M. "Tuched Nothing to Drink: Frontier Army Leisure." *Periodical: Journal of the Council on America's Military Past* 12 (January 1981): 11–23.

King, James T. "The Sword and the Pen: The Poetry of the Military Frontier." *Nebraska History* 47 (September 1966): 229–45.

Lent, John A. "The Press on Wheels: A History of *The Frontier Index* of Nebraska, Colorado, Wyoming, Elsewhere." *Annals of Wyoming* 43 (Fall 1971): 165–204.

McDermott, John D. "The *Frontier Scout:* A View of Fort Rice in 1865." *North Dakota History* 61 (Fall 1994): 25–35.

McKale, William. "Military Photography." *Journal of the West* 28 (January 1989): 83–88.

McMurtrie, Douglas C. "The Fourth Infantry Press at Fort Bridger." *Annals of Wyoming* 13 (October 1941): 437–51.

Nottage, James H. "A Centennial History of Artist Activities in Wyoming, 1837–1937." *Annals of Wyoming* 48 (Spring 1976): 77–100.

Railsback, Thomas C. "Military Bands and Music at Old Fort Hays, 1867–1889." *Journal of the West* 22 (July 1983): 28–35.

Railsback, Thomas C., and John P. Langellier. *The Drums Would Roll: A Pictorial History of U.S. Army Bands on the American Frontier, 1866–1900.* New York: Arms and Armour Press, 1987.

COMMUNITY RELATIONSHIPS

Athearn, Robert G. "Frontier Critics of the Western Army." *Montana, Magazine of Western History* 5 (Spring 1955): 16–28.

Bland, Thomas A. "Abolish the Army." *Council Fire* (March 1879): 36.

Bluthardt, Valerie C., ed. "Town Building on the Texas Frontier." *Fort Concho Report* 18 (Winter 1986–1987): 1–46.

Burlingame, Merrill. "The Influence of the Military in the Building of Montana." *Pacific Northwest Quarterly* 29 (April 1938): 135–50.

Caldwell, Jo Anne. "Community at a Crossroads: San Angelo and the Closing of Fort Concho, 1889." *Fort Concho Report* 20/21 (Winter 1988–Spring 1989): 5–21.

Carlson, Paul H. "The Discovery of Silver in West Texas." *West Texas Historical Association Year Book* 54 (1978): 55–64.

Christian, Garna L. "Sword and Plowshare: The Symbiotic Development of Fort Bliss and El Paso, Texas, 1849–1918." PhD diss., Texas Tech University, 1977.

Crandall, Genia Rood. "Fort Hartsuff and the Local Pioneer Life: A School Teacher's Recollections of Fort Hartsuff." *Nebraska History* 12 (April–June 1929): 140–57.

Dinges, Bruce J. "Colonel Grierson Invests on the West Texas Frontier." *Fort Concho Report* 16 (Fall 1984): 2–13.

Fleming, William F. "San Antonio: The History of a Military City, 1865–1880." PhD diss., University of Pennsylvania, 1963.

Freedom, Gary S. "The Role of the Military and the Spread of Settlement in the Northern Great Plains, 1866–1891." *Midwest Review* 9 (Spring 1987): 1–11.

Haskew, Eula. "Stribling and Kirkland of Fort Griffin." *West Texas Historical Association Year Book* 32 (October 1956): 55–69.

Price, George F. "The Necessity for Closer Relations between the Army and the People, and the Best Method to Accomplish the Result." *Journal of the Military Service Institution of the United States* 6 (December 1885): 303–30.

Robinson, Charles M. *The Frontier World of Fort Griffin: The Life and Death of a Western Town.* Spokane, WA: Arthur H. Clark, 1992.

Ruhlen, George. "Quitman's Owners: A Sidelight on Frontier Reality." *Password* 5 (April 1960): 54–64.

Rust, Thomas C. "Settlers, Soldiers, and Scoundrels: Economic Tension in a Frontier Military Town." *Military History of the West* 31 (Fall 2001): 117–38.

Smith, Duane A. "'Where a Bird Could Hardly Obtain a Footing': George Armstrong Custer and the Stevens Mine." *Colorado Heritage,* Spring 1997, 25–37.

Smith, Julia Cauble. "The Shafter Mining District." *Permian Historical Annual* 28 (December 1988): 75–84.

Smith, Thomas T. *The U.S. Army and the Texas Frontier Economy, 1845–1900.* College Station: Texas A&M University Press, 1999.

Stewart, Miller J. "To Plow, to Sow, to Reap, to Mow: The U.S. Army Agriculture Program." *Nebraska History* 63 (Summer 1982): 194–215.

Twichel, Thomas. "Fort Logan and the Urban Frontier." *Montana, Magazine of Western History* 17 (Autumn 1967): 44–49.

Unsworth, Michael E., ed. *Military Periodicals: United States and Selected International Journals and Newspapers.* Westport, CT: Greenwood Press, 1990.

Ware, James H. "San Angelo and San Antonio: A Comparative Study of the Military City in Texas, 1865–1898." MA thesis, Southwest Texas State University, 1973.

Williams, Mary L. "Empire Building: Colonel Benjamin H. Grierson at Fort Davis, 1882–1885." *West Texas Historical Association Year Book* 61 (1985): 58–73.

SUPPLY AND CONTRACTS

Ballew, Elvis Joe. "Supply Problems of Fort Davis, Texas, 1867–1880." MA thesis, Sul Ross State University, 1971.

Caperton, Thomas J., and LoRheda Fry. "U.S. Army Food and Its Preparation during the Indian Wars, 1865–1900, with Selected Recipes." *El Palacio* 80 (Winter 1974): 29–45.

Davis, W. N. "The Sutler at Fort Bridger." *Western Historical Quarterly* 2 (January 1971): 37–54.

Delo, David Michael. *Peddlers and Post Traders: The Army Sutler on the Frontier.* Salt Lake City: University of Utah Press, 1992.

Foote, Morris C. "The Post Mess." *Journal of the Military Service Institution of the United States* 14 (1893): 519–24.

Greene, Jerome A. "Army Bread and Army Mission on the Frontier, with Special Reference to Fort Laramie, Wyoming, 1865–1890." *Annals of Wyoming* 47 (Fall 1975): 191–219.

Innis, Ben. "Bottoms Up! The Smith and Leighton Yellowstone Store Ledger of 1876." *North Dakota History* 51 (Summer 1984): 24–38.

Ivey, James. "'The Best Sutler's Store in America': James E. Barrow and the Formation of Trader's Row at Fort Union, New Mexico, 1867–1891." *New Mexico Historical Review* 70 (July 1995): 299–327.

Kane, Randy. "'An Honorable and Upright Man': Sidney R. DeLong as Post Trader at Fort Bowie." *Journal of Arizona History* 19 (Autumn 1978): 297–314.

Lee, J.G.C. "Suggestions for Consideration, Relative to the Quartermaster's Department, United States Army." *Journal of the Military Service Institution* 15 (March 1894): 257–80.

Mattes, Merrill J. "The Sutler's Store at Fort Laramie." *Annals of Wyoming* 18 (July 1946): 93–137.

McChristian, Douglas C. "The Commissary Sergeant: His Life at Fort Davis." *Military History of Texas and the Southwest* 14, no. 1 (1978): 21–32.

Miller, Darlis A. "The Perils of a Post Sutler: William H. Moore at Fort Union, New Mexico, 1859–1870." *Journal of the West* 32 (April 1993): 7–18.

———. *Soldiers and Settlers: Military Supply in the Southwest, 1861–1885.* Albuquerque: University of New Mexico Press, 1989.

Risch, Erna. *Quartermaster Support of the Army: A History of the Corps, 1775–1939.* Washington, DC: U.S. Government Printing Office, 1962.

Spring, Agnes Wright, ed. "Old Letter Book: Discloses Economic History of Fort Laramie, 1858–1871." *Annals of Wyoming* 13 (October 1941): 237–330.

Tapson, Alfred J. "The Sutler and the Soldier." *Military Affairs* 21 (Winter 1957): 175–81.

Welty, Raymond L. "Supplying the Frontier Military Posts." *Kansas Historical Quarterly* 7 (May 1938): 154–69.

TRANSPORTATION AND COMMUNICATION

Albright, George L. *Official Explorations for Pacific Railroads.* Berkeley: University of California Press, 1921.

Allin, Lawrence C. "'A Mile Wide and an Inch Deep': Attempts to Navigate the Platte River." *Nebraska History* 63 (Spring 1982): 1–15.

———. "'A Thousand and One Little Delays': Training the Missouri River at Omaha, 1877–1883." *Nebraska History* 66 (Winter 1985): 349–71.

Athearn, Robert G. "The Firewagon Road." *Montana, Magazine of Western History* 20 (April 1970): 2–19.

———. *Union Pacific Country.* Chicago: Rand McNally, 1971.

Austerman, Wayne R. *Sharps Rifles and Spanish Mules: The San Antonio–El Paso Mail, 1851– 1881.* College Station: Texas A&M University Press, 1985.

Cabaniss, Archibald A. "Troop and Company Pack-Trains." *Journal of the U.S. Cavalry Association* 3 (September 1890): 248–52.

Daly, Henry W. *Manual of Instructions in Pack Transportation.* West Point, NY: U.S. Military Academy Press, 1901.

Ellis, L. Tuffly, ed. "Lieutenant A. W. Greely's Report on the Installation of Military Telegraph Lines in Texas, 1875–1876." *Southwestern Historical Quarterly* 69 (July 1965): 65–87.

Essin, Emmett M., III. "Mules, Packs and Packtrains." *Southwestern Historical Quarterly* 74 (July 1970): 52–63.

Fine, Harry L. "Fort Laramie: Post Office in the Old West." *Posta: Postal History Journal* 8 (November 1977): 2–5.

Franks, Kenny, ed. "Ostriches for the Cavalry!" *Military History of Texas and the Southwest* 11, no. 4 (1973): 281–83.

Freedom, Gary S. "Moving Men and Supplies: Military Transportation on the Northern Great Plains, 1866–1891." *South Dakota History* 14 (Summer 1984): 114–33.

Gray, John S. "Veterinary Service on Custer's Last Campaign." *Kansas Historical Quarterly* 43 (Autumn 1977): 249–63.

Greene, A. C. *900 Miles on the Butterfield Trail.* Denton: University of North Texas Press, 1994.

Hammer, Kenneth M. "Railroads and the Frontier Garrisons of Dakota Territory." *North Dakota History* 46 (Summer 1979): 24–34.

Hedren, Paul L. "A Footnote to History: The U.S. Army at Promontory, Utah, May 10, 1869." *Utah Historical Quarterly* 49 (Fall 1981): 363–73.

Holcomb, Freeborn P. "The Use of the Bicycle in the Army." *Journal of the United States Cavalry Association* 15 (January 1905): 598–604.

Howell, Charles W. "An Army Engineer on the Missouri in 1867." *Nebraska History* 53 (Summer 1972): 253–91.

Hutton, Paul A. "'Fort Desolation': The Military Establishment, the Railroad, and Settlement on the Northern Plains." *North Dakota History* 56 (Spring 1989): 21–30.

McChristian, Douglas C. "Apaches and Soldiers: Mail Protection in West Texas." *Periodical: Journal of the Council on America's Military Past* 13, no. 3 (1985): 3–17.

Miles, Susan. "The Post Office War." *Fort Concho Report* 12 (Spring 1980): 5–13.

Miller, Darlis A. "Civilians and Military Supply in the Southwest." *Journal of Arizona History* 23 (Summer 1982): 115–38.

"Ostriches for Our Cavalry." *Army and Navy Journal* 16 (August 1879): 955–56.

Remington, Frederic. "Stirrups or Pedals? The Colonel of the First Cycle Infantry." *American West* 11 (September 1974): 10–13, 58–59.

Rolak, Bruno J. "General Miles' Mirrors: The Heliograph in the Geronimo Campaign of 1886." *Journal of Arizona History* 16 (Summer 1975): 145–60.

Rue, Norman L. "Words by Wire: Construction of the Military Telegraph in Arizona Territory, 1873–1877." MA thesis, University of Arizona, 1967.

Walker, Henry P. *The Wagonmasters: High Plains Freighting from the Earliest Days of the Santa Fe Trail to 1880.* Norman: University of Oklahoma Press, 1966.

EXPLORATION AND SCIENCE

Almy, Kenneth J., ed. "Thof's Dragon and the Letters of Capt. Theophilus H. Turner, M.D., U.S. Army." *Kansas History* 10 (Autumn 1987): 170–200.

Bartlett, Richard A. *Great Surveys of the American West.* Norman: University of Oklahoma Press, 1962.

Bell, William Gardner. "John Gregory Bourke: A Soldier Scientist in the Southwest." In *Military History of the Spanish-American Southwest: A Seminar,* ed. Bruno J. Rolak. Fort Huachuca, AZ: Fort Huachuca Museum, 1976.

Bonney, Orrin H., and Lorraine Bonney. *Battle Drums and Geysers: The Life and Journals of Lt. Gustavus Cheyney Doane, Soldier and Explorer of the Yellowstone and Snake River Regions.* Chicago: Swallow Press, 1970.

Brodhead, Michael J. "The Military Naturalist: A Lewis and Clark Heritage." *We Proceeded On* 9 (November 1983): 6–10.

———. "Notes on the Military Presence in Nevada, 1843–1988." *Nevada Historical Quarterly* 32, no. 4 (1989): 261–77.

———. "Of Mice and Mastodons: Contributions to the Literature of Mammology by Officers and Men of the United States Army in the Nineteenth Century." *Archives of Natural History* 18 (1991): 363–74.

———. *A Soldier-Scientist in the American Southwest: Being a Narrative of the Travels of Elliot Coues.* Tucson: Arizona Historical Society, 1973.

Falk, Stanley L. "Soldier-Technologist: Major Alfred Mordecai and the Beginnings of Science in the United States Army." PhD diss., Georgetown University, 1958.

Goetzmann, William H. *Army Exploration in the American West, 1803–1863.* New Haven, CT: Yale University Press, 1959.

———. *Exploration and Empire: The Explorer and the Scientist in the Winning of the American West.* New York: Alfred A. Knopf, 1971.

Halpern, Katheryn Spencer, and Susan Brown McGreevy, eds. *Washington Matthews: Studies of Navajo Culture, 1880–1894.* Albuquerque: University of New Mexico Press, 1996.

Hedren, Paul L. *With Crook in the Black Hills: Stanley J. Morrow's 1876 Photographic Legacy.* Boulder, CO: Pruett, 1985.

Jackson, Donald. *Custer's Gold: The United States Cavalry Expedition of 1874.* New Haven, CT: Yale University Press, 1966.

Kime, Wayne R., ed. *The Black Hills Journals of Colonel Richard Irving Dodge.* Norman: University of Oklahoma Press, 1996.

Knecht, Robert Lee. "Ado Hunnius, Great Plains Cartographer." MA thesis, Emporia State University, 1987.

Krause, Herbert, and Gary D. Olson. *Prelude to Glory: A Newspaper Accounting of Custer's 1874 Expedition to the Black Hills.* Sioux Falls, SD: Brevet Press, 1974.

Manning, Thomas J. *Government in Science: The U.S. Geological Survey, 1867–1894.* Lexington: University Press of Kentucky, 1967.

McAndrews, Eugene V., ed. "An Army Engineer's Journal of Custer's Black Hills Expedition, July 2, 1874–August 23, 1874." *Journal of the West* 13 (January 1974): 78–85.

O'Hara, Susan Pritchard, and Gregory Graves. *Saving California's Coast: Army Engineers at Oceanside and Humboldt Bay.* Spokane, WA: Arthur H. Clark, 1991.

Richmond, Henry R., III. *The History of the Portland District, Corps of Engineers, 1871–1969.* Portland, OR: U.S. Army Corps of Engineers, 1970.

Ronda, James P. *Beyond Lewis and Clark: The Army Explores the West.* Tacoma: Washington State Historical Society, 2003.

Scheufele, Roy W. *The History of the North Pacific Division, U.S. Army Corps of Engineers, 1888–1965.* Portland, OR: U.S. Army Corps of Engineers, 1969.

Schubert, Frank N. *Vanguard of Expansion: Army Engineers in the Trans-Mississippi West, 1819–1879.* Washington, DC: Office of the Chief of Engineers, n.d.

Stegner, Wallace. "The Scientist As Artist: Clarence E. Dutton and the Tertiary History of the Grand Cañon District." *American West* 15 (May–June 1978): 17–29.

Turcheneske, John A., Jr. "Historical Manuscripts as Sources for Anthropological Study: The Ethnological Correspondence of John Gregory Bourke." *New Mexico Historical Review* 59 (July 1984): 267–87.

———. "John G. Bourke—Troubled Scientist." *Journal of Arizona History* 20 (Autumn 1979): 323–44.

Willingham, William F. *Army Engineers and the Development of Oregon: A History of the Portland District, U.S. Army Corps of Engineers, 1929–1973.* Washington, DC: U.S. Government Printing Office, 1983.

MORALE AND DESERTIONS

Ambrose, David C. "The Major Reasons for Army Desertions at Fort Davis, Texas, 1882–1885." *Panhandle-Plains Historical Review* 45 (1972): 38–45.

Anderson, E. "The Pay of Our Soldiers Affecting Desertion and Re-enlistment." *American Review of Reviews* 33 (1906): 330–40.

Bergey, Ellwood. *Why Soldiers Desert from the United States Army.* Philadelphia: W. F. Fell, 1903.

Carter, Robert G. *On the Trail of Deserters.* Washington, DC: Gibson Brothers, 1920.

Daubenmier, Judy. "Empty Saddles: Desertion from the Dashing U.S. Cavalry." *Montana, Magazine of Western History* 54 (Autumn 2004): 2–17.

Duke, Escal F. "O. M. Smith, Frontier Pay Clerk." *West Texas Historical Association Year Book* 45 (1969): 45–57.

McAnaney, William D. "Desertion in the United States Army." *Journal of the Military Service Institution of the United States* 10 (1889): 450–65.

McChristian, Douglas C. "The Bug Juice War." *Annals of Wyoming* 49 (Fall 1977): 253–61.

McDermott, John D. "Were They Really Rogues?: Desertion in the Nineteenth-Century U.S. Army." *Nebraska History* 78 (Winter 1997): 165–74.

Murray, Robert A. "Prices and Wages at Fort Laramie, 1881–1885." *Annals of Wyoming* 36 (April 1964): 19–21.

Pope, J. Worden. "Desertion and the Military Prison." *Cosmopolitan Magazine* 10 (November 1890): 111–20.

Walker, Henry P. "Bugler! No Pay Call Today! The Year the Army Went Payless." *Montana, Magazine of Western History* 21 (Summer 1971): 34–43.

EDUCATION

Allensworth, Allen. "Military Education in the United States." In *National Education Association Journal of Proceedings and Addresses,* 224–34. New York: J. J. Little, 1891.

Ambrose, Stephen E. *Duty, Honor, Country: A History of West Point.* Baltimore: Johns Hopkins University Press, 1966.

Annual Report of the U.S. Military Post Library Association, 1871–72. New York: Headquarters of the Library Association, 1872.

Brereton, T. R. *Educating the U.S. Army: Arthur L. Wagner and Reform, 1875–1905.* Lincoln: University of Nebraska Press, 2000.

Edens, Walter. "Wyoming's Fort Libraries: The March of Intellect." *Annals of Wyoming* 51 (Fall 1979): 54–62.

Iverson, William L. "U.S. Military Post Schools, 1821–1921." PhD diss., Stanford University, 1936.

King, Charles. "The Leavenworth School." *Harper's New Monthly Magazine* 76 (April 1888): 777–92.

Miewald, Robert D. "The Army Post Schools: A Report from the Bureaucratic Wars." *Military Affairs* 39 (February 1975): 8–11.

Mullins, George G. "Education in the Army." *United Service* 2 (April 1880): 478–85.

Nenninger, Timothy K. *The Leavenworth Schools and the Old Army: Education, Professionalism, and the Officer Corps of the United States Army, 1881–1918.* Westport, CT: Greenwood Press, 1978.

Raines, Edgar F., Jr. "Major General J. Franklin Bell, U.S.A.: The Education of a Soldier, 1856–1899." *Register of the Kentucky Historical Society* 83 (Autumn 1985): 315–46.

Reeves, Ira L. *Military Education in the United States.* Burlington, VT: Free Press, 1914.

Riter, Maria Inez Corlett. "Teaching School at Old Fort Laramie." *Annals of Wyoming* 51 (Fall 1979): 24–25.

Sehon, John L. "Post Schools in the Army." *Journal of the Military Service Institution of the United States* 14 (May 1892): 522–34.

Sharpe, Alfred C. "Post Schools." *Journal of the Military Service Institution of the United States* 12 (November 1891): 1177–88.

Smith, Thomas T. "West Point and the Indian Wars." *Military History of the West* 24 (Spring 1994): 24–55.

Stewart, Miller J. "A Touch of Civilization: Culture and Education in the Frontier Army." *Nebraska History* 65 (Summer 1984): 257–82.

Weaver, E. M. "The Military Schools of the United States." *United Service* 3 (May 1890): 457–69.

White, William Bruce. "ABCs for the American Enlisted Man: The Army Post School System, 1866–1898." *History of Education Quarterly* 8 (Winter 1968): 479–96.

MEDICAL ISSUES

Ashburn, Percy M. *A History of the Medical Department of the United States Army.* Boston: Houghton Mifflin, 1929.

Billings, John S. *A Report on Barracks and Hospitals, with Descriptions of Military Posts.* War Department Surgeon General's Office Circular, no. 4. Washington, DC: U.S. Government Printing Office, 1870.

———. *Report on the Hygiene of the United States Army, with Descriptions of Military Posts.* War Department Surgeon General's Office Circular, no. 8. Washington, DC: U.S. Government Printing Office, 1875.

Breeden, James O. "The Army and Public Health." In *The United States Army in Peacetime,* ed. Robin Higham and Carol Brandt. Manhattan, KS: Military Affairs/Aerospace Historian, 1975.

Brown, Harvey E., comp. *The Medical Department of the United States Army from 1775 to 1873.* Washington, DC: Surgeon General's Office, 1873.

Buecker, Thomas R., ed. "A Surgeon at the Little Big Horn: The Letters of Dr. Holmes O. Paulding." *Montana, Magazine of Western History* 32 (Autumn 1982): 34–49.

Chappell, Gordon S. "Surgeon at Fort Sidney: Captain Walter Reed's Experiences at a Nebraska Military Post, 1883–1884." *Nebraska History* 4 (Fall 1973): 419–43.

Clary, David A. "The Role of the Army Surgeon in the West: Daniel Weisel at Fort Davis, Texas, 1868–1872." *Western Historical Quarterly* 3 (January 1972): 53–66.

Corbusier, William T. *Verde to San Carlos: Recollections of a Famous Army Surgeon and His Observant Family on the Western Frontier, 1869–1886.* Tucson, AZ: Dale Stuart King, 1968.

Craig, Stephen C. "Medicine for the Military: Dr. George M. Sternberg on the Kansas Plains, 1866–1870." *Kansas History* 21 (Autumn 1998): 188–206.

Davidson, Wilson T. *Years of an Army Doctor: An Autobiography.* San Antonio, TX: Naylor, 1944.

Gibson, John M. *Soldier in White: The Life of General George Miller Sternberg.* Durham, NC: Duke University Press, 1958.

Gillett, Mary C. *The Army Medical Department, 1865–1917.* Washington, DC: Center for Military History, U.S. Army, 1995.

———. "United States Army Surgeons and the Big Horn–Yellowstone Expedition of 1876." *Montana, Magazine of Western History* 39 (Winter 1989): 16–27.

Grange, Roger T., Jr. "Treating the Wounded at Fort Robinson." *Nebraska History* 45 (September 1964): 273–94.

Hedren, Paul L. "The Sioux War Adventures of Dr. Charles V. Petteys, Acting Assistant Surgeon." *Journal of the West* 32 (April 1993): 29–37.

Hume, Edgar Erskine. *Ornithologists of the United States Army Medical Corps.* Baltimore: Johns Hopkins University Press, 1942.

Kalisch, Philip A., and Beatrice J. Kalisch. "Indian Territory Forts: Charnel Houses of the Frontier, 1839–1865." *Chronicles of Oklahoma* 50 (Spring 1972): 65–81.

Kelly, Carla. "'The Buffalo Carcass on the Company Sink': Sanitation at a Frontier Army Fort." *North Dakota History* 69, no. 2–4 (2002): 50–60.

Kennedy, W.J.D. *On the Plains with Custer and Hancock: The Journal of Isaac Coates, Army Surgeon.* Boulder, CO: Johnson Books, 1996.

Kimball, Maria Brace. *A Soldier-Doctor of Our Army: James P. Kimball, Late Colonel and Assistant Surgeon-General, U.S. Army.* Boston: Houghton Mifflin, 1917.

Luce, Edward S., ed. "The Diary and Letters of Dr. James DeWolf, Acting Assistant Surgeon, U.S. Army: His Record of the Sioux Expedition of 1876 as Kept until His Death." *North Dakota History* 25 (April–July 1958): 33–81.

Mattison, Ray H., ed. "The Diary of Surgeon Washington Matthews, Fort Rice, D.T." *North Dakota History* 21 (January 1954): 5–74.

Neilson, John. "'I Long to Return to Fort Concho': Acting Assistant Surgeon Samuel Smith's Letters from the Texas Military Frontier, 1878–1879." *Military History of the West* 24 (Fall 1994): 122–86.

———, ed. "Military Medicine on the Frontier: Charles M. Gandy in Texas, 1886–1890." *Fort Concho Report* 21, no. 2 (1989): 22–36.

———. "Soldiers and Surgeons: Army Medical Practice at Fort Concho, Texas, 1867–1889." *West Texas Historical Association Year Book* 59 (1993): 45–58.

Notson, William M. "Fort Concho, 1868–1872: The Medical Officer's Observations." *Military History of Texas and the Southwest* 12 (Fall 1975): 125–49.

Olch, Peter D. "Medicine in the Indian-Fighting Army, 1866–1890." *Journal of the West* 21 (July 1982): 32–41.

Omer, George E., Jr. "An Army Hospital: From Dragoons to Rough Riders—Fort Riley, 1853–1903." *Kansas Historical Quarterly* 23 (Winter 1957): 337–67.

Palmieri, Anthony, and Chris Humberson. "Medical Incidents in the Life of Dr. John H. Finfrock." *Annals of Wyoming* 53 (Fall 1981): 64–69.

Paulding, Holmes Offley. *Surgeon's Diary with the Custer Relief Column.* Edited by W. Boyes. Washington, DC: WJBM Associates, 1974.

Poor, Robert. "Washington Matthews: An Intellectual Biography." MA thesis, University of Nevada-Reno, 1975.

Potter, James E. " 'He…Regretted Having to Die That Way': Firearms Accidents in the Frontier Army, 1806–1891." *Nebraska History* 78 (Winter 1997): 175–86.

Powers, Ramon S., and Gene Younger. "Cholera and the Army in the West: Treatment and Control in 1866–1867." *Military Affairs* 39 (April 1975): 49–54.

Riley, Paul. "Dr. David Franklin Powell and Fort McPherson." *Nebraska History* 51 (Summer 1970): 153–71.

Roberson, Jere W., ed. "A View from Oklahoma, 1866–1868: The Diary and Letters of Dr. James Reagles, Jr., Assistant Surgeon, U.S. Army." *Red River Valley Historical Review* 3 (Fall 1978): 19–46.

Steele, Volney. "Doctors at the Battle of the Big Hole." *Military History of the West* 32 (Spring 2002): 25–33.

Sternberg, Martha L. *George Miller Sternberg, a Biography.* Chicago: American Medical Association, 1920.

Wengert, James W. "The Contract Surgeon." *Journal of the West* 36 (January 1997): 67–76.

Wier, James A. "19th Century Army Doctors on the Frontier and in Nebraska." *Nebraska History* 61 (Summer 1980): 192–214.

Williams, Mary L. "Care of the Dead (and Lack of It) at 19th Century Posts." *Periodical: Journal of the Council on America's Military Past* 13, no. 1 (1984): 14–30.

Wood, Laura N. *Walter Reed: Doctor in Uniform.* New York: Julian Messner, 1943.

CHAPLAINS

Beecher, George Allen. *A Bishop of the Great Plains.* Philadelphia: Church Historical Society, 1950.

Gamble, Richard D. "Army Chaplains at Frontier Posts, 1830–1860." *Historical Magazine of the Protestant Episcopal Church* 27, no. 4 (1958): 287–304.

Matthews, James T. "Using the Deity's Name in Reverence: The Chaplains at Fort Concho." *Panhandle-Plains Historical Review* 68 (1995): 37–44.

Office of the Chief of Chaplains. *American Army Chaplaincy: A Brief History.* Washington, DC: Chaplains Association, 1946.

Pfaller, Louis L. "Eli Washington John Lindesmith: Fort Keogh's Chaplain in Buckskin." *Montana, Magazine of Western History* 27 (January 1977): 14–25.

Reaves, Stacy Webb. " 'No Pretensions of Piety': The Army Post Chaplain in the American West, 1866–1895." PhD diss., Oklahoma State University, 1984.

Schmidt, Carol. "The Chaplains of Fort Concho." Pts. 1 and 2. *Fort Concho Report* 16 (Spring 1984): 27–32; 16 (Summer 1984): 31–40.

Seraile, William. "Saving Souls on the Frontier: A Chaplain's Labor." *Montana, Magazine of Western History* 42 (Winter 1992): 29–41.

Smith, Richard K. "For God…for Country…for the Territories." *Arizona Highways* 49 (April 1973): 8–12.

Stratton, David H. "The Army and the Gospel in the West." *Western Humanities Review* 8 (Spring 1954): 247–62.

SIGNAL CORPS AND WEATHER SERVICE

Bates, Charles C., and John F. Fuller. *America's Weather Warriors, 1814–1985.* College Station: Texas A&M University Press, 1986.

Crimmins, Martin L. "General Albert J. Myer: The Father of the Signal Corps." *West Texas Historical Association Year Book* 29 (1953): 47–66.

Hawes, Joseph M. "The Signal Corps and Its Weather Service, 1870–1890." *Military Affairs* 30 (Summer 1966): 68–76.

Hughes, Frederic J., Jr. "Albert James Myer: Army Physician and Climatologist." *Transactions of the American Clinical and Climatological Association* 81 (1969): 119–29.

Hume, Edgar Erskine. "The Foundation of American Meteorology by the United States Army Medical Department." *Bulletin of the History of Medicine* 8 (January–May 1940): 202–38.

Marshall, Max L., ed. *The Story of the U.S. Army Signal Corps.* New York: Franklin Watts, 1965.

Raines, Rebecca Robbins. *Getting the Message Through: A Branch History of the U.S. Army Signal Corps.* Washington, DC: Center for Military History, U.S. Army, 1996.

Scheips, Paul J. "'Old Probabilities': A. J. Myer and the Signal Corps Weather Service." *Arlington Historical Magazine* 5 (October 1974): 29–43.

Whitnah, Donald R. *A History of the United States Weather Bureau.* Urbana: University of Illinois Press, 1961.

RELIEF EFFORTS FOR CIVILIANS

Buecker, Thomas R. "'Can You Send Us Immediate Relief?' Army Expeditions to the Northern Black Hills, 1876–1878." *South Dakota History* 25 (Summer 1995): 95–115.

Cooling, B. Franklin. "The Army and Flood and Disaster Relief." In *The United States Army in Peacetime,* ed. Robin Higham and Carol Brandt. Manhattan, KS: Military Affairs/Aerospace Historian, 1975.

Fite, Gilbert C. "The United States Army and Relief to Pioneer Settlers, 1874–1875." *Journal of the West* 6 (January 1967): 99–107.

Kenner, Charles. "Guardians in Blue: The United States Cavalry and the Growth of the Texas Range Cattle Industry." *Journal of the West* 34 (January 1995): 46–54.

Kepfield, Sam S. "Grasshoppers, Destitution, and Public Relief in Western Nebraska, 1874–1875." *Journal of the West* 34 (July 1995): 93–100.

———. "'A Great Deal Like Smallpox': 'Destitution Business' and State Drought Relief in Nebraska, 1890–1895." *Heritage of the Great Plains* 26 (Summer 1993): 37–46.

Olson, Gary D., ed. "Relief for Nebraska Grasshopper Victims: The Official Journal of Lieutenant Theodore E. True." *Nebraska History* 48 (Summer 1967): 119–40.

Skaggs, Jimmy M. "Military Operations on the Cattle Trails." *Texas Military History* 6 (Summer 1967): 137–48.

PROTECTING NATIONAL PARKS

Anderson, George. "Work of the Cavalry in Protecting the Yellowstone National Park." *Journal of the United States Cavalry Association* 10 (March 1897): 3–10.

Archibald, James F. J. "A Cavalry March to the Yosemite." *Illustrated American* 7 (November 1896): 718–22.

Baldwin, Kenneth H. *Enchanted Enclosure: The Army Engineers and the Yellowstone National Park, a Documentary History.* Washington, DC: Office of the Chief of Engineers, U.S. Army, 1976.

Bartlett, Richard A. "The Army, Conservation, and Ecology: The National Park Assignment." In *The United States Army in Peacetime,* ed. Robin Higham and Carol Brandt. Manhattan, KS: Military Affairs/Aerospace Historian, 1975.

———. *Nature's Yellowstone: The Story of an American Wilderness That Became Yellowstone National Park in 1872.* Albuquerque: University of New Mexico Press, 1974.

———. *Yellowstone: A Wilderness Besieged.* Tucson: University of Arizona Press, 1985.

Fletcher, Marvin E. "Army Fire Fighters." *Idaho Yesterdays* 16 (Summer 1972): 12–15.

Haines, Aubrey L. *Yellowstone National Park: Its Exploration and Establishment.* Washington, DC: U.S. Department of the Interior, National Park Service, 1974.

———. *The Yellowstone Story: A History of Our First National Park.* 2 vols. Yellowstone National Park, WY: Yellowstone Library and Museum Association, 1977.

Hampton, H. Duane. "The Army and the National Parks." *Montana, Magazine of Western History* 22 (July 1972): 64–79.

———. *How the U.S. Cavalry Saved Our National Parks.* Bloomington: Indiana University Press, 1971.

Hutton, Paul A. "Phil Sheridan's Crusade for Yellowstone." *America History Illustrated* 19 (February 1985): 7, 10–15.

Lockwood, John A. "Uncle Sam's Troopers in the National Parks of California." *Overland Monthly* 33 (April 1899): 356–68.

McClure, N. F. "The Fourth Cavalry in the Yosemite National Park." *Journal of the United States Cavalry Association* 10 (June 1897): 113–21.

Meyerson, Harvey. *Nature's Army: When Soldiers Fought for Yosemite.* Lawrence: University Press of Kansas, 2001.

Remington, Frederic. "Policing the Yellowstone." *Harper's Weekly* 39 (January 1895): 35–38.

PROTECTING INDIAN LANDS

Anderson, Grant K. "The Black Hills Exclusion Policy: Judicial Challenges." *Nebraska History* 58 (Spring 1977): 1–24.

Anderson, Harry H. "A History of the Cheyenne River Agency and Its Military Post, Fort Bennett, 1868–1891." *South Dakota Report and Historical Collections* 28 (1956): 390–551.

Bocock, Pamela S. "Camp Guthrie: Urban Outpost in the Territory, 1889–1891." *Chronicles of Oklahoma* 62 (Summer 1984): 166–89.

Bunky [Irving Geffs]. *The First Eight Months of Oklahoma City.* Oklahoma City: McMaster, 1890.

Dyer, Mrs. D. B. *"Fort Reno," or Picturesque "Cheyenne and Arrapahoe Army Life" before the Opening of "Oklahoma."* New York: G. W. Dillingham, 1896.

Green, Donald E. "The Oklahoma Land Run of 1889: A Centennial Re-interpretation." *Chronicles of Oklahoma* 67 (Summer 1989): 116–49.

Hoig, Stan. *The Oklahoma Land Rush of 1889.* Oklahoma City: Oklahoma Historical Society, 1984.

McDermott, John D. "The Military Problem and the Black Hills, 1874–1875." *South Dakota History* 31 (Fall/Winter 2001): 188–210.

Parker, Watson. "The Majors and the Miners: The Role of the U.S. Army in the Black Hills Gold Rush." *Journal of the West* 11 (January 1972): 79–113.

Payne, John Scott. "Conflict in Dakota Territory: Episodes of the Great Sioux War." *South Dakota History* 23 (Spring 1993): 1–47.

Rister, Carl Coke. *Land Hunger: David L. Payne and the Oklahoma Boomers.* Norman: University of Oklahoma Press, 1942.

Turner, Alvin O. "Order and Disorder: The Opening of the Cherokee Outlet." *Chronicles of Oklahoma* 71 (Summer 1993): 154–73.

CIVIL STRIFE

Badinelli, Don F. "Struggle in the Choctaw Nation: The Coal Miners Strike of 1894." *Chronicles of Oklahoma* 72 (Fall 1994): 292–311.

Ball, Larry D. "The United States Army and the Big Springs, Nebraska, Train Robbery of 1877." *Journal of the West* 34 (January 1995): 34–45.

———. "The United States Army As a Constabulary on the Northern Plains." *Great Plains Quarterly* 13 (Winter 1993): 21–32.

Birkhimer, William E. *Military Government and Martial Law.* Kansas City, MO: Franklin Hudson, 1914.

Blow, William N. "Use of Troops in Riots." *Journal of the Military Service Institution of the United States* 25 (July 1899): 45–57.

Carroll, Murray L. "Governor Francis E. Warren, the United States Army, and the Chinese Massacre at Rock Springs." *Annals of Wyoming* 59 (Fall 1987): 16–27.

Coakley, Robert W. *The Role of Federal Military Forces in Domestic Disorders, 1789–1878.* Washington, DC: Center for Military History, U.S. Army, 1988.

Cooper, Jerry M. *The Army and Civil Disorder: Federal Military Intervention in Labor Disputes, 1877–1900.* Westport, CT: Greenwood Press, 1980.

———. "The Army As Strikebreaker—The Railroad Strikes of 1877 and 1894." *Labor History* 18 (Spring 1977): 179–96.

———. "Federal Military Intervention in Domestic Disorders." In *The United States Military under the Constitution of the United States, 1789–1989,* ed. Richard H. Kohn. New York: New York University Press, 1991.

De Lorme, Roland L. "The Long Arm of the Law: Crime and Federal Law Enforcement in the Northern Tier Territories." In *Centennial West: Essays on the Northern Tier States,* ed. William L. Lang. Seattle: University of Washington Press, 1991.

Drees, James David. "The Army and Horse Thieves." *Kansas History* 11 (Spring 1988): 35–53.

Fulton, Maurice G. *A History of the Lincoln County War.* Edited by Robert N. Mullin. Tucson: University of Arizona Press, 1968.

Furman, H.W.C. "Restrictions upon the Use of the Army Imposed by the Posse Comitatus Act." *Military Law Review* 7 (January 1960): 85–129.

Gould, Lewis L. "Francis E. Warren and the Johnson County War." *Arizona and the West* 9 (Summer 1967): 131–42.

Gresham, John C. "Civil Employment of Troops." *United Service* 7 (May 1892): 476–82.

Hacker, Barton C. "The United States Army As a National Police Force: The Federal Policing of Labor Disputes, 1877–1898." *Military Affairs* 33 (April 1969): 255–64.

Karlin, Jules A. "The Anti-Chinese Outbreaks in Seattle, 1885–1886." *Pacific Historical Review* 29 (1948): 103–30.

———. "The Anti-Chinese Outbreak in Tacoma, 1885." *Pacific Historical Review* 23 (August 1954): 271–83.

Kavass, Igor I., and Adolph Sprudzs. *Military Aid to the Civil Power.* Fort Leavenworth, KS: General Service Schools Press, 1925.

Keleher, William A. *Violence in Lincoln County, 1869–1881.* Albuquerque: University of New Mexico Press, 1957.

Laurie, Clayton D. "'The Chinese Must Go': The United States Army and the Anti-Chinese Riots in Washington Territory, 1885–1886." *Pacific Northwest Quarterly* 81 (January 1990): 22–29.

Laurie, Clayton D. "Civil Disorder and the Military in Rock Springs, Wyoming: The Army's Role in the 1885 Chinese Massacre." *Montana, Magazine of Western History* 40 (Summer 1990): 44–59.

———. "Extinguishing Frontier Brushfires: The U.S. Army's Role in Quelling the Pullman Strike in the West, 1894." *Journal of the West* 32 (April 1993): 54–63.

———. "Filling the Breach: Military Aid to the Civil Power in the Trans-Mississippi West." *Western Historical Quarterly,* Summer 1994, 149–62.

———. "The United States Army and the Labor Radicals of the Coeur d'Alenes: Federal Military Intervention in the Mining Wars of 1892–1899." *Idaho Yesterdays* 37 (Summer 1993): 12–29.

Laurie, Clayton D., and Ronald H. Cole. *The Role of Federal Military Forces in Domestic Disorders, 1877–1945.* Washington, DC: Center for Military History, U.S. Army, 1997.

Lieber, G. Norman. *The Use of the Army in Aid of the Civil Power.* Washington, DC: U.S. Government Printing Office, 1898.

Molineux, E. L. "Riots in Cities and Their Suppression." *Journal of the Military Service Institution of the United States* 4 (1883): 335–70.

Murray, Robert A. "The United States Army in the Aftermath of the Johnson County Invasion." *Annals of Wyoming* 38 (April 1966): 59–75.

Nolan, Frederick. *The Lincoln County War: A Documentary History.* Norman: University of Oklahoma Press, 1992.

Otis, Elwell S. "The Army in Connection with the Labor Riots of 1877." Pts. 1 and 2. *Journal of the Military Service Institution of the United States* 5 (1884): 292–323; 6 (1884): 117–39.

Regan, James. "Military Duties in Aid of the Civil Power." *Journal of the Military Service Institution of the United States* 18 (March 1896): 285–97.

Smith, Helena Huntington. *The War on Powder River: The History of an Insurrection.* New York: McGraw-Hill, 1966.

Thayer, Russell. "Movements of Troops in Cities in Cases of Riots or Insurrection." *United Service* 1 (January 1879): 92–99.

Wade, Louise Carroll. "'Hell Hath No Fury Like a General Scorned': Nelson A. Miles, the Pullman Strike, and the Beef Scandal of 1898." *Illinois Historical Quarterly* 79, no. 3 (1986): 162–84.

Walker, Henry P. "When the Law Wore Army Blue." *Military Collector and Historian* 29 (Spring 1977): 4–14.

Wallace, William. "The Army and the Civil Power." *Journal of the Military Service Institution of the United States* 17 (September 1895): 235–66.

Welty, Raymond L. "The Policing of the Frontier by the Army, 1860–1870." *Kansas Historical Quarterly* 7 (August 1938): 246–57.

Wilson, Frederick T. *Federal Aid in Domestic Disturbances, 1789–1903.* 57th Cong., 2nd sess., 1903. S. Doc. 209.

INDIAN RELATIONS

Athearn, Robert G. "War Paint against Brass: The Army and the Plains Indian." *Montana, Magazine of Western History* 6 (July 1956): 11–22.

Bentley, Charles A. "Captain Frederick W. Benteen and the Kiowas." *Chronicles of Oklahoma* 56 (Fall 1978): 344–47.

Brodhead, Michael J. "Elliott Coues and the Apaches." *Journal of Arizona History* 14 (Summer 1973): 87–94.

Crook, George. "The Apache Problem." *Journal of the Military Service Institution of the United States* 7 (September 1886): 257–69.

D'Elia, Donald J. "The Argument over Civilian or Military Indian Control, 1865–1880." *Historian* 24 (February 1962): 207–25.

Dobak, William A. "The Army and the Buffalo: A Demur." *Western Historical Quarterly* 26 (Summer 1995): 197–202.

Dunlay, Thomas W. "General Crook and the White Man Problem." *Journal of the West* 18 (April 1979): 3–10.

Ellis, Richard N. "The Humanitarian Generals." *Western Historical Quarterly* 3 (April 1972): 169–78.

———. "The Humanitarian Soldiers." *Journal of Arizona History* 10 (Summer 1969): 53–66.

Gibbon, John. "Our Indian Question." *Journal of the Military Service Institution of the United States* 2 (1881): 101–20.

King, James T. "'A Better Way': General George Crook and the Ponca Indians." *Nebraska History* 50 (Fall 1969): 239–56.

———. "George Crook: Indian Fighter and Humanitarian." *Arizona and the West* 9 (Winter 1967): 333–48.

Leonard, Thomas C. "Red, White and the Army Blue: Empathy and Anger in the American West." *American Quarterly* 26 (May 1974): 176–90.

———. "The Reluctant Conquerors: How the Generals Viewed the Indians." *American Heritage* 27 (August 1976): 34–41.

Miles, Nelson A. "Our Indian Question." *Journal of the Military Service Institution of the United States* 2 (1881): 278–92.

Pratt, Richard Henry. *Battlefield and Classroom: Four Decades with the American Indian, 1867–1904.* Edited by Robert M. Utley. New Haven, CT: Yale University Press, 1964.

Rickards, Colin. "The Christian General Investigates the Camp Grant Massacre." In *The English Westerners' 10th Anniversary Publication.* London: English Westerners Society, 1964.

Smith, Sherry L. *The View from Officer's Row: Army Perceptions of Western Indians.* Tucson: University of Arizona Press, 1990.

———. "A Window on Themselves: Perceptions of Indians by Military Officers and Their Wives." *New Mexico Historical Review* 64 (October 1989): 447–61.

Smits, David D. "The Frontier Army and the Destruction of the Buffalo: 1865–1883." *Western Historical Quarterly* 25 (Autumn 1994): 313–38.

Utley, Robert M. "A Chained Dog: The Indian-Fighting Army." *American West* 10 (July 1973): 18–24, 61.

———. "The Frontier Army: John Ford or Arthur Penn?" In *Indian–White Relations: A Persistent Paradox,* ed. Jane F. Smith and Robert Kvasnicka. Washington, DC: Howard University Press, 1976.

Walker, Henry P. "George Crook, 'The Gray Fox': Prudent, Compassionate Indian Fighter." *Montana, Magazine of Western History* 17 (April 1967): 2–13.

INDIAN SCOUTS AND SOLDIERS

Ball, Eve. "The Apache Scouts: A Chiricahua Appraisal." *Arizona and the West* 7 (Winter 1965): 315–28.

Beck, Paul N. "Military Officers' Views of Indian Scouts, 1865–1890." *Military History of the West* 23 (Spring 1993): 1–19.

Carriker, Robert C. "Mercenary Heroes: The Scouting Detachment of the Indian Territory Expedition, 1874–1875." *Chronicles of Oklahoma* 51 (Fall 1973): 309–24.

Coopersmith, Clifford P. "Indians in the Army: Professional Advocacy and Regularization of Indian Military Service, 1889–1897." *Military History of the West* 26 (Fall 1996): 159–85.

Downey, Fairfax, and J. N. Jacobsen Jr. *The Red-Bluecoats: The Indian Scouts.* Fort Collins, CO: Old Army Press, 1973.

Dunlay, Thomas W. *Wolves for the Blue Soldiers: Indian Scouts and Auxiliaries with the United States Army, 1860–1890.* Lincoln: University of Nebraska Press, 1982.

Feaver, Eric. "Indian Soldiers, 1891–95: An Experiment on the Closing Frontier." *Prologue* 7 (Summer 1975): 109–18.

Greene, Jerome A. "The Crawford Affair: International Implications of the Geronimo Campaign." *Journal of the West* 2 (June 1972): 143–53.

Grinnell, George B. *Two Great Scouts and Their Pawnee Battalion.* Cleveland, OH: Arthur H. Clark, 1928.

Hatfield, Shelley Bowen. "The Death of Emmet Crawford: Who Was to Blame?" *Journal of Arizona History* 29 (Summer 1988): 131–48.

Lee, Robert. "Warriors in Ranks: American Indian Units in the Regular Army, 1891–1897." *South Dakota History* 21 (Fall 1991): 263–316.

Nalty, Bernard C., and Truman R. Strobridge. "Captain Emmet Crawford: Commander of Apache Scouts, 1882–1886." *Arizona and the West* 6 (Spring 1964): 30–40.

Porter, Kenneth W. "The Seminole Negro-Indian Scouts 1870–1881." *Southwestern Historical Quarterly* 55 (January 1952): 358–77.

Powell, William H. "The Indian As a Soldier." *United Service* 3 (March 1890): 229–38.

———. "Soldier or Granger?" *United Service* 3 (November 1889): 445–53.

Rope, John, and Grenville Goodwin. "Experiences of an Indian Scout." Pts. 1 and 2. *Arizona Historical Review* 3 (January 1936): 31–68; (April 1936): 31–73.

Tate, Michael L. "Soldiers of the Line: Apache Companies in the U.S. Army, 1891–1897." *Arizona and the West* 16 (Winter 1974): 343–64.

Thrapp, Dan L. *Al Sieber, Chief of Scouts.* Norman: University of Oklahoma Press, 1964.

Vance, Zebulon V. "The Indian Soldier." *Journal of the Military Service Institution of the United States* 14 (November 1893): 1203–7.

Weist, Katherine M. "Ned Casey and His Cheyenne Scouts: A Noble Experiment in an Atmosphere of Tension." *Montana, Magazine of Western History* 27 (January 1977): 26–39.

White, William Bruce. "The American Indian As Soldier, 1890–1919." *Canadian Review of American Studies* 7 (Spring 1976): 15–25.

INDIAN WARS

Aleshire, Peter. *The Fox and the Whirlwind: General George Crook and Geronimo, a Paired Biography.* New York: John Wiley, 2000.

Andrist, Ralph K. *The Long Death: The Last Days of the Plains Indians.* New York: Collier Books, 1964.

Athearn, Robert. "The Fort Buford 'Massacre.'" *Mississippi Valley Historical Review* 41 (March 1955): 675–84.

———. "Major Hough's March into Southern Ute Country, 1879." *Colorado Magazine* 25 (May 1948): 97–109.

Bourke, John G. *An Apache Campaign in the Sierra Madre: An Account of the Expedition in Pursuit of the Hostile Chiricahua Apaches in the Spring of 1883.* New York: Charles Scribner's Sons, 1886.

———. *Mackenzie's Last Fight with the Cheyennes: A Winter Campaign in Wyoming and Montana.* New York: Argonaut Press, 1966.

Bradley, James H. *The March of the Montana Column: A Prelude to the Custer Disaster.* Norman: University of Oklahoma Press, 1961.

Brill, Charles J. *Custer, Black Kettle, and the Fight on the Washita.* Norman: University of Oklahoma Press, 2001.

Brown, Dee. *Bury My Heart at Wounded Knee: An Indian History of the American West.* New York: Holt, Rinehart, and Winston, 1970.

Carroll, John M., ed. *The Papers of the Order of Indian Wars.* Fort Collins, CO: Old Army Press, 1975.

Carter, Robert G. *Tragedies of Cañon Blanco: A Story of the Texas Panhandle.* Washington, DC: Gibson Brothers, 1919.

Chalfant, William Y. *Cheyennes at Dark Water Creek: The Last Fight of the Red River War.* Norman: University of Oklahoma Press, 1997.

Chandler, Melbourne C. *Of Garryowen in Glory: A History of the Seventh U.S. Cavalry Regiment.* Annandale, VA: Turnpike Press, 1960.

Clow, Richmond L. "General Philip Sheridan's Legacy: The Sioux Pony Campaign of 1876." *Nebraska History* 57 (Winter 1976): 461–77.

Collins, Charles. *Apache Nightmare: The Battle of Cibecue Creek.* Norman: University of Oklahoma Press, 1999.

Courtney, Bradley G. "'One of the Most Remarkable Marches Ever Made': The Lawton Expedition and the American Military Pursuit of Geronimo's Band of Chiricahua Apaches." *Military History of the West* 34 (2004): 1–28.

Cozzens, Peter, ed. *Eyewitness to the Indian Wars, 1865–1890.* Vol. 5, *The Army and the Indian.* Mechanicsburg, PA: Stackpole, 2005.

Crimmins, Martin L. "Colonel Buell's Expedition into Mexico in 1880." *New Mexico Historical Review* 10 (April 1935): 133–42.

Daly, Henry W. "The Geronimo Campaign." *Journal of the United States Cavalry Association* 19 (July 1908): 68–103.

Davison, Stanley R., ed. "The Bannock-Paiute War of 1878: Letters of Major Edwin C. Mason." *Journal of the West* 11 (January 1972): 128–42.

Debo, Angie. *Geronimo: The Man, His Time, His Place.* Norman: University of Oklahoma Press, 1976.

De Keim, B. Randolph. *Sheridan's Troopers on the Border: A Winter Campaign on the Plains.* Philadelphia: Claxton, Remsen, and Haffelfinger, 1870.

Dillon, Richard. *Burnt-Out Fires: California's Modoc Indian War.* Englewood Cliffs, NJ: Prentice Hall, 1973.

Dinges, Bruce J. "The Victorio Campaign of 1880: Cooperation and Conflict on the United States–Mexico Border." *New Mexico Historical Review* 62 (January 1987): 81–94.

Ege, Robert J. *"Tell Baker to Strike Them Hard": Incident on the Marias, 23 Jan. 1870.* Bellevue, NE: Old Army Press, 1970.

Farrow, Edward S. *Mountain Scouting: A Hand-Book for Officers and Soldiers on the Frontiers.* New York: E. S. Farrow, 1881.

Faulk, Odie B. *Crimson Desert: Indian Wars of the American Southwest.* New York: Oxford University Press, 1974.

Finerty, John F. *War-Path and Bivouac, or the Conquest of the Sioux: A Narrative of Stirring Personal Experiences and Adventures in the Big Horn and Yellowstone Expedition of 1876, and in the Campaign on the British Border in 1879.* Norman: University of Oklahoma Press, 1961.

Garfield, Marvin. "The Military Post As a Factor in the Frontier Defense of Kansas, 1865–1869." *Kansas Historical Quarterly* 1 (November 1931): 50–62.

Gates, John M. "Indians and Insurrectos: The U.S. Army's Experience with Insurgency." *Parameters: The Journal of the U.S. Army War College* 13 (March 1983): 59–68.

Gibbon, John. "Arms to Fight Indians." *United Service* 1 (April 1879): 237–44.

Gray, John S. *Centennial Campaign: The Sioux War of 1876.* Ft. Collins, CO: Old Army Press, 1976.

Greene, Jerome A., ed. *Battles and Skirmishes of the Great Sioux War, 1876–1877: The Military View.* Norman: University of Oklahoma Press, 1993.

———, ed. *Lakota and Cheyenne: Indian Views of the Great Sioux War, 1876–1877.* Norman: University of Oklahoma Press, 1994.

———. *Morning Star Dawn: The Powder River Expedition and the Northern Cheyennes, 1876.* Norman: University of Oklahoma Press, 2003.

———. *Nez Perce Summer, 1877: The U.S. Army and the Nee-Me-Poo Crisis.* Helena: Montana Historical Society Press, 2000.

———. *Slim Buttes, 1876: An Episode in the Great Sioux War.* Norman: University of Oklahoma Press, 1982.

Haley, James L. *The Buffalo War: The History of the Red River Indian Uprising of 1874.* Garden City, NY: Doubleday, 1976.

Hammer, Kenneth, ed. *Custer in '76: Walter Camp's Notes on the Custer Fight.* Norman: University of Oklahoma Press, 1976.

Hatfield, Shelley Bowen. *Chasing Shadows: Apaches and Yaquis along the United States–Mexico Border, 1876–1911.* Albuquerque: University of New Mexico Press, 1998.

Hedren, Paul L. *First Scalp for Custer: The Skirmish at Warbonnet Creek, Nebraska, July 17, 1876.* Glendale, CA: Arthur H. Clark, 1980.

———, ed. *The Great Sioux War, 1876–77: The Best from* Montana, Magazine of Western History. Helena: Montana Historical Society Press, 1991.

———. "An Infantry Company in the Sioux Campaign, 1876." *Montana, Magazine of Western History* 33 (Winter 1983): 30–39.

Hoig, Stan. *The Battle of the Washita: The Sheridan-Custer Indian Campaign of 1867–69.* Garden City, NY: Doubleday, 1976.

Kaywaykla, James, and Eve Ball. *In the Days of Victorio: Recollections of a Warm Springs Apache.* Tucson: University of Arizona Press, 1970.

Kessel, William B., and Robert Wooster. *Encyclopedia of Native American Wars and Warfare.* New York: Facts on File, 2005.

King, Charles. *Campaigning with Crook: The Fifth Cavalry in the Sioux War of 1876.* Norman: University of Oklahoma Press, 1964.

Knight, Oliver. *Following the Indian Wars: The Story of the Newspaper Correspondents among the Indian Campaigns.* Norman: University of Oklahoma Press, 1960.

Lane, Jack C., ed. *Chasing Geronimo: The Journal of Leonard Wood, May–September, 1886.* Albuquerque: University of New Mexico Press, 1970.

Leckie, William H. *The Military Conquest of the Southern Plains.* Norman: University of Oklahoma Press, 1963.

———, ed. "Special Issue on the Red River War, 1874–1875." *Red River Valley Historical Review* 3 (Spring 1978): 143–276.

Marshall, J. T. *The Miles Expedition of 1874–1875: An Eyewitness Account of the Red River War.* Edited by Lonnie J. White. Austin, TX: Encino Press, 1971.

McDermott, John D. *A Guide to the Indian Wars of the West.* Lincoln: University of Nebraska Press, 1998.

Michno, Gregory F. *Encyclopedia of Indian Wars: Western Battles and Skirmishes, 1850–1890.* Missoula, MT: Mountain Press, 2003.

Monnett, John H. *The Battle of Beecher Island and the Indian War of 1867–1869.* Niwot: University Press of Colorado, 1992.

Monnett, John H. *Tell Them We Are Going Home: The Odyssey of the Northern Cheyennes.* Norman: University of Oklahoma Press, 2001.

Moriarty, James Robert, III. "The Congressional Medal of Honor during the Indian Wars." In *Troopers West: Military and Indian Affairs on the American Frontier,* ed. Ray Brandes. San Diego, CA: Frontier Heritage Press, 1970.

Murray, Keith A. *The Modocs and Their War.* Norman: University of Oklahoma Press, 1959.

Nye, Wilbur S. *Plains Indian Raiders: The Final Phases of Warfare from the Arkansas to the Red River.* Norman: University of Oklahoma Press, 1968.

Olson, James C. *Red Cloud and the Sioux Problem.* Lincoln: University of Nebraska Press, 1965.

Paul, R. Eli, ed. *The Nebraska Indian Wars Reader, 1865–1877.* Lincoln: University of Nebraska Press, 1998.

Rankin, Charles E., ed. *Legacy: New Perspectives on the Battle of the Little Bighorn.* Helena: Montana Historical Society Press, 1996.

Roberts, David. *Once They Moved Like the Wind: Cochise, Geronimo, and the Apache Wars.* New York: Simon and Schuster, 1993.

Robinson, Charles M., III. *A Good Year to Die: The Story of the Great Sioux War.* New York: Random House, 1995.

Russell, Don. "How Many Indians Were Killed?" *American West* 10 (July 1973): 42–47, 61–63.

Sheffy, L. F., ed. "Letters and Reminiscences of Gen. Theodore L. Baldwin: Scouting After Indians on the Plains of West Texas." *Panhandle-Plains Historical Review* 11 (1938): 6–19.

Sklenar, Larry. "Medals for Custer's Men." *Montana, Magazine of Western History* 50 (Winter 2000): 54–65.

———. *To Hell with Honor.* Norman: University of Oklahoma Press, 2000.

Spotts, David L. *Campaigning with Custer and the Nineteenth Kansas Volunteer Cavalry on the Washita Campaign, 1868–69.* Edited by E. A. Brininstool. Los Angeles: Wetzel, 1928.

Stands In Timber, John, and Margot Liberty. *Cheyenne Memories.* New Haven, CT: Yale University Press, 1967.

Stanley, Henry M. *My Early Travels and Adventures in America.* London: S. Low Marston, 1895.

Stewart, Edgar I. *Custer's Luck.* Norman: University of Oklahoma Press, 1955.

Taylor, Joe F., comp. *The Indian Campaign on the Staked Plains, 1874–1875: Military Correspondence from War Department Adjutant General's Office, File 2815-1874.* Canyon, TX: Panhandle-Plains Historical Society, 1962.

Thompson, Gerald. *The Army and the Navajo: The Bosque Redondo Reservation Experiment, 1863–1868.* Tucson: University of Arizona Press, 1976.

Thompson, Neil Baird. *Crazy Horse Called Them Walk-a-Heaps: The Story of the Foot Soldier in the Prairie Indian Wars.* Saint Cloud, MN: North Star Press, 1979.

Thompson, Richard A. *Crossing the Border with the 4th Cavalry: Mackenzie's Raid into Mexico, 1873.* Waco, TX: Texian Press, 1986.

Thrapp, Dan L. *The Conquest of Apacheria.* Norman: University of Oklahoma Press, 1967.

———, ed. *Dateline Fort Bowie: Charles Fletcher Lummis Reports on an Apache War.* Norman: University of Oklahoma Press, 1979.

———. *General Crook and the Sierra Madre Adventure.* Norman: University of Oklahoma Press, 1972.

Utley, Robert M. *The Lance and the Shield: The Life and Times of Sitting Bull.* New York: Henry Holt, 1993.

———. *The Last Days of the Sioux Nation.* New Haven, CT: Yale University Press, 1963.

Vaughn, J. W. *The Reynolds Campaign on Powder River.* Norman: University of Oklahoma Press, 1961.

———. *With Crook at the Rosebud.* Harrisburg, PA: Stackpole, 1956.

Wallace, Ernest. "Colonel Ranald S. Mackenzie's Expedition of 1872 across the South Plains." *West Texas Historical Association Year Book* 38 (October 1962): 4–22.

———, ed. *Ranald S. Mackenzie's Official Correspondence Relating to Texas, 1871–1873.* Lubbock: West Texas Museum Association, 1967.

Wallace, Ernest, and Adrian S. Anderson. "R. S. Mackenzie and the Kickapoos: The Raid into Mexico in 1873." *Arizona and the West* 7 (Summer 1965): 105–26.

Webb, George W. *Chronological List of Engagements between the Regular Army of the United States and Various Tribes of Hostile Indians during the Years 1790 to 1898, Inclusive.* St. Joseph, MO: Wing, 1939.

White, Lonnie J., ed. *Hostiles and Horse Soldiers: Indian Battles and Campaigns in the West.* Boulder, CO: Pruett, 1972.

FORT HISTORIES

Adams, Gerald M. *The Post Near Cheyenne: A History of Fort D. A. Russell, 1867–1930.* Boulder, CO: Pruett, 1989.

Annin, William E. "Fort Robinson during the 1880's: An Omaha Newspaperman Visits the Post." *Nebraska History* 55 (Summer 1974): 181–202.

Baker, Robert Orr. *The Muster Roll: A Biography of Fort Ripley, Minnesota.* Saint Paul, MN: H. M. Smyth, 1972.

Bierschale, Margaret. *Fort McKavett, Texas: Post on the San Saba.* Salado, TX: Anson Jones Press, 1966.

Brandes, Ray. *Frontier Military Posts of Arizona.* Globe, AZ: Dale Stuart King, 1960.

Brown, Dee. *Fort Phil Kearny: An American Saga.* New York: G. P. Putnam's Sons, 1962.

Buecker, Thomas R. "The 1887 Expansion of Fort Robinson." *Nebraska History* 68 (Summer 1987): 83–93.

———. "Fort Niobrara, 1880–1906: Guardian of the Rosebud Sioux." *Nebraska History* 65 (Fall 1984): 300–25.

———. *Fort Robinson and the American West, 1874–1899.* Norman: University of Oklahoma Press, 2003.

Cagle, Eldon, Jr. *Quadrangle: The History of Fort Sam Houston.* Austin, TX: Eakin Press, 1985.

Carriker, Robert C. *Fort Supply, Indian Territory: Frontier Outpost on the Plains.* Norman: University of Oklahoma Press, 1970.

Cashion, Ty. "Life on Government Hill: Fort Griffin before the Boom." *West Texas Historical Association Year Book* 70 (1994): 113–25.

———. *A Texas Frontier: The Clear Fork Country and Fort Griffin, 1849–1887.* Norman: University of Oklahoma Press, 1996.

Crimmins, Martin L. "Camp Peña Colorado, Texas." *West Texas Historical and Scientific Society Bulletin* 56 (1935): 8–22.

Cusack, Michael F. *Fort Clark: The Lonely Sentinel.* Austin, TX: Eakin Press, 1985.

De Noyer, Charles. "The History of Fort Totten." *Collections of the State Historical Society of North Dakota* 3 (1910): 178–236.

Dobak, William A. *Fort Riley and Its Neighbors: Military Money and Economic Growth.* Norman: University of Oklahoma Press, 1998.

Dunn, Adrian R. "A History of Old Fort Berthold." *North Dakota History* 30 (October 1963): 157–240.

Edwards, Paul M. "Fort Wadsworth and the Friendly Santee Sioux, 1864–1892." *South Dakota Department of History Report and Historical Collections* 31 (1962): 74–156.

Emmett, Chris. *Fort Union and Winning of the Southwest.* Norman: University of Oklahoma Press, 1965.

Frazer, Robert W. *Forts of the West: Military Forts and Presidios and Posts Commonly Called Forts West of the Mississippi River to 1898.* Norman: University of Oklahoma Press, 1965.

Goplen, Arnold O. "Fort Abraham Lincoln: A Typical Frontier Military Post." *North Dakota History* 13 (October 1946): 176–221.

Graham, Roy Eugene. "Federal Fort Architecture in Texas during the Nineteenth Century." *Southwestern Historical Quarterly* 74 (October 1970): 165–88.

Green, Bill. *The Dancing Was Lively: Fort Concho, Texas, a Social History, 1867 to 1882.* San Angelo, TX: Fort Concho Sketches, 1974.

Greene, Jerome A. *Fort Randall on the Missouri, 1856–1892.* Pierre: South Dakota State Historical Society Press, 2005.

Grinstead, Marion C. *The Life and Death of a Frontier Fort: Fort Craig, New Mexico, 1854–1885.* Socorro, NM: Socorro County Historical Society, 1973.

Hafen, LeRoy R., and Francis Marion Young. *Fort Laramie and the Pageant of the West, 1834–1890.* Glendale, CA: Arthur H. Clark, 1938.

Haley, J. Evetts. *Fort Concho and the Texas Frontier.* San Angelo, TX: San Angelo Standard-Times, 1952.

Hamilton, Allen Lee. *Sentinel of the Southern Plains: Fort Richardson and the Northwest Texas Frontier, 1866–1878.* Fort Worth: Texas Christian University Press, 1988.

Hardeman, Nicholas P. "Brick Stronghold of the Border: Fort Assinniboine, 1879–1911." *Montana, Magazine of Western History* 29 (April 1979): 54–67.

Harvey, Mark. "Securing the Confluence: A Portrait of Fort Buford, 1866 to 1895." *North Dakota History* 69, no. 2–4 (2003): 34–49.

Hedren, Paul L. *Fort Laramie and the Great Sioux War.* Norman: University of Oklahoma Press, 1998.

———. "On Duty at Fort Ridgely, Minnesota: 1853–1867." *South Dakota History* 7 (Spring 1977): 168–92.

Hoagland, Alison K. *Army Architecture in the West: Forts Laramie, Bridger, and D. A. Russell, 1849–1912.* Norman: University of Oklahoma Press, 2004.

Hoeckman, Steven. "The History of Fort Sully." *South Dakota Historical Collections* 26 (1952): 222–77.

Hoig, Stan. *Fort Reno and the Indian Territory Frontier.* Fayetteville: University of Arkansas Press, 2000.

Holmes, Louis A. *Fort McPherson, Nebraska, Cottonwood, N.T.: Guardian of the Tracks and Trails.* Lincoln, NE: Johnsen, 1963.

Hunt, Elvid. *History of Fort Leavenworth, 1827–1927.* Fort Leavenworth, KS: General Service Schools Press, 1926.

Hurt, R. Douglas. "Fort Wallace, Kansas, 1865–1882: A Frontier Post during the Indian Wars." *Red River Valley Historical Review* 1 (Summer 1974): 132–45.

Jackson, Brenda K. "Holding Down the Fort: A History of Dakota Territory's Fort Randall." *South Dakota History* 32 (Spring 2002): 1–27.

Jennings, Jan. "Frank R. Grodavent: Western Army Architect." *Essays and Monographs in Colorado History* 11 (1990): 2–23.

Kyvig, David E. "Policing the Panhandle: Fort Elliott, Texas, 1875–1890." *Red River Valley Historical Review* 1 (Autumn 1974): 222–32.

Lavender, David. *Fort Laramie and the Changing Frontier.* Washington, DC: U.S. Department of the Interior, 1983.

Lee, Robert. *Fort Meade and the Black Hills.* Lincoln: University of Nebraska Press, 1991.

Libby, Orin G. "Fort Abercrombie, 1857–1877." *Collections of the State Historical Society of North Dakota* 2 (1908): 1–163.

Lindmier, Tom. *Drybone: A History of Fort Fetterman, Wyoming.* Glendo, WY: High Plains Press, 2002.

Loudon, Betty, ed. "Pioneer Pharmacist J. Walter Moyer's Notes on Crawford and Fort Robinson in the 1890s." *Nebraska History* 58 (Spring 1977): 89–117.

Mattison, Ray H. "Fort Rice, North Dakota's First Missouri River Military Post." *North Dakota History* 20 (April 1953): 87–108.

———. "Old Fort Stevenson—A Typical Missouri River Military Post." *North Dakota History* 18 (April–July 1951): 53–91.

Mayes, William G., Jr. "Did Murphy Blunder? The Closing of Fort Hays, Kansas." *Journal of the West* 15 (July 1976): 38–48.

McChristian, Douglas C. "Fort Laramie—After the Army: Part I, the Auction." *Annals of Wyoming* 73 (Summer 2001): 12–23.

Murray, Robert A. "Fort Fred Steele: Desert Outpost on the Union Pacific." *Annals of Wyoming* 44 (Fall 1972): 139–206.

Nye, Wilbur S. *Carbine and Lance: The Story of Old Fort Sill.* Norman: University of Oklahoma Press, 1942.

Oliva, Leo E. *Fort Hays, Frontier Army Post, 1865–1889.* Topeka: Kansas State Historical Society, 1980.

———. *Fort Larned on the Santa Fe Trail.* Topeka: Kansas State Historical Society, 1982.

Oswald, John M. "History of Fort Elliott." *Panhandle-Plains Historical Review* 32 (1959): 1–59.

Outline Descriptions of the Posts in the Military Division of the Missouri. Chicago: Military Division of the Missouri, 1876.

Pirtle, Caleb, III, and Michael F. Cusack. *Fort Clark: The Lonely Sentinel on Texas's Western Frontier.* Austin, TX: Eakin Press, 1985.

Reed, Bill. *The Last Bugle Call: A History of Fort McDowell Arizona Territory, 1865–1890.* Parsons, WV: McClain, 1977.

Remele, Larry, ed. *Fort Totten: Military Post and Indian School, 1867–1959.* Bismarck: State Historical Society of North Dakota, 1986.

Rister, Carl Coke. *Fort Griffin on the Texas Frontier.* Norman: University of Oklahoma Press, 1956.

Robinson, Willard B. *American Forts: Architectural Form and Function.* Urbana: University of Illinois Press, 1977.

Robrock, David P. "A History of Fort Fetterman, Wyoming, 1867–1882." *Annals of Wyoming* 48 (Spring 1976): 5–76.

Ruhlen, George. "Fort Hancock—Last of the Frontier Forts." *Password* 4 (January 1959): 19–30.

———. "Quitman: The Worst Post at Which I Ever Served." *Password* 12 (Fall 1966): 107–26.

Schubert, Frank N. *Buffalo Soldiers, Braves and Brass: The Story of Fort Robinson, Nebraska.* Shippensburg, PA: White Mane, 1993.

Scobee, Barry. *Fort Davis, Texas, 1583–1960.* El Paso, TX: Hill, 1963.

Sharp, Walter C., Jr. "Fort Omaha and the Winning of the West." MA thesis, University of Nebraska at Omaha, 1967.

Smith, Cornelius C., Jr. *Fort Huachuca: The Story of a Frontier Post.* Washington, DC: U.S. Government Printing Office, 1976.

Strate, David K. *Sentinel to the Cimarron: The Frontier Experience of Fort Dodge, Kansas.* Dodge City, KS: Cultural Heritage and Arts Center, 1970.

Sutton, Mary. "Glimpses of Fort Concho through the Military Telegraph." *West Texas Historical Association Year Book* 32 (1956): 122–34.

Thomson, William D. "History of Fort Pembina: 1870–1895." *North Dakota History* 36 (Winter 1969): 5–39.

Uglow, Loyd M. *Standing in the Gap: Army Outposts, Picket Stations, and the Pacification of the Texas Frontier, 1866–1886.* Fort Worth: Texas Christian University Press, 2001.

Upton, Richard, ed. *Fort Custer on the Big Horn, 1877–1898: Its History and Personalities as Told and Pictured by Its Contemporaries.* Glendale, CA: Arthur H. Clark, 1973.

Wertenberger, Mildred, comp. "Fort Totten, Dakota Territory, 1867." *North Dakota History* 34 (Spring 1967): 125–46.

Whisenhunt, Donald W. *Fort Richardson: Outpost on the Texas Frontier.* Southwestern Studies Monograph, no. 20. El Paso: Texas Western Press, 1968.

Williams, Clayton. *Texas' Last Frontier: Fort Stockton and the Trans-Pecos, 1861–1895.* Edited by Ernest Wallace. College Station: Texas A&M University Press, 1982.

Wooster, Robert. *Frontier Crossroads: Fort Davis and the West.* College Station: Texas A&M University Press, 2006.

INDEX

ABOUT THE AUTHOR

MICHAEL L. TATE is Professor of History at University of Nebraska, Omaha. Among his previously published books are *The Frontier Army in the Settlement of the West* and *Indians and Emigrants on the Overland Trails: Myths Reexamined.*